INFORMATION SOURCES
IN ADVERTISING HISTORY

INFORMATION SOURCES
IN ADVERTISING HISTORY

Edited and Compiled by
Richard W. Pollay

GREENWOOD PRESS
Westport, Connecticut • London, England

Library of Congress Cataloging in Publication Data

Pollay, Richard W
  Information sources in advertising history.

  Includes index.
1. Advertising—History—Bibliography. I. Title.
Z7164.C81P66 [HF5811]   016.6591   78-75259
ISBN 0-313-21422-0

Library of Congress Catalog Card Number: 78-75259
ISBN: 0-313-21422-0

First published in 1979

Greenwood Press, Inc.
51 Riverside Avenue, Westport, Connecticut 06880

Printed in the United States of America

10 9 8 7 6 5 4 3 2 1

TO THE HIGH PRIESTS AND HUMBLE HISTORIANS WITH
THE HOPE THAT BOTH GROUPS WILL HAVE THE SELF
CONFIDENCE THAT RISKS HERESY IN THE PURSUIT OF TRUTH.

"Research on a great social institution can never be conducted
from a position of the Establishment. The only useful inquiry is an
objective one. But to be objective, the researcher can hardly fail to
be critical in spirit, to question all articles of faith, and therefore
risk appearing heretical to the high priests of the institutions which
are the objects of his research as well as its patrons."

Leo Bogart

"Where Does Advertising Research Go From Here?"
Journal of Advertising Research, Vol. 9, no. 1 (1969), p. 12.

CONTENTS

FOREWORD

Advertising is exciting. A growing recognition of the fact that a history of advertising could provide a realistic mirror of the cultural and economic history of the times is also exciting. The fact that a beginning is being made in accumulating sources in advertising history is even more exciting.

Four steps will be required in order to produce an adequate history of advertising. First, an appropriate set of concepts for selecting and organizing the essential material must be developed. Second, a compilation of the publicly available relevant source material is necessary. Third, and most difficult, is the enlisting of cooperation by people in the advertising business to record, selectively and objectively, the privileged material so essential to a revealing history. Fourth, of course, is the dedication of an inspired writer equipped with a style and the editorial judgment required for the task.

Dr. Richard W. Pollay has accomplished the first two steps, and perhaps the fourth, in his *Information Sources in Advertising History*. The contents of this volume are organized and indexed in a manner that both displays the varieties of types of literature extant on advertising and also anticipates the research questions and needs of future scholars. Despite its relatively voluminous size, the bibliographic section also shows selectivity in its purposeful omission, for example, of ephemera, the short-lived publicity materials published by agencies and associations. This and other exclusions keep the work within manageable proportions, with the directories serving to steer future scholars directly to the agencies and associations for this kind of supplemental material.

The work, as it stands, represents a huge accomplishment for the benefit of all those who will help in the documenting of advertising's major role in modern society. It has intelligently processed and organized the extensive contents of the major public and university libraries on the subject. This difficult spade work will permit users of the work to orient themselves rapidly in this immense literature and to locate those materials most germane to their interests.

Information Sources in Advertising History includes many bibliographies and directories. These extensive and annotated lists have been flavored by the inclusion of three unique essays, making the book much more than a compendium of titles. The author, himself a curator and promoter of marketing museums, has made this book a standard work for all who wish to proceed toward the goal of an up-to-date history.

One needs to keep in mind that advertising will have to be a central focus of any history of twentieth-century business. But the businesses that advertise have their focus on the present and the future, not on the past. A history of advertising will be sparse without the records held by the companies active in advertising. It is hoped that this book will provide incentive as well as guidance for company archivists now privy to internal information. It will direct their selection and organization of private business records that, upon later release, will enable any historian better to reflect the times of which he writes.

Dr. Pollay's motivation in the tedious culling and documenting of historical sources was not merely to enable some historians to write a revealing contribution. The inspiration to produce these sources must have come from his prominent part in promoting a twentieth-century history of advertising. His teaching and writing have made a compelling case for early achievement of a history. This has made almost mandatory the accumulation of all available sources. His book represents completion of that task and should stand as a landmark awaiting only the recording and ultimate release of relevant internal advertising decisions and practices.

Those interested in joining a movement to bring about a true history of advertising will find much guidance in the London-based "History of Advertising Trust" and its *Journal of Advertising History*. They will also find guidance and leadership in the activities of the author of this book. His contributions and insight go far beyond the accumulation of sources. As a writer and teacher he has already given great momentum to the development of an advertising history. He has also demonstrated that he has the great talent needed to succeed in such an exciting and worthy adventure as writing the history of twentieth-century advertising.

Darrell B. Lucas

ACKNOWLEDGMENTS AND DISCLAIMERS

The citations included in the bibliography were collected over a number of years during which I examined the impressive resources of many major libraries, particularly the libraries of Harvard, Columbia, the University of Chicago, and the municipal public libraries of Boston, Chicago, New York, and the Library of Congress in Washington, D.C. These were supplemented with references drawn from *America: History and Life: A Guide to Periodical Literature* and Eugene P. Sheehy's *Guide to Reference Books,* Chicago: American Library Association, 1976. Surprisingly, several additions were also made from my personal library, a collection of books on advertising assembled by patient scrounging in secondhand bookstores, a process which apparently unearths materials not in even the largest libraries.

In my judgment, the bibliography is best for materials before 1960. During the 1960's and 1970's I have witnessed an explosion of literature in consumerism, which naturally included much discussion of advertising, and in consumer behavior, a field which has emerged as an intellectual discipline unto itself, complete with texts, case books, research methodologies, professional associations, journals like the *Journal of Marketing Research,* the *Journal of Consumer Research,* the *Journal of Consumer Affairs,* and the *Journal of Consumer Policy.* The explosion of literature in these fields has been so vast that it would take a volume the size of this one just to document the past two decades' intellectual product, much less the professional activities and publications.

The Archives list, which I hope is an especially valuable aid to the research of others, is as exhaustive as possible. Mail and telephone surveys were conducted with all repositories that I knew existed either from consulting the *National Union Catalogue of Manuscript Collections,* the *Directory of Special Libraries and Information Centers, Encyclopedia of*

Associations, The Special Library's Association Directory of Members, or
from hearsay leads provided by sundry correspondents. My apologies to
possessors and potential users of any materials I have omitted, whether
through my oversight or the lack of a timely response to the survey. Any
such omissions called to my attention, along with any new acquisitions,
will be included in my personal files and in any subsequent revision or
supplements to this work. The same should be said for any works unin-
tentionally omitted from the bibliography.

Despite the size of the bibliographic sections that follow, and the
length of the list of archival resources available, this collection-finding
aid has some boundary limitations that deserve discussion. In order to
make the project manageable, I had to exclude topics from the domain
of literature and resources covered; this exclusion may prove to be a
frustration to some researchers.

For example, the topic of public relations is covered only superficially,
since excellent bibliographies already exist (See Cutlip, 1.013). The works
of major figures, Edward Bernays for example, and academic studies of
public relations are included however, especially where the efforts described are companions to advertising. Few of the myriad articles in
periodicals, either academic or professional, are individually cited in the
bibliography and neither are conference proceedings or miscellaneous
papers of associations. The periodical literature of the advertising trade
can be easily accessed with assistance from *Journalism Quarterly* (1.026)
and from the bibliographic essay of Quentin Schultze contained in this
work. Papers of associations are best found through direct contact with
the associations and their library staff. The articles cited here are those
known to me which are in obscure locations or explicitly historical in nature.

Nor does the bibliography contain much in the way of the manifold
pamphlets, speeches, and other promotional ephemera issued by advertising agencies seeking to attract business. The exceptions to this rule are
those publications that give historical information or address themselves
specifically and informatively to a particular problem, like that of media
selection.

Works on the production of advertisements, be that type-setting or
artistic renderings, are not included. This literature is not well maintained
in public or university libraries, making accession difficult. I implicitly
presume that the impact of changes in these technologies is not as significant as the impact of the changing technologies of psychological research,
media placement, or management. Lastly, this work contains few citations
to publications that are solely facsimiles. There has been an abundance
of these in recent years, since they are produceable by anyone with the
most elemental of photographic and printing equipment, but the collections are invariably idiosyncratic and unannotated, making them virtually
useless as research resources.

This work could not have come to be without the moral and tangible support of countless people. My gratitude to all of those who responded to our surveys, all correspondents, and the many unnamed librarians and nonprofessional staff of the research centers I used in assembling this work. Certain individuals, however, deserve particular mention for the quality of their contributions. The contributing authors of the bibliographic essays, of course, made a crucial contribution. Barbara Pearce and Barbara Gibson of the University of British Columbia Library taught me much about the value of finding aids and reference books. I received support and encouragement from professional librarians like Marsha Appel of The American Association of Advertising Agencies, N. Terry Munger of J. Walter Thompson (New York), Johnn Patton, the President of the Marketing and Advertising Division of the Special Libraries Association, who kindly arranged for the use of their mailing list, Elisabeth Proudfit of the Advertising Research Foundation Library, and Edward Strable of J. Walter Thompson Company (Chicago).

Various other scholars have also been particularly helpful and encouraging at various stages in the development of this project. Particular mention is deserved by Robert Bartels (Ohio State University), Jim Baughman (Harvard), Alfred Chandler (Harvard), Stanley Hollander (Michigan State), Otis Pease (University of Washington), P. Glenn Porter (Harvard, and more recently Elutherian Mills), and Larry Rosenberg (New York University). Special thanks are offered to David Dunbar, Editor of the *Journal of Advertising History* and the Secretary of the History of Advertising Trust, London, with regrets that neither time nor resources permitted this work to be inclusive of materials for Great Britain.

Special thanks go to those agencies whose financial contributions helped underwrite the cost of producing this work. The Ministry of Labour for the Province of British Columbia provided funds for the summer employment of library school students as assistants. Funds for sundry office supplies and expenses and a part-time research assistant were provided by the UBC Humanities and Social Sciences Grants Committee. The bulk of the expenses, including most travel and secretarial costs, were covered by a grant from the Social Science and Humanities Research Council of Canada, Ottawa. My gratitude to these facilitators is immeasurable. Without their support this work would not exist.

I am most indebted to those stalwart individuals who worked closely with me during the final months of this project. Debby Kirchner and Karen Walker displayed not only professional library skills but also patience and initiative in looking after the details of our correspondence with individuals, archives and libraries, and in transforming my scratches and scrawls into uniform citations and annotations. Nancy Carpenter provided timely and continuing professional and personal encouragement. Last, and very far from least, the skilled typing and intelligent secretarial skills of Betty Ruebart and Pat Haynes transformed my rough drafts and card catalogs into a finally finished product. Whatever shortcomings the work may have are my responsibility alone and have been minimized by the efforts of those assisting me.

Richard W. Pollay
Director, History of Advertising Project

University of British Columbia
Vancouver, B.C.   V6T   1W5

I.
Overview

1.
TYPES OF LITERATURE ON ADVERTISING IN HISTORY:
Inadequacies and Needs

Richard W. Pollay

It has often been remarked that conventional history pays inordinate tribute to the personalities and actions of politicians and in comparison virtually ignores all but the most infamous of businessmen and their behavior. To some extent this is a failure on the part of historians to adjust their focus of concern to reflect the increasing importance of economic activity in shaping society's evolution. But the continuation of the traditional attention to politicians and heads of state is not only the result of historical bias. The blame for the inadequate chronicling of business activity lies not only with historians but also with the business sector itself, for good history can be written only to the extent that business firms keep historical records, provide scholars with access to those records, and permit the citation and publishing of results.

The typical business firm is ahistorical in temperament, possessed as it is with a managerial focus on contemporary problems and strategies for the future. They keep relatively skimpy records for only brief periods of time. Suspicious of scholars, firms who manifest any historical interest are more likely to hire a professional journalist to write a vanity history of "struggle and triumph" for publicity purposes - with the result narrow in perspective and of dubious candidness. The result of this behavior is that what little is believed of business behavior is often the result of exposé, and is probably greatly distorted compared to what would be known if firms kept and made available systematic records.

The ideas contained here have been expressed by the author elsewhere on numerous occasions. Readers will note many similarities in substance and style between this and some of the author's recent publications addressed to different audiences, in particular: "The Importance, and the Problems of Writing the History of Advertising," *Journal of Advertising History*, Vol. 1 #1 (December 1977); and "Wanted: Contributions to the History of Advertising," *Journal of Advertising Research*, Vol. 18 #5 (October, 1978). For a discussion on the records and documents needed for research in the area see the author's "Maintaining Archives for the History of Advertising," *Special Libraries*, Vol. 69 #4 (April 1978).

It is clear to even a casual observer that the history of the 20th century must be in large part a history of the growth and development of
business from the 19th century model of family-owned, community-based
primitive factories to the interurban, multinational megacorporations of
today. There is no part of society, including its problems and politics,
that is not strongly colored by this change. Already many serious scholars are beginning the plunge into the source materials saved by those
firms with foresight, but to date few of the firms who are actively maintaining archives, or who have opened them up to scholars, are major advertising agencies or marketing firms.

This is most unfortunate, for advertising is one of the key technologies
that permits, and perhaps even creates, the scale of corporations we now
experience.

Advertising Can't Be Ignored

It is inevitable that advertising will be a central focus of the history of the 20th century. Not only because advertising as we know it has
evolved and matured within the 20th century, thereby making the 20th century unique. Not only because its size and centrality to the economy
make it a significant industry in its own right. Not only because its
social visibility, and presumed social influence, may be great - that is,
because advertising is both pervasive and persuasive. But also because
advertising is at the interfaces between pragmatics and art, between
psychology and economics, between the producers and consumers of society,
making it a key element in our economic history and in our social, tech-
nological, artistic and cultural histories as well. The history of advertising is, therefore, perhaps one of the keys to the appropriate understanding of the evolution of our complex urban society. Advertising is
a "tremendous institution which deserves study in its own right, and because of its influence on the most vital concerns and powers and values
of our society." (Bogart, 1969).

The potential richness of advertising as a source material through
which great insight might be obtained has long been recognized. A late
19th century issue of *Harper's Weekly* said that advertisements are: "a
true mirror on life, a sort of fossil history from which the future
chronicler, if all other historical monuments were to be lost, might
fully and graphically re-write the history of our time."

A quarter of a century later Salmon (1923), herself a historian, said
that a newspaper without advertising "would deprive society of the most
flawless mirror of itself and the historian of the most unimpeachable
evidence at his command." James Webb Young, (1949), one of the few advertising leaders ever to gain wide respect in the academic community,
noted that "any anthropologist who attempted to describe our culture with
advertising left out, would, I suggest, be as nearsighted as one who left
corn out of the story of the Mayas - or the camel out of that of the
Bedouin tribes." And most recently Wood, whose *Story of Advertising*
(1958) is undervalued by historians, commented in his preface that
"...advertising is the story of the people. In first hand actuality, advertising describes their desires, tastes, habits, weaknesses, hopes and
pretensions. In advertising can be seen the actuality of what people
have been like in their day-to-day living through the centuries and what

we are like now. There can be found few more accurate representations of
a time and the people in it than the advertising amid which and, willy-
nilly, by which they live." (pp. v-vi).

The historical treatment of advertising is inevitable because of its
centrality to our economy, and to be encouraged because advertising is
such a faithful mirror to our culture. In addition, "the study of a
single advanced marketing culture and the role which marketing has played
in its economic development would yield patterns of change in marketing
attitudes and techniques which might lead to useful generalizations"
about the ways in which underdeveloped nations might best adapt to the
industrialized world's productivity. (Myers and Smalley, 1959, p. 395).

But Advertisers Can't Write Their Own History

One might think that the history of advertising is most likely to be
written by members of the advertising profession. After all, they certainly have a high degree of familiarity with the subject from personal
experience, are well skilled at wrapping words around ideas, and are
hardly averse to writing for public consumption, as the many quality
books written by members of the industry attest. But these books are not
history. This is hardly a criticism since few are historical in style or
purpose, but the result is that they do not influence history's treatment
of advertising, and often for good reason.

The most common style of book is the semi-autobiographical, *My Life in
Advertising* (Hopkins, 1927), published in the golden sunset years of a
distinguished advertising agent's career. Whether the book is a discussion of *Me and Other Advertising Geniuses* (Brower, 1974) or *The Huckster's
Revenge* (Manchee, 1959), the content is of limited historical value.
While these two works are less self-serving or vengeful than their titles
might make them appear, they, like others of this genre, suffer from being
idiosyncratic, the experience of only one individual. Some of the books
of this style are shamelessly self-glorifying. In addition the perspective of the author is almost exclusively "the view from the top." Lastly,
the content of most of these works is typically little more than a compilation of entertaining anecdotal highlights, salted with both wit and
wisdom, but without a compelling conceptual coherence.

Even the best of the lot have limited usefulness as history. For example, Ogilvy's *Confessions of an Advertising Man* (1963) is thoughtful,
articulate, well organized and generally good enough to be required reading of every serious advertising professional. Yet despite these virtues
it is not history, nor is it even very much grist for the historian's
mill. This is so because he has distilled his experience into operational advice for other advertisers, not a description of advertising's evolution or its functions in society.

Perhaps because advertising men are inclined to write their own memoirs,
there are relatively few formal biographies of advertising leaders. With
the exception of the legendary P. T. Barnum, "Almost all the other major
figures in the history of American advertising lack adequate biographies"
(Boorstin, 1964, p. 291). The best known recent biography is John
Gunther's story of Albert D. Lasker (1960) which Boorstin (1964) found to
be "a disappointing, thin and pious account of one of the most interesting

figures in modern American social history." So even historians sympathetic to the importance of advertising and its leaders find little of
value in biographical works.

There is, of course, also the occasional book written by an advertiser
or a journalist with a historical theme. Watkin's *100 Greatest Advertisements* (1941) and Rowsome's *They Laughed When I Sat Down* (1959) spring
immediately to mind. They were produced and marketed as coffee table
books, of interest primarily because of their illustrations, and are
treated as such by scholars - despite the well informed editorial content.
Seldin's *The Golden Fleece* (1963) uses an historical theme very successfully in describing post World War II marketing in America, as does
Turner (1953) in portraying advertising's earlier history, but these books
too are generally ignored by scholars. Seldin's work was mismarketed and
got nowhere near the circulation it deserved and has since become rare
and obscure. Turner's work was marketed with the objective of trade
sales and not academic impact.

These works, and all of the many volumes written by advertisers, are
relatively ignored regardless of their quality because of an academic
distrust in their validity or representativeness. While some of this
cavalier dismissal may be a manifestation of a bias, an alienation and
basic distrust of advertisers by academics, much of it is justified.
The historian must conscientiously dismiss those works obviously evangel-
ical or anecdotal. He also requires works that are well annotated and
indexed so that they are suitable for validation and reference. Some may
argue that the academic's insistence of a certain formal style is little
more than an insistence that the historical product be packaged a certain
way. This probably undervalues the legitimacy of the historians preferences, but be that as it may, there seems to be little reason to resist
the product preferences of the consumer. For until the professional
historian is the consumer, whatever is written is not really a part of
history, for history is what historians read, write and believe it to be.
And as time passes on history is *only* what historians write.

And Historians Haven't ...Yet!

Given the importance of advertising to the history of the 20th century,
the calls to action periodically heard among historians, and their tendency to ignore the writings of practitioners, historians are to be em-
barrassed by the relative paucity of respectable studies. While the
annotated bibliography, which follows in this book, includes many, many
titles, many of these are brief articles, repetitive early textbooks, and
anecdotal reflections by agents through the ages. There are very, very
few sources which are comprehensive and authoritative enough to command
the attention of historians. The two studies most commonly cited both
date from before World War II. They are Presbrey's (1929) chronicle of
the first half century of modern advertising and Hower's (1939) more
focused history of N. W. Ayer & Son. Besides these two there are few
studies of major significance. So great is the void that one still finds
frequent references to Sampson's history published in *1874*!!

Daniel Boorstin, a preeminent American historian, author of the trilogy,
The Americans (1973), former head of the Smithsonian Institution, now the
Librarian of Congress, noted that "Advertising, one of the most character-

istic and most vigorous of American institutions, has been less adequately chronicled than almost any other major institution," (p. 630), and elsewhere that "Advertising despite its importance in the American economy and in our daily life, has attracted surprisingly few historians." (1964, p. 289).

Ralph Hower, one of the few who has been attracted, surveyed his colleagues at the Harvard Business School in 1935 and found that "the one topic on which information is especially wanted is a history of marketing." But Ralph Hidy, also from Harvard's Business School, noted in his more recent review of business history (1970) that there the history of all of marketing was subject to "considerable discussion but little action."

There are the adventurous young historians who from time to time produce a dissertation or an article in a learned journal. The dissertations, no matter what their quality, go largely uncirculated and unread even in academic circles, as Pope's (1976) respectable pioneer scholarly effort demonstrates. Articles in scholarly presses are of necessity limited in scope, as witness McMahon's (1972) study of the adoption of psychological concepts by the advertising industry in the 20's and 30's, or Curti's (1967) study over a longer time span of an even smaller focus of concern: the changing notions of human nature as displayed in the pages of *Printers' Ink*. Even though these studies meet even the most demanding standards of academic acceptability, their contribution and influence on the thinking of historians is as small as their narrowness of interest. And historians, like the rest of us, have the bias of considering a book as significantly more substantial and important than any article no matter how thoughtful.

Unfortunately the books written are often not that thoughtful. The most recent book to be published among historians on advertising is Stuart Ewen's *Captains of Consciousness*. As the title suggests, the book takes a very critical stance with respect to advertising. Employing a Marxist perspective he argues that "the formulators of the consumer market and the propagandists who publicized it hoped to instill an authoritarian obedience to the dictates of daily life in the machine age." (p. 96). He chastises other critical perspectives, like Vance Packard's (1957), as "inadequate" because it portrays the faults of advertising as eccentric rather than systematic. (pp. 188-189). His central theme is that "While much of the thinking in the American industrial 'war rooms' maintained an adherence to traditional 'democratic' rhetoric, the basic impulse in advertising was one of control, of actively channeling social impulses," assuming a "manipulative approach to the problem of popular consciousness," and undertaking "the imperialization of the psyche." (p. 81).

It is only a small consolation that his rhetoric is clearly just that, and that his Marxist perspective is intellectually unequal to the task of describing advertising's historical role, and that it offers no striking insights. Nor is it very consoling to note that at least one academic book reviewer found the work "hampered, indeed crippled, by severe conceptual and methodological shortcomings." (Tedlow, 1976). It would be more consoling were it not for the fact that the intellectual vacuum is great and that works like this fill some of the void. No matter how inadequately or inaccurately they do so, they will be read, and sometimes quoted, and what they say may long be noted.

On Facilitating the Needed Research

From the serious historian's point of view virtually all of the literature available on the history of advertising is either anecdotal, evan-
gelical, trivial or rhetorical. So why, you might ask, hasn't some competent serious scholar leapt into the breach and written a *magnum opus*
guaranteed to win fame even if not fortune. Why, indeed, have historians
given advertising such short shrift. The question is a difficult one,
and the answer complex.

Part of the answer lies in the cultural bias against marketing that
pervades even the most fundamental of our economic concepts. The prejudice against marketing (Steiner, 1977) is pervasive and historians are
no more likely to be enthralled with the thought of their daughter marry-
ing a marketing or advertising man than anyone. There is also a bias
among most historians against all elements of popular culture.

"There is an insistent tendency among solemn social scientists to think
of any institution which features rhymed and singing commercials, intense
and lachrymose voices urging highly improbable enjoyments, caricatures of
the human esophagus in normal or imparied operation, and which hints im-
plausibly at opportunities for antiseptic seduction, as inherently trivial." (Galbraith, 1967, p. 218).

These factors, while significant, are probably of small influence compared to two others. Academics of any kind are rarely given access to
the inner workings of advertisers and agencies. This is certainly true
even for business school professors, much less the more suspected liberal
arts, history professor. No matter how understandable this "stonewalling"
might be, it is none-the-less unfortunate. With alienation and suspicion
flowing both ways between academics and the professional advertising
community, both doors and minds get closed. The validity of the way
history will treat advertising is probably what suffers most. Perhaps
also lost is an opportunity to improve advertising by learning from valid
histories. Instead of "stonewalling," it would be preferable to follow
Bogart's (1969) suggestion that "we should be enlisting the support of
... historians."

Even if access to records were free and unrestricted, the task of pro-
cessing the information intelligently is formidable. The relevant source
materials are scattered in diverse locations; little pockets of valuable
information secreted in remote corners and files of multitudinous agencies and clients. Since the industry is both large and lives by its
words, the volume of materials one might conceivably be called upon to
consult is immense. Worse still, the increasing sophistication of advertising is reflected in the growth of specialized methods, technical
language and strategic concepts that may be taken for granted by those
immersed in the industry, but which are obscure and virtually unintelli-
gible to the layman. The typical academic historian is surely just that
- a layman - with respect to business practice in general, or advertising
practice in specific.

Yet another factor which inhibits adequate treatment of advertising by
historians, and by no means the least, stems from the very fact that
there is such a void in the literature. Whatever is written about advertising is sure to be the focus of much attention. Business, economic

and social historians will all seize upon the work with critical eager-
ness. The advertising community is sure to discuss and publicize the
work. Like any book on advertising it would even stand a chance of
catching the popular interest and becoming widely read indeed. But the
limelight can be harsh and is perhaps likely to be so. Both the academic
and professional communities are notable for their quickness to criticism.
Academics are critical by force of intellectual habit and justify this as
a necessary means in "the pursuit of truth." The advertising community
has a track record of hypersensitive retaliatory responses to even vague-
ly implied criticisms; the wailing of so much wounded pride at being
described as something less than paragons of virtue, and thereby inhibiting an honest, balanced (and interesting to read) history. So extensive
criticism seems inescapable, especially when one considers the nearly
impossible task of impressing both audiences simultaneously.

Thus far I have argued that it is inevitable that advertising be discussed at length as the history of the twentieth century gets written;
that the treatment of advertising by conventional historians to date has
been less than adequate; that the biographical or anecdotal writings of
advertising agents will not greatly influence history's treatment of advertising no matter how voluminous, witty or wise those writings might
be; and that there are many serious problems inhibiting competent scholarly treatment.

Not all of those problems are easily solved, but there are certainly
some things that can be done to encourage future researchers. The successful treatment of advertising seems to depend on three basic elements:
(1) an appropriate set of concepts, or theoretical framework, with which
to select, organize and discuss advertising, (2) a competent, credible
author-scholar, and (3) a broad base of information to draw upon. Few
of the works to date have had any of these elements, much less all three,
so it is small wonder the resulting books are of little import.

The first is probably the most critical element in determining the
character of the final product, for it is through use of a conceptual
structure that the researcher selects, organizes, discusses and generally
gives meaning to otherwise diverse, chaotic observations. It is the concepts that bring order out of the chaos by highlighting the communalities
of events happening simultaneously and the continuity of events happening
across time. It is the concepts employed that determine what questions
the researcher asks, what "data" he observes and what he ignores, and
ultimately what he sees. A useful and valid set of concepts provides
both coherence and insight, by exposing patterns of development and by
permitting inference and the perception of implications.

One of the major disappointments of the work to date has been the lack
of a convincing conceptual structure. Some books have little structure
at all, being content to be anecdotal and journalistic. Others have an
unambiguous set of conceptual tools but tools inappropriate to the task.
Like Ewen's (1976) use of concepts evolving from 19th century Marxist
thought, the result is that no matter how hard the author tries, the tools
do not provide a satisfactory "explanation" of the reality, provide no
insight into the practice and often end up "rules" with more exceptions
than adherences. Worse still, they can be dangerously misleading. While
it is not easy to judge at this time, before the research is done, what
concepts will be most helpful in making sense out of the history of ad-

vertising, it is clear there are concepts more likely to be appropriate
than those used by authors like Ewen. To give the simplest and most
obvious example, much could be made of "the marketing concept," an idea
now so ingrained in the profession that we overlook its import. The
history of advertising, when seen as the shift from the selling concept
of flogging what the factory makes to the concept of marketing what the
consumer desires, takes on a new clarity. The marketing concept allows
the understanding of the functions of consumer research and market seg-
mentation strategies, activities which, although often painted as manipulative in intent, might well be increasing the efficiency and service of
marketing.

   Finding an author-researcher who possesses the necessary credibility
may not be easy, for the individual needs credibility with two disparate
groups - the professional advertising community and the community of
academic historians. For the latter, credibility would depend on having
the necessary union card (a Ph.D.), a university appointment (preferably
current), and a track record of quality scholarly publications, especially
on historical topics. The advertising community would want reassurance
that the individual knows about advertising through more than just the
consumer's viewpoint and is generally well informed about trade practices.
This combination of requirements suggests that the man for the job is
more likely to be found among scholars who have made most of their careers
within the professional advertising community, or among those who have
spent their careers studying and teaching marketing and advertising in a
university. If one also requires a demonstration of interest in matters
historical, the number of candidates who come to mind shrinks to a tiny
handful, and several of these men are preoccupied with other research
interests which would prevent the long commitment that a thorough piece
of historical research would require.

   But of all the necessary components to the successful treatment of advertising by history, none is more essential than the existence of a rich
and organized supply of archival information. If by chance today's acad-
emies of learning do not provide us with the appropriate concepts or the
needed volume of competent scholars, then patience should bring the re-
ward of a never ending stream of new scholars with new ideas. But no one
can create new archival materials. Once the records are lost or destroyed
they are lost forever. While patience may be rewarded with the occasional
uncovering of hitherto unknown collections of material, on the whole the
passage of time witnesses the decay and destruction of material. It is
also obvious that the number or competence of researchers, and the bril-
liance of their research ideas, all go for naught in the absence of adequate information upon which the historical hypothesis may be tested.

   It is toward closing the gap between researchers and available information that this book is dedicated, not only archival information but also
the potential wealth of information in selected secondary sources. Hopefully this will facilitate scholarly efforts and publications.

REFERENCES

1. Bogart, Leo, "Where does Advertising Research Go From Here?", *Journal of Advertising Research*, Vol. 9 #1 (March 1969), pp. 3-12.

2. Boorstin, Daniel J., *The Image: A Guide to Pseudo-Events in America*, New York: Harper and Row, 1964.

3. Boorstin, Daniel J., *The Americans: The Democratic Experience*, New York: Random House, 1973.

4. Brower, Charlie, *Me and Other Advertising Geniuses*, Garden City: Doubleday, 1974.

5. Curti, Merle, "The Changing Concept of 'Human Nature' in the Literature of American Advertising," *Business History Review*, Vol. 41 #4 (Winter 1967), pp. 335-357.

6. Ewen, Stuart, *Captains of Consciousness: Advertising and the Social Roots of the Consumer Culture*, New York: McGraw-Hill, 1976.

7. Galbraith, John Kenneth, *The New Industrial State*, Boston: Houghton-Mifflin, 1967.

8. Gunther, John, *Taken at the Flood: The Story of Albert D. Lasker*, New York: Harper and Bros., 1960.

9. *Harper's Weekly*: the quotation cited was reprinted in *Printers' Ink*, Vol. 20 (August 25, 1897), p. 42.

10. Hidy, Ralph W., "Business History: Present Status and Future Needs," *Business History Review*, Vol. 44 (1970), p. 495.

11. Hopkins, Claude, *My Life in Advertising*, New York: Harper & Row, 1927.

12. Hower, Ralph M., "Wanted: Material on the History of Marketing," *Bulletin of the Business Historical Society*, Vol. 9 #5 (October 1935), pp. 79-81.

13. Hower, Ralph M., *History of an Advertising Agency: N. W. Ayer & Son at Work, 1869-1939*, Cambridge: Harvard University Press, 1939.

14. McMahon, A. Michael, "An American Courtship: Psychologists and Advertising Theory in the Progressive Era," *American Studies*, Vol. 13 (1972) pp. 5-18.

15. Manchee, Fred, *The Huckster's Revenge: The Truth About Life on Madison Avenue*, New York: Thomas Nelson and Sons, 1959.

16. Myers, Kenneth H., Jr. and Orange A. Smalley, "Marketing History and Economic Development," *Business History Review*, Vol. 33 (1959), pp. 387-401.

17. Ogilvy, David, *Confessions of an Advertising Man*, New York: Atheneum, 1963.

18.   Packard, Vance, *The Hidden Persuaders*, New York: David McKay, 1957.

19.   Pease, Otis, *The Responsibilities of American Advertising*, New Haven: Yale University Press, 1958.

20.   Pollay, Richard W., "Notes on Sources for the History of Marketing and Advertising in North America," Working Paper #434, Faculty of Commerce, University of British Columbia, Vancouver, B. C.

21.   Pollay, Richard W., "Maintaining Archives for the History of Advertising," paper read to the 1977 Annual Conference of the Special Libraries Association.

22.   Pope, Daniel Andrew, "The Development of National Advertising, 1865-1920," unpublished Ph.D. dissertation, Columbia University, 1973.

23.   Presbrey, Frank, *History and Development of Advertising*, Garden City: Doubleday, 1929.

24.   Rowsome, Frank Jr., *They Laughed When I Sat Down*, New York: Bonanza, 1959.

25.   Salmon, Lucy Maynard, *The Newspapers and the Historian*, New York: Oxford University Press, 1923.

26.   Sampson, Henry, *The History of Advertising from its Earliest Years*, London: Chato and Windis, 1874.

27.   Seldin, Joseph, *The Golden Fleece: Advertising in American Life*, New York: Marzani and Munsell, 1963.

28.   Steiner, Robert L., "The Prejudice Against Marketing," *Journal of Marketing*, Vol. 40 (July 1976), pp. 2-9.

29.   Tedlow, Richard S., Review of Ewen's *Captains of Consciousness* in *Business History Review*, Vol. 50 #3 (Autumn 1976), pp. 399-400.

30.   Turner, E. S., *The Shocking History of Advertising*, New York: E. P. Dutton & Co., 1953.

31.   Watkins, Julian, *The 100 Greatest Advertisements*, New York: Moore, 1941.

32.   Wood, James Playstead, *The Story of Advertising*, New York: Ronald, 1958.

33.   Young, James Webb, *Some Advertising Responsibilities in a Dynamic Society*, New York: J. Walter Thompson Co., 1949.

II.
Bibliographic Essays

1.
SOME SOURCES
OF ECONOMIC
DATA ON ADVERTISING

Julian L. Simon

Reader, beware. This essay offers clues, not inclusiveness. It covers some topics more thoroughly than others. And the listings on any one sort of data are usually only a few examples from ongoing series. Furtheremore, the coverage for the years 1963-1970 is much more thorough than for the years before 1963. The reader who wants a historical series will have to back-track from the contemporary data. Nevertheless, it is hoped that this essay is helpful and better than nothing.

From one point of view the researcher in the economics of advertising is well off. The data available to him are plentiful as compared with other industries. One reason for this is that the basic facts about advertising - how many advertising messages are sent out by various advertisers - are public, out in the open. One can watch a competitor's advertising and record what he does, and the competitor cannot conceal the broad outlines of his advertising efforts. This naturally has led to the rise of commercial organizations that measure all firms' advertising, and these published measurements are basic data for the researcher.

Several of the standard texts do an excellent job of listing these commercial services. Probably the most recent and comprehensive is Bogart (1967, Chapter 10 and pp. 324-327). An older book which also gives a comprehensive listing is Burton (1959, Chapter XXIII). Although some of the publications in Burton are now out of print, they are still available in agencies and libraries and are useful historically. A number are also

This essay originally appeared in 1970 as Appendix D of the author's *Issues in the Economics of Advertising*, and is reprinted with the permission of the author and the publisher, the University of Illinois Press. This essay benefited from the assistance of Eleanor Blum, who wrote some of it. She should not be held responsible for any of its many shortcomings, however. Seymour Banks was good enough to correct and up-date several of the data-source descriptions, and his wording has been used in such places without further note. Estelle Popkin also contributed several very helpful pieces of information. ©1970 by the Board of Trustees of the University of Illinois.

described in Blum (1963, and currently being updated). The reader may
also want to consult the chapter on "Competitive Advertising Expenditures" in Brown, et al. (1957, Chapter 12). There is also a good section, "Advertising Expenditures and Activity for Companies and Products,"
in *Media Analysis Principles and Practices,* a mimeographed publication
of Leo Burnett Company, presently being rewritten, which may or may not
be available upon request. Two excellent articles are by Daley (1963)
and Ziegler (1964), though not completely up to date as of now.

Also, the researcher is fortunate that the field has an exceptionally
good trade journal, *Advertising Age* (*AA* hereafter), which publishes excerpts of most of the data of value that are available anywhere. Many
of the data we mention are in *AA*.

In spite of these advantages, advertising data can be hard to come by,
especially complete data. The purpose of this essay is to lead the
researcher to some of the more obscure sources of information and to
point out certain gaps in the field.

Advertising Expenditures by Firms and Brands

In England expenditure data for firms and brands have been compiled for
over 30 years by the *Statistical Review of Press Advertising*. In the
United States, however, there are several organizations that collect this
type of data, and they have changed from time to time; the areas of
their coverage have changed also.

For newspapers, *Media Records* (Media Records, In., 370 Seventh Avenue,
N.Y.) compiles data by individual firm and by brand as it appears
throughout the year in almost 400 newspapers (more in the past), and presents it in detailed form. The forms in which the data were presented as
of 1962:

Media Records Quarterly Blue Book: Linage record of 420 /380 as of 1969/
    newspapers in 140 cities, by classification, accumulative year to date
    quarterly; linage used by each. Covers 75 percent of the total daily
    circulation, and 92 percent of total Sunday circulation in the United
    States.

Monthly City Report is compiled for newspaper publishers in each city
    showing a complete record of each advertiser's use of linage in all
    the newspapers in that city for the past month and accumulative year
    to date total.

Quarterly City Report of General and Automotive Advertising shows amount
    of space used by every individual General and Automotive advertiser in
    each paper in the city for the accumulated 3,6, 9 and 12 months'
    periods respectively.

Annual City Report is identical with monthly city report except carries
    accumulated twelve months' figures for each Display account in Retail,
    General, Automotive, and Financial Advertising.

Retail Advertising Performance Report lists in descending order according to population size, all cities measured, showing for each total Retail linage of the eight most important subclassifications of Retail advertising for current month.

First Fifty Report lists leading papers for Retail, General, Automotive, Financial, Department Stores, Classified and Total Advertising. Since 1930.

Chain Store Report is an annual report of chain store linage in newspapers of each Media Records city in which chain had retail outlets.

Advertising Trend Chart. Monthly. 52 city base, January 1928, to date, for the following classifications: Retail General, Automotive, Financial, Total Display, Classified, Department Store, and Total Advertising.

Other monthly reports and special services available upon request.

Although the *Media Records* data are very useful, the coverage is far from complete - not all newspapers are covered, and coverage differs each year. Another difficulty is that firms whose expenditures in a given medium are not large are not mentioned in the published data. (The minimum changes from year to year.) A yearly abridgement of the data, *Expenditures of National Advertisers in Newspapers* (Bureau of Advertising of the American Newspaper Publishers Association, 485 Lexington Ave., New York) lists amounts spent by those national advertisers who invested $25,000 or more in newspapers measured by *Media Records*. The Bureau of Advertising also has begun recently to publish a monthly newspaper advertising report which gives percentage changes in revenue for national, retail, classified and total for the report month versus the same month a year previous and for the current and previous year's totals to date. It also contains seasonally adjusted annual advertising revenues in millions of dollars for the same four classifications. Finally, it gives percentage changes in general and automotive linage from 14 cities as measured by Media Research for the report month and year to date versus the corresponding periods of the previous year. This may be obtained from the Research Department, Bureau of Advertising, ANPA.

For consumer magazines: Leading National Advertisers (P.O. Box 525, Norwalk, Conn.) prepares for Publishers Information Bureau (575 Lexington Ave., New York) a compilation by advertiser of the expenditures in more than 100 of the largest consumer magazines.

For television: Two formerly allied firms compete in the production of network television activity and expenditure data. Both Leading National Advertisers and Broadcast Advertisers Reports (formerly LNA-BAR) monitor ABC, CBS, and NBC broadcasts and estimate expenditures for the advertisers and individual brands. BAR recently began to prepare a spot-television expenditure report on the basis of one week's monitored data per month in each of the top 75 markets. The data are projected to a monthly figure and cumulated quarterly. The Rorabaugh report was produced by LNA until January 1, 1969. It estimated spot-television expenditures in all markets on the basis of station logs. Currently, Rorabaugh estimates only TV spot expenditures for markets not monitored by BAR.

These services are well known, expensive, and difficult for libraries to obtain unless connected with an advertising agency, a fact which can make it difficult for researchers to obtain them. Less well known and much less expensive is LNA's *National Advertising Investments* which abridges data in PIB, LNA-BAR and Rorabaugh. All companies investing in these media $20,000 or more in the first six months, and $25,000 or more in the twelve month period, are included. Media covered are approximately 100 of the consumer mass magazines; five newspaper supplements; net time and program expenditures on the three major TV networks; and spot TV expenditures on 400 stations. The tables preceding this data are also useful. One table ranks the 100 top advertisers, giving comparative figures covering five years, another table shows the ten top-ranking companies in each of the four media. The data in *National Advertising Investments* are nowhere near as detailed as the data in the more comprehensive services, but they will often serve the researcher's purpose.

For radio: Since 1966, Radio Expenditure Reports, a firm located in Larchmont, N.Y., has compiled for the Radio Advertising Bureau (RAB) quarterly data on advertisers' expenditures on network and national spot radio. These reports contain a complete list, arranged by product category, of national spot advertisers (companies and some brands) and their estimated expenditures. Also the top 100 national spot advertisers are listed alphabetically with expenditures broken down by brand. Network advertisers' expenditures are listed by company and brand.

For business publications: *The Rome Report of Business Publication Advertising* (Rome Research Company, 1960 Broadway, New York), formerly *Brad Vern's Report*, gives the expenditures of hundreds of companies which placed advertising in 630 business publications. A similar publication, more condensed and not so well known but which nevertheless lists much of the same data is *Leading Advertisers in Business Publications* (American Business Press, Inc., Business Press Advertising Bureau, Information Division, 205 E. 42nd St., New York). Since 1950 it has provided advertising expenditures by company for the majority of the periodicals having their primary listing in Standard Rate & Data's *Business Publication Rates & Data*. The 1967 edition contains data on almost 2,500 advertisers investing $35,000 or more.

Standard Directory of Advertisers (National Register Publishing Co., 5201 Old Orchard Road, Skokie, Ill.), a classified guide to 17,000 corporations, occasionally gives advertising appropriations. Generally only the total amount is given, although sometimes there is a breakdown by media.

Thus, a great deal of raw data exists. But the data are not complete, even for any given brand in any one medium. Brands whose expenditures in a given medium are small are not mentioned in the published data. (The minimum amount which merits inclusion changes from year to year.) A good discussion of the difficulties in obtaining complete data is Ziegler (1964, p. 122), which tells what supplementary steps must be taken to gather comprehensive broadcast data. Brown, Lessler and Weilbacher (1957, Chapter 12) discusses the problems in connection with both print and broadcast media.

The researcher who wants to know the total expenditure for one or more particular firms must compile the expenditures from each medium separately.

This is a great nuisance, and sometimes downright impossible, because one often cannot lay one's hands on all this data in even the best library. The totals were published, however, for the "100 largest" or "125 largest" advertisers each year, for many years by *Printers' Ink* (PI hereafter) which has recently become *Marketing/Communications*, and then by *AA* (e.g., August 26, 1968, the 13th year in the *AA* series. However, these data are most frustrating and can be misleading for several reasons. First, they are for firms and not for brands or products; second, the measured expenditures include some media expenditures one year and exclude the media the next year -- e.g., radio and farm magazines; third, the retrospective data exclude years for which the firm was not in the top 100 (or 25, or whatever). The recent *AA* run-downs also include data from company balance sheets where possible, and although this is helpful in estimating total advertising and sales, this kind of data is of far more interest to businessmen than to academic students of the advertising industry. (The data on the 100 or the 25 largest advertisers in *particular* media, carried in the same annual issue of *AA* as the "125 largest" is even more ubiquitous and even less useful.)

Advertising Expenditures by Industries

The academic researcher has two further difficulties: aggregating into industries, and getting data on past years.

For most industries no one organization pulls together the expenditures of the various firms, either in particular media or all together. There are certain welcome exceptions. *Advertising Age* carries data for automobiles (e.g., June 2, 1967, p. 42; September 18, 1967, p. 63; September 9, 1968, p. 106; January 2, 1966, p. 62; October 9, 1961, p. 70). The *Printers' Ink* "Battle of the Brands" series in 1964 and 1965 gives data for one or more years for razor blades, pet foods, insurance, hair products, frozen foods, gas and oil, cereals, detergents, coffee and business machines. Products sold in drugstores get the best coverage of all, compiled in *Drug Trade News* and carried in a June issue each year since 1956 (e.g., June 18, 1956, p. 24ff.). *Merchandising Week* is another useful source, with data on the various classes of major and minor appliances and consumer electronics goods (e.g., June 14, 1965, July 19, 1965; May 31, 1965). Each year Travel Research International publishes data on major public carriers and selected travel services in U.S. media. And the Magazine Advertising Bureau makes available the expenditures in various media of states and leading associations (e.g., Air Transport Association). All of the compilations contain data both by industry and by individual brand. Data for a few industries are broken down by media in *Survey of Current Business* and *Statistical Abstract*. The product breakdown of industrial advertising in business publications is compiled by American Business Press and published in *Industrial Marketing* (e.g., July, 1968, pp. 66-70). *National Advertising Investments* (page 12 of the January-June 1968 issue compares January-June 1968 vs. the same period in 1967; page 9 of the January-December 1968 issue compares January-December 1968 vs. 1967) has a table which summarizes industry class expenditures for the current and preceding year. (The Data include only expenditures of firms that spent at least $35,000 in the year.)

The researcher can get some idea about various industry expenditures from data published by the Internal Revenue Service in *Statistics of Income* and in the unpublished (but available on microfilm) *Source Book of*

Statistics of Income. *Advertising Age* presents these data yearly for many industries as ratio of sales. But again the definitions of the industries are not always what is desired. More troublesome still, the Internal Revenue Service definition of advertising expenditures, from tax returns, often produces estimates far from those obtained by checking services, and the differences are predictable neither in size nor even in direction.

Very detailed monthly and yearly linage data have been provided for many years on individual department store items -- e.g., towels -- by the *Neustadt Red Book of Seasonal Patterns,* sold by George Neustadt Statistical Advertising. Average prices for past years are also included.

National Total Advertising Expenditure -- U.S.

In light of these problems at the firm and industry levels, it is not surprising that the aggregate statistics for the United States are less than perfectly reliable or meaningful. The trouble is compounded by the lack of coverage for some media (which change from year to year), such as point-of-purchase advertising, and the casual coverage of others, such as direct mail, which is estimated from Post Office data on mail volume. The first regular compilation of aggregate data was by L. D. H. Weld under the auspices first of *Printers' Ink* and later the McCann-Erickson Advertising Agency. The handiest source for this series back to 1867 is *Historical Statistics of the U.S.*, and from 1958 onwards, the current *U.S. Statistical Abstract*. The problems of working with these data, plus some attempts to patch them up for particular purposes, have been discussed by other writers. The interested reader should consult Borden (1942, Appendices I and II), Backman (1967, pp. 161-167) and Blank (1963). Recently Yang has tried to improve the aggregate estimates by working with both the *purchases* of advertising as measured by the IRS tax data on reported advertising expenses and the *sales* of advertising, from IRS data on the advertising media, and then reconciling the two. These estimates are available back to 1947, and are discussed in Yang (1965).

Amounts of Advertising in the Various Media

We have discussed how data for the various media are used to estimate aggregate expenditures. However, these data are sometimes of interest for themselves. In addition to the sources already mentioned, both *Survey of Current Business* and the back of *PI (Marketing/Communications)* give the most current figures, including monthly estimates. *Business Statistics* goes into even more detail, giving both dollar figures and statistically adjusted indices. The latest edition should be considered the basic source for all aggregate and major-media expenditure data. Even more important, the descriptions of the sources of the data (found in the back of the book) are the most comprehensive and detailed listings available, past and present. This is where the researcher should begin his search for most advertising data.

The *Directory of Specialized Media,* prepared by Ted Bates and Company, New York, gives a standardized report -- description, geographic availability, audience data, costs, advertiser acceptance (users) and suppliers -- on a wide (and wild) variety of media -- spectaculars, skywriting, truck posters, handbills, matchbooks, shirtboards, milk containers, shopping carts, hotel TV, commuter-clock spectaculars, ethnic, outdoor, etc., etc.

Estimates for the "unmeasured" media are occasionally made by their own trade publications, e.g., *Premium Practices*, and often picked up by *AA* (e.g., September 23, 1968, p. 50 for premiums, p. 102 for trading stamps). The Transit Advertising Measurement Bureau publishes estimates for that medium and for advertisers in it each year. Aggregates are in *AA* (e.g., November 29, 1965). The *Census of Manufacturers* is another source of data on media receipts (e.g., the 1958 and 1963 data in *AA*, September 13, 1965). Linage data for middle-western newspapers are given monthly and retrospectively in the Inland Daily Press Association's *Bulletin*.

Sometimes, too, the researcher needs to know data for a specific media vehicle -- a television network or station, or a given magazine. Data on pages of advertising each month and cumulatively through the year in most consumer and farm magazines are a monthly feature of *Advertising Age*. So, too, are network billing figures originating from LNA-BAR. *Media Records* gives linage figures for specific newspapers. And *Editor and Publisher* publishes yearly advertising linage figures from more than 700 newspapers not covered by *Media Records*. (The May 24, 1969, issue gives these data as well as some republished *Media Records* data.) *Broadcasting Yearbook* contains data from the Federal Communications Commission on billings of television stations in a number of countries (e.g., 1969 edition, p. A-128ff.).

For individual business publications, *Industrial Marketing* carries a rich collection of information each year (e.g., July 1968, pp. 65-72). It gives annual data both in pages and in dollars, retrospective to 1955 and also 1950 and 1945; dollar volume by field, such as power and power utilities, for 1955 and also 1950 and 1945; and expenditures by Standard Industrial Classification groups in 1966 and 1967. Also, each issue gives total advertising volume in business publications monthly and cumulatively in terms of pages, and breaks the data down by types -- industrial, "class," and so on -- as well as by individual publications.

Estimates of total industrial advertising volume, made by American Business Press, appear in *Advertising Age* (e.g., June 20, 1966, p. 84).

A report on Yellow Pages advertising expenditure (a nontrivial half-billion dollars in 1963) appeared in *Media/Scope* (February 1964, pp. 48-51).

Advertising Rates and Circulation

The prices of advertising in the various domestic and foreign media are readily available through a number of sources. The Standard Rate & Data Series (SRDS) covers most of the major media. It provides comprehensive data on most vehicles in major media, including each type of offer made by the vehicle. (For an example, see the *New York Times* rate display shown on pp. 148-9.) Separate publications cover daily U.S. newspapers, weekly papers audited by ABC, spot and network radio and television, consumer magazines (including newspaper-distributed ones), farm publications, business publications, direct mail, and transit advertising. All broadcasting stations and print media which accept advertising on a large scale are included.

A microfilm record spanning forty-five years, of all media rates and data compiled and published by Standard Rate and Data Service, Inc., (SRDS) [is in] the Mass Communications History Center of the State Historical Society of Wisconsin. . . . The 730 reels of 16 mm. microfilm contain more than a million pages of information. . . . [The] Society will maintain a continuing record of media information by microfilming annually the January and July issues of all SRDS publications which will be donated to the Center by the firm [SHSW Press release].

The Audit Bureau of Circulation provides quarterly circulation figures for newspapers and magazines, and the American Research Bureau does so for broadcast media. Information about both rates and circulation is generally comprehensive but varies according to medium, as does the frequency; the series for major media like broadcasting, magazines and daily newspapers are issued bimonthly. International editions are available for Canada, England, France, Italy, Mexico and West Germany. However, because ABC audits so few weekly newspapers, coverage here is far from complete, but fortunately can be supplemented by the annual *National Directory of Weekly Newspapers* (American Newspaper Representatives, Inc., 404 Fifth Ave., New York). SRDS also has international editions for Canada, England, France, Italy, Mexico and West Germany.

Data on circulation and rate trends for some major media are collected from time to time by the Association of National Advertisers, Inc. (155 East 44th St., New York). *Magazine Circulation and Rate Trends* began in 1940 under the title *Magazine Circulation Analysis* and is continuous through 1967; *Business Publication Circulation and Rate Trends* began in 1946 and is continuous through 1966; *Newspaper Circulation and Rate Data* also began in 1946 and is continuous through 1968; *Television Circulation and Rate Trends* began in 1959 and is continuous through 1968; *Outdoor Advertising Circulation and Rate Trends* began in 1959 and is continuous through 1966. All five series are updated irregularly at periods varying from one to four years.

Further information on outdoor advertising rates can be found in three other references, each of which is annual: *Outdoor Rate and Market Service* (Outdoor Advertising Association of America, 24 West Erie St., Chicago); *Outdoor Buyers Guide*, sections II, IV and V (Institute of Outdoor Advertising, 625 Madison Ave., New York); and *Poster Rate Book* (v. 1-2), (National Outdoor Advertising Bureau, Inc., 711 Third Ave., New York). The first of these contains information on markets, districts, cities and towns, including coverage intensities, service costs and poster discount plans. The second tells outdoor rates and markets in Section II, discount plans in Section IV, and TAB circulation Audits in Section V. The third gives rates and allotments in over 10,000 U.S. towns and markets.

Circulation '68, published annually since 1962 by American Newspaper Markets, Inc., compiles data on the geographic distribution of newspapers, i.e., the circulation by newspapers and major magazines in various states, counties, and metropolitan areas.

Radio Programming Profile (BF Communication Services, Inc., 341 Madison Ave., New York) gives audience and program data for a number of radio stations. It is updated by quarterly supplements. Coverage includes only the AM stations in the country's top 100 markets.

The considerable amount of change in television prices from week to week is shown in *AA* (February 27, 1967, p. 20). In contrast, the prices listed for magazines and newspapers are fairly firm, but prices for large blocks of advertising in all media, and especially television, are subject to considerable haggling. Therefore published rates may be misleading. (For further price sources see Chapter 6 of original).

Advertising price data should support many kinds of studies of price behavior of interest to students of industrial organization, e.g., studies of prices in markets of different degrees of concentration and at different points on the business cycle. The course of advertising rates taken together is shown by indexes of media cost formerly in *Printers' Ink* and now in *Media/Scope*. A survey of such rates from 1940 to 1965 and an analysis of them is in Backman (1967, Appendix B).

Advertising Audience Breakdowns

The *audiences* of advertising media are of great importance for advertisers, and hence the media have spent a lot of money providing audience data. This topic is therefore a voluminous one. It will not be covered here because it is well covered at length elsewhere. A large number of studies are done for particular media and their markets. Many of the current ones are listed in *Advertising Age's* yearly "Market Data Section," e.g., May 20, 1968, the 21st such yearly section, while others are available upon application to the particular media.

Audiences are also measured more broadly by a variety of organizations for the various media. Rundowns are given in Burton (1959, Chapter 23) and Bogart (1967, Chapter 10 and p. 326). And all of Lucas and Britt's book (1963) is about this topic.

Consumer Market and Magazine Report (Daniel Starch and Staff, Boston Post Road and Beach Avenue, Mamaroneck, N.Y.), popularly known as the Starch Report, annually publishes a demographic and product rundown on readership for about 100 mass consumer magazines. W.R. Simmons and Associates Research, Inc. (235 East 42nd St., New York) has since 1963 published annual reports on readership of approximately 40 mass consumer magazines, each report differing somewhat from the others both in title and content. *Brand Rating Index* also supplies useful audience data of this sort.

Sales Data

Many advertising studies require sales data as well as advertising data. Industry and aggregate sales data require an entire bibliography of their own. Most information comes from government sources, including income-tax data and censuses of business. A magnificent source for the number of steel items of various types sold yearly (e.g., bicycles) is in *Steel* magazine (e.g., March 27, 1961), the 13th annual).

Data on sales of individual brands and firms are harder to come by. For those commodities that are taxed or licensed directly, e.g., cars, cigarettes, liquor and beer, data are sometimes available. *AA* usually manages to find and publish these, often picking them up from other trade sources. *PI* also has run a series of articles entitled "Battle of the Brands" (e.g., on cereal, June 24, 1966) which has compiled some brand-share data over time. Other sources are purchase panels, some of which are commercial (e.g., Nielsen, Pulse, Trendex and Sales-Area Marketing Inc.) while others are run by particular media in their own areas for the benefit of their advertisers (e.g., *Chicago Tribune, Milwaukee Journal*, and Scripps-Howard papers in various cities). Brand-usage studies are done for particular products in particular geographic and media cate-gories by the media. Many are listed as available in *AA*'s "Market Data Section" (e.g., May 20, 1968), but you are not likely to be able to get either a comprehensive picture of the present or a historical picture of the past from these piecemeal sources.

Miscellaneous

The above paragraphs have attended mostly to on-going series or still-current compilations. Now we shall briefly list some valuable special compilations, followed by a variety of statistics relating more or less tangentially to the advertising business.

1. Data on the billings of the largest agencies, both in the United States and world-wide, are compiled annually, by *AA* (e.g., February 26, 1968, p. 34 ff., and March 25, 1968, p. 45 ff.).

2. Billings of advertising agencies in each main city and for various types of agency activity are compiled from the Census Bureau and pub-lished in *AA* (e.g., August 2, 1965, pp. 79, 86, 115.)

3. *The World of Advertising* (*AA*, January 15, 1963) was a useful sup-plement of *AA* which pulled together many pieces of data found elsewhere.

4. Comparative advertising agency income accounts are published yearly in *AA* (e.g., August 12, 1968, p. 44), including a ten-year retrospective picture. The income accounts are also broken by size of agency (e.g., *AA*, Jan. 2, 1967; *World of Advertising*, Jan. 15, 1963, p. 50). The na-ture of agency operations is also illuminated by the balance sheets of publicly-owned agencies (e.g., Foote-Cone-Belding, in *AA*, August 2, 1965; Wells, Rich, Greene, in *AA*, August 26, 1968, p. 254; Grey, in *AA*, August 30, 1965, p. 32). Stock prices of agencies and other advertising-related businesses are published weekly in the back of *AA*.

5. Crum (1927) compiled enormous amounts of data up to the 1920s on various categories of newspaper advertising. Most of it does not seem to be very useful today, however.

6. Advertising agency salaries are released from time to time by one or another employment agency catering to the advertising industry, and reported in *AA* (e.g., by Jack Baxter, *AA* Supplement, *World of Advertising*, January 15, 1963, p. 387).

7. *Advertisers' Guide to Marketing* was from 1954 to 1965 a most valu-able annual supplement of *PI*, republishing data published earlier in the year in *PI*. But as *PI* began going downhill, both generally and from the point of view of statistical publication, the annual also began to carry less and less information of value.

8. *AA* is a wonderful trade journal and is certainly a great boon to the researcher, publishing most of the data of value that are available anywhere which do not require too much space. Unfortunately, the index is not consistently informative throughout its history.

9. *Television Factbook* yearly presents various data pertaining to television, including (in the 1968-69 issue):

a) Television ownership. Broken by 1967 market geography and by color, multiset, UHF (pp. 21a, ff.); by size rank (pp. 40a, ff.), by state and countries (pp. 65a, ff. 1946-68, pp. 56a-57a).

b) Television station aggregate financial data, 1946-66 (pp. 44a). By market, 1961-66 (pp. 45a, ff.).

c) CATV subscribers, by market (p. 57a).

d) TV time sales, 1949-66 (pp. 55a).

e) TV set production and sales, 1946-67 (pp. 55a, 58a, 62a); tube sales, 1947-67 (p. 59a); sales to dealers (pp. 609, 61a).

10. The number of television sets in use in various countries in the world is picked up from the USIA and other sources by *AA* (e.g., May 31, 1965, p. 69, and June 26, 1967).

11. Radio data may be found in *Television Factbook*, too:

a) Radio set production, 1922-1967 (p. 58a); sales (p. 62a).

b) Radio station aggregate financial data, 1946-66 (p. 54a).

12. The percentages of sales spent in 1955 for advertising in eight media for 521 major companies, summarized into industries (e.g., gasoline and oil), are in a *Printers' Ink* publication (1957, pp. 53-61).

13. *Standard Directory of Advertising Agencies* (National Register Publishing Co., 5201 Old Orchard Road, Skokie, Ill.), an annual, lists all agencies in the United States, with top personnel, and accounts carried, and in some cases approximate billings. This is especially useful for charting the development of an agency. (To find out which agency a given company uses, consult a companion volume mentioned previously, *Standard Directory of Advertising*.)

REFERENCES

1. Abrams, Mark, "Statistics of Advertising," *Journal of the Royal Statistical Society*, 1952, 115 (pt. 2), pp. 258-264.

2. Backman, Jules, *Advertising and Competition*, New York: New York University Press, 1967.

3. Blank, David M., "A Note on the Golden Age of Advertising," *Journal of Business*, Vol. 36, (January 1963), pp. 33-38.

4. Blum, Eleanor, *Reference Books in the Mass Media*, Urbana: University of Illinois Press, 1963.

5. Bogart, Leo, *Strategy in Advertising*, New York: Harcour, Brace & World, 1967.

6. Borden, Neil Hopper, *The Economic Effects of Advertising*, Chicago: Irwin, 1942.

7. Brown, Lyndon Osmond, R. S. Lessler and W. M. Weilbacher, *Advertising Media: Creative Planning in Media Selection*, New York: Ronald, 1957.

8. Burton, Philip Ward, *The Profitable Science of Making Media Work*, New London: Printers' Ink, 1959.

9. Crum, William Leonard, *Advertising Fluctuations: Seasonal and Cyclical*, Chicago: Shaw, 1927.

10. Daley, James B., Jr., "Services that Measure Competitive Advertising Expenditures," *Media/Scope*, Vol. 7, (May 1963), pp. 57-58, 62-66.

11. Lucas, Darrell Blaine, and Steuart H. Britt, *Measuring Advertising Effectiveness*, New York: McGraw-Hill, 1963.

12. Yang, Charles Yneu, "Variations in the Cyclical Behavior of Advertising," *Journal of Marketing*, Vol. 28, No. 2 (April 1964), pp. 25-30.

13. _____, "Input-Output Concept is Basis of Improved Estimates on Advertising Expenditures in the U.S.," *Advertising Age*, Vol. 36 (March 1965), pp. 79-84.

14. Ziegler, Isabel, "Procuring Competitive Information," *Media/Scope*, Vol. 8, (December 1964), p. 122.

2.
COMMERCIAL AND PROFESSIONAL SOURCES OF DATA FOR ADVERTISING RESEARCH

Margaret A. Muller

This essay will attempt to aid historians and other scholars and business researchers in identifying the major U.S. commercial, trade and professional data sources for in depth advertising and media research. Some of the sources in this chapter duplicate those presented in the previous chapter, "Some Sources of Economic Data in Advertising" by Julian L. Simon. They are included here to supplement, update and clarify what is currently available, because new sources have come into existence and others have ceased publication since 1970.

This essay will cover general advertising directories and indexes; media research sources; print advertising readership; television commercial research sources; advertising campaign searches; advertising expenditure sources; audience and intermedia analysis studies; computer media analysis and other specialized research services.

In order to make this essay useful to researchers, addresses, telephone numbers, and approximate costs have been included where possible. The reader may also wish to consult a recent and broader bibliographic survey "Advertising Information Sources," by M. Balachandran in *RSR (Reference Services Review)*, Vol. 5, No.2, April/June, 1977, p.27-32 which covers ninety-six sources in some detail.

General Advertising Research Sources

Basic to any discussion of advertising sources and useful as a starting point for many historical searches is the *Standard Directory of Advertisers* and the *Standard Directory of Advertising Agencies*, more commonly known to those in the ad business as the "Advertiser Red Book" and

The author is Assistant Librarian, Information Center, J. Walter Thompson Company, 875 N. Michigan Avenue, Chicago, Illinois 60611. The author wishes to thank Robert Warrens, Vice President, Associate Media Director, Media Information and Support, J. Walter Thompson Co. for providing background materials and computer systems information.

"Agency Red Book" respectively. Published since 1916 the directories can
be useful in tracking down agency changes, doing tradename searches, determining when a new product was introduced, analyzing agency organizational developments, etc. Larger agency libraries do keep extensive back
files and the publisher will do a retrospective search for a fee. The
directories cover over 17,000 advertisers who make annual appropriations
for national advertising campaigns listing their personnel, address, products, tradenames, agency, account executive, budget appropriations, advertising media used and over 4,000 advertising agencies, listing their
estimated billings, top personnel by title, accounts by office, along
with a geographical agency index, a media buying service and sales promotion agency section, and recently a "Special Market Index" listing agencies by specialization -- Black, Spanish, financial, direct response, etc.

The *Standard Directory of Advertisers* (Classified Edition) is arranged
by fifty-two product classifications and is published annually in April
with nine monthly cumulative supplements and a pocket-sized *Geographical
Index* for $127. A complete Geographical Edition is also published annu-
ally in August and is arranged by state and city. A weekly *Ad Change*
bulletin is also available for $50. The *Standard Directory of Adverti-
sing Agencies* is published three times a year (February, June and October) with nine monthly updates for $97. Contact the National Register
Publishing Company, Inc., 5201 Old Orchard Road, Skokie, Illinois 60077,
312-966-8500 for additional information.

For data on regional and smaller advertiser companies and agencies,
the National Register Publishing Company also publishes for the Chicago
area only *The Chicago Metro Book; Eight County Chicago Area* covering
3,500 companies with significant advertising budgets and over 300 advertising agencies. Also the various special issues published by A/S/M
Communications Inc. in *ANNY, SAM,* and *Mac* are useful. For example, *SAM
(Serving Advertising in the Midwest),* SAM Publications, 435 N. Michigan
Avenue, Chicago, Illinois 60611, 312-467-6500 issues a "Client/Agency
Review" annually, *MAC (Western Advertising News),* 6565 Sunset Blvd., Los
Angeles, California 90028, 212-465-2173 publishes an "Annual Budget Re-
port of Western Advertising," and "Agency/Client Directory," and *ANNY
(Advertising News of New York),* 230 Park Avenue, New York, New York 10017,
212-661-8080 has a "Year End Review" and a "Mid-Year Review."

In the past, most general historical literature searches for advertising research questions were begun by consulting the *Business Periodicals
Index* (formerly *Industrial Arts Index*). Currently, however, there are
several specialized indexes available. Crain Communications did publish
a useful paperbound *Advertising Age Editorial Index* annually from 1973
to 1975, but it ceased publications in 1976. Since 1977 their "Cite
Service" is offered to companies and agencies on a yearly fee basis de-
pending on the size of the company (approximately $150 to $250 yearly).
No student or university fee structures are available, but one time
limited searches can be arranged for about $25 plus photocopying costs.
Advertising Age is indexed in depth and retrieved by means of microfiche
(1976 to present); but historical searches are possible through clip
files back to 1949. Another journal, *Crain's Chicago Business* which began publication in 1978 will also be included in the "Cite Service" soon.
For further details contact Cite Service Department, Crain Communications
Inc., 740 Rush Street, Chicago, Illinois 60611, 312-649-5328 or 5329.
Predicasts Inc.'s *F & S Index of Corporations and Industries* is indexed

by company and product SIC codes (Standard Industrial Classifications). The SIC code for advertising is 7310000. Another lesser known source is the *Topicator; Classified Guide to Advertising/Communications/Marketing Press* which has been published annually since 1965 to present by Thompson Bureau, 5395 South Miller Street, Littleton, Colorado 80123, 303-973-23 37, ($50). Individual annual indexes in journals are also useful in searching for specific information, e.g. *Broadcasting* produces a detailed separate annual index and the *Journal of Advertising Research* has an annual index in the December issue.

Computerized on-line bibliographic data bases (currently there are more than 100 available) can be another extremely useful means of quickly doing retrospective searches on specific advertising research questions. Some of the more important on-line data bases that cover advertising and related journals are:

Data Base	Coverage	Approximate connect costs depending on vendor used
F & S Indexes (Predicasts)	Jan., 1972 -	$90/hour
Prompt (Predicasts)	Jan., 1972 -	$90/hour
PTS Weekly (Predicasts	Current month	$90/hour
Inform (Abstracted Business Information)	August, 1971 -	$40-$65/hour
Management Contents	September, 1975	$35-$65/hour
Information Bank (New York Times)	Jan., 1969 -	$90/hour
Magazine Index	July, 1977 -	$45/hour

The American Association of Advertising Agencies' Member Information Service recently began offering their members access to on-line data bases charging for computer and communication time.

Other useful basic sources include two fairly recent special issues published by *Advertising Age: The New World of Advertising* (November 21, 1973) discusses topics such as how the advertising business works covering agencies, advertising media, associations, regulations, etc., and *How It Was In Advertising: 1776-1976* (April 19, 1976) which contains much historical data as well as reproductions of ads. Also the annual conference proceedings from advertising associations are very good sources for unpublished research, e.g., The Advertising Research Foundation, 3 East 54th Street, New York, New York 10022, 212-751-5656, annually publishes conference proceedings, the Association of National Advertisers, 155 E. 44th Street, New York, New York 10017, 212-697-5950, issues conference workshop papers, the American Association of Advertising Agencies, 200 Park Avenue, New York, New York 10017, 212-682-2500 periodically releases papers presented at its various regional and annual conferences,

the American Academy of Advertising, c/o Dept. of Advertising, Michigan
State University, East Lansing, Michigan 48224 publishes annually its
conference proceedings.

Media Research Sources

A very useful starting point for many media research questions is a
small pamphlet recently published by Newsweek Inc. entitled *Media Research
Index: 1950-1977* which lists and describes the major primary and syndicated media research studies 1950 to 1977. Reports are listed by year
and identified by category -- general, intermedia, magazine, newspapers,
radio, television. Also two indexes list studies chronologically by
media category and alphabetically by author or source of study. It is
available gratis from Newsweek Inc., 444 Madison Avenue, New York, New
York 10022, 212-350-2000. Another recent comprehensive source listing
over 7,000 advertising research studies, journal articles, books,
conference proceedings, in-house reports papers, etc., is *Evaluating
Advertising; A Bibliography of the Communications Process,* by Benjamin
Lipstein and William J. McGuire published by the Advertising Research
Foundation (ARF), 1978, 362p., $65 for members and $95 for non-members.
Covering research done during the past fifteen years, the sources are
organized under 270 subject categories and a topical index pertaining to
testing advertising copy, primarily television. Many of the items included are accompanied by abstracts giving brief summaries of the study
findings. For studies prior to 1960, the ARF's *Sources of Published
Advertising Research* by Thornton C. Lockwood and Charles Raymond, 1960,
65p. (out of print) should be consulted. Also useful are two bibliographic articles by Neil Bruce Holbert: "Key Articles in Advertising
Research (1960-1971)" in the *Journal of Advertising Research,* Vol.12,
No.5, October, 1972, p.5-13 and "More Key Articles in Advertising Research (1972-1976) in the *Journal of Advertising Research,* Vol.17, No.4,
August, 1977, p.33-42.

Two annotated bibliographies of articles, speeches and books published
by the ARF cover specialized areas: *Measuring Payout; An Annotated Bibliography On the Dollar Effectiveness of Advertising* (1965-1972), 1973,
39p. $5.00 and *Copy Testing; An Annotated Bibliography* (1960-1972), 1972,
46p. $5.00 covers copy content, timing and frequency effects, and relation
to position, time and frequency effects.

The various advertising media and associations also do special intermedia effectiveness studies frequently employing outside research companies such as Alfred Politz and Audits and Surveys. For example, Newsweek, Inc. recently released "Eyes On; A Comparison of Television Commercial Audience With Magazine Advertising Page Audience" conducted by
Audits and Surveys. However, caution must be used with many of these
types of studies because of possible self-interest bias. Also a new
book *The Media Book* edited by Ed Papazian (152 East 52nd Street, New
York, New York 10022, $75) looks promising. It contains four basic sec-
tions on magazine, newspaper, television and radio research and a special
section comparing the four media directly both quantitatively and quali-
tatively analyzing landmark studies of the past two decades.

Print Advertising Readership

An area frequently asked about is the important topic of print advertisement readership -- how is the readership of an ad influenced by its size, color, shape, position, how often should an ad be repeated, etc. Sources in this area are dated, but two that are useful for business and trade journals are the research reports periodically published by McGraw-Hill and Cahners. The *Laboratory of Advertising Performance (Lap)*, McGraw-Hill Publishing Company, 1221 Avenue of the Americas, New York, New York 10020, 212-997-3608, covers such topics as magazine readership, coverage and circulation; the elements of advertising (color, repetition, frequency, size, bleed, continuity, position, copy, headline, left and right hand pages; measurements of advertising effectiveness (inquiries, seasonal ads); and business and industrial advertising research. *Cahners Advertising Research Reports*, Cahners Publishing Company, 221 Columbus Avenue, Boston, Massachusetts 02116, 212-536-7780, is similar to *LAP* in setup and covers many of the same type of subjects. For consumer magazines and newspapers, *Starch Tested Copy*, a newsletter which was published periodically from 1937 to 1968 by Daniel Starch & Staff (now called Starch INRA Hooper, Inc., 566 E. Boston Post Road, Mamaroneck, New York 10543, 914-698-0800), covered topics such as -- how does repetition of advertisements affect readership, is preferred position worth it, why people read ads through, readership of multi-gate and gatefold ads, etc. Also the book, *Measuring Advertising Readership and Results* by Daniel Starch (McGraw-Hill, 1966, 270p.), is a basic and valuable reference source. Some of the subjects covered include readership and thickness of issues, readership and position, readership of advertisements in color, size, shape, layout, inherent human interests, repetition, measuring advertising effects, etc. Starch INRA Hooper publishes annually *Adnorms Report* which gives readership averages by publication, size of ad, color and type of products for ads "Starched" during the previous two years. Also Available on a rental basis is their *Ad-Files Data Bank* of over two million ads "Starched" since 1937. Meldrum & Fewsmith Inc., 1220 Huron Road, Cleveland, Ohio 44115, periodically publishes a *Readership Digest* which provides concise information on all 32 major readership services (e.g., Starch, Readex).

Television Commercial Research

Some of the major research companies that are involved in pretesting and on-air testing of television commercials periodically release overall research findings. For example, Burke Marketing Research Inc., 1529 Madison Rd., Cincinnati, Ohio 45206, 513-961-8000 issues a loose-leaf binder of on-air research results -- *Related Recall Norms for Day-After Recall Tests of Television Commercials*. Included are charts on effectiveness of commercial length, testing among children, use of music, testing daytime programs, commercials showing competitive brands, cartoon vs. live action, testimonials, humor, etc. Another service, TeleResearch Inc., 5455 Wilshire Blvd., Los Angeles, California 90036, 213-937-2551 has published a newsletter, *Tele/Scope*, since 1967 covering topics such as research on the pros and cons of pretesting advertising in rough form, how do consumers feel about today's typical commercial, etc. Recently McCollum/Spielmen/&Co., Inc., 235 Great Neck Rd., Great Neck, New York 11021 announced their intention of issuing a bimonthly newsletter, *TOP-LINE*, covering such topics as use of celebrity/presenters, is music a plus, do integrated commercials work?

Advertising Campaign Searches

Many advertising agency libraries maintain historical files of print

ads on their client's products as well as competitive brands, and some
are involved in ordering television storyboards and kinescopes of television commercials. One useful service for locating examples of print
advertisements is the monthly *Advertisers Page Index* published by Leading National Advertisers Inc., Box 525, Norwalk, Connecticut 06856, 203-
838-4396 and *PIB Magazine Advertising Analysis*, Publisher's Information
Bureau Inc., 575 Lexington Avenue, New York, New York 10022, 212-PL2-00
55, which covers 104 consumer magazines and national newspaper supplements. For each brand a monthly advertising schedule is provided with
issue date and page number of ad, indication of regional placement, and
space description (size, color). A service that provides tearsheets of
ads in newspapers is the Advertising Checking Bureau, Inc., 434 South
Wabash Avenue, Chicago, Illinois 60605, 312-922-2841. Photoboards, kinescopes, color videocassetes of television commercials and radio commercials can be ordered from companies such as Radio TV Reports, Inc., 41
East 42nd Street, New York, New York 10017, 212-697-5100.

Advertising Expenditure Reports

   Collections of advertising expenditure reporting services are expensive
and normally are maintained by the advertising agency's media research
department. Due to the proprietary nature of the information they provide, these detailed reports usually are unavailable to outside researchers. However, much of this data is summarized and reproduced in many of
the media trade journals. *Media Decisions* (Decisions Publications Inc.,
342 Madison Avenue, New York, New York 10017, 212-953-1888) has published
annually since 1972 in the July issue a "Directory of Top 200 Advertised
Brands," listing advertising expenditures in eight media and advertiser/
agency decision makers for each brand. Also each issue usually has a
"Brand Report" analysis of advertising expenditures for a specific brand,
consumer product or service, e.g., beer, airlines. A relatively new
journal, *Marketing Communications* (not to be confused with *Printer's Ink*
and *Marketing/Communications)* published by United Business Publications
Inc., 475 Park Avenue South, New York, New York 10016 issued in June,
1978 its first annual "The Big Spenders" which is a roundup of the top
225 brands, their marketing teams and agencies; however no expenditures
are provided. *Advertising Age* publishes annually many useful statistics
such as:

* "Comparison of Advertising Volume of Major Media, 1935--" (date of
  issue varies). Compiled by McCann-Erickson, Inc. and *Advertising
  Age*.

* "The Top 100 Leading National Advertisers" (August). Tabulates
  advertising expenditures by company by nine media.

* "Advertising Expenditures As a Percent of Sales" (by company)
  (August).

* "Estimates of Average Advertising to Sales and Advertising to Gross
  Profit Margin by Industry" (September). Based on annual study by
  Schonfeld & Associates Inc., 120 S. La Salle St., Chicago, Ill.
  60603, $225. Previous studies in *Advertising Age* were based on
  Internal Revenue Service unpublished data.

* "Newspaper Advertising Expenditures for 30 Top Markets" (June).

Based on Media Records Inc. data arranged by product and brand.

* "Annual Compilation of Agency Data" (March). U.S. agency profiles ranked by size, gross income, billings.

* "Annual Survey of Foreign Agencies" (April). Foreign agency profiles, gross income, billings.

* *Advertising Age Europe* periodically reports foreign advertising expenditures.

Editor and Publisher, 575 Lexington Avenue, New York, New York 10022 annually publishes in the May issue "Total Advertising Lineage in 1,113 Newspapers". Statistics are presented by category (retail, general, automotive, financial, and classified). The *Public Relations Journal*, Public Relations Society of America, 845 Third Avenue, New York, New York 10022, annually reports in the November issue corporate advertising expenditures. Both *Broadcasting*, Broadcasting Publications Inc., 1735 De Sales St., N.W., Washington, D.C. and *Television/Radio Age*, Television Educational Corp., 1270 Avenue of the Americas, New York, New York 10020 periodically compile advertising expenditure reports for television and radio and annually report FCC figures for radio and television revenue with market by market breakouts. *Incentive Marketing*, Hartman Communications Inc., 633 Third Avenue, New York, New York 10017 annually reports in its December "Facts Issue" estimates of incentive usage expenditures (e.g., coupons, sweepstakes, contests, trading stamps, premiums). Many of the trade journals periodically report advertising expenditures for specific product categories with brand expenditure breakouts, for example, *Product Marketing*, Charleson Publishing Co., 124 E. 40th Street, New York, New York 10016, annually publishes in the September issue advertising expenditures for major health and beauty aids manufacturers and *Advertising Age*, for example, annually reports in October "Ad Costs for Beer, Ales, Malt Liquor."

Competitive advertising reports do have an important use in the development of a brand's budget strategy and planning and it is also important to realize that the reports represent reasonable approximations of actual expenditures; errors in the reporting procedures of the various services and coverage limitations have to be taken into consideration. Currently the standard industry sources are as follows. *World Advertising Expenditures* is available annually since 1966 and covers total advertising expenditures for over eighty countries and has detailed media breakdowns for over 70 countries. The report is sponsored by the International Advertising Association and Starch INRA Hooper and is published by Starch for $50. Total U.S. advertising expenditures are reported in the Leading National Advertisers, Inc. (LNA) annual *Ad $ Summary* reports which lists expenditures for all brands (approximately 24,000) that were active in six major media (consumer magazines, national newspaper supplements, network and spot television, network radio and outdoor) for the top 1,000 companies by media and for the top ten brands in each of 243 product categories. The approximate cost of this summary is $75 from LNA, 347 Madison Avenue, New York, New York 10017, 212-490-9155. More detailed reports are available quarterly ($125 per year) with year-to-date totals as part of LNA's Multi-Media Report Service, for example, *Company/Brand $* and *Class/Brand $*. All active brands in each product classification are listed with advertising expenditures by media for companies and brands spending over $25,000 a year.

Newspaper advertising expenditures are reported quarterly with year-to-date totals in *Media Records National Brand Investments* by Media Records Inc., 370 Seventh Avenue, New York, New York 10001, 212-736-7490. It is based on a page-by-page analysis of advertising appearing in approximately 242 daily and Sunday newspapers published in about 86 cities. Statistics represent actual lineage measured and converted to dollar estimates by product and brand, by city and by newspaper.

Consumer magazines and national newspaper supplements are provided by Publishers Information Bureau, Inc.'s *PIB Magazine Advertising Analysis*. Reports are monthly with year-to-date summaries based on a page-by-page analysis of 104 magazine and newspaper supplements giving advertising schedules, detailing space used and dollar expenditure by product classification, parent company and brand, and class totals by magazines, newspaper supplements and media totals. Also available is the *LNA Regional Advertising Service* which analyzes sectional and geographical split-run advertising appearing in 35 consumer magazines. LNA also publishes the *LNA Agency Report* and *Agency Supplement Report: Advertising Agency Billings in Twenty-Three Magazines* which gives detailed billings by brand and company for the top 25 agencies and total billings for the top 50 agencies, *LNA Magazine Ranking Report* which ranks the leading fifteen magazines by dollar volume and pages within product classes, and *Magazine Totals by Parent Company*.

For business and trade journals, the American Business Press, Inc., 205 E. 42nd Street, New York, New York 10017 annually reports dollar investment of about 1600 companies. Although not published in 1977, Media Records did publish the *Media Records Report of Business Publications Advertising* semi-annually which was a compilation of advertising appearing in approximately 700 business publications representing 116 publishing classifications. Information is listed alphabetically by advertiser company giving the publications schedule, number of insertions run, total space run and dollar expenditures. Farm publications expenditures are reported annually by the Agricultural Marketing Information Service (AGRICOM).

Network television expenditures are reported and estimated by *Broadcast Advertisers Report* (BAR), 500 Fifth Avenue, New York, New York 10036, 212-221-2630. Reports are available weekly and monthly with quarterly and year-to-date summaries showing brand, product, company, daypart, day schedule, length of commercial and program used. National spot television expenditure data is similar to BAR and reported by Broadcast Advertisers Report's *BARCUME*. It is available monthly with quarterly and year-to date summaries by individual market for 75 top television markets. Another report *BARCUME Retail/Local Spot TV* includes national and regional chain stores and other retail, local services, and merchants' expenditures.

Network radio expenditures are also reported by BAR based on continuous monitoring by individuals using audio magnetic tape recordings of three networks (ABC, CBS, NBC) and is available weekly and monthly with quarterly summaried and year-to-date totals. Spot radio expenditures are estimated by *Radio Expenditure Reports* (RER), 200 Palmer Avenue, Larchmont, New York 10533, 914-834-0833, based on information from stations and station representatives (about 1,000 in the 150 top markets) through the joint efforts of RER and the Radio Advertising Bureau. Projected expenditures are reported quarterly.

Outdoor expenditures are projected by *LNA Outdoor Advertising Expenditures* from reports submitted by participating plant operators and prepared in cooperation with the Outdoor Advertising Association of America. Expenditures are given for product, company, and brand by market quarterly with year-to-date summaries.

Audience Analysis - Circulation and Rates

Important to the advertising media planning and selection process is the analyzing of audience data and costs. As a starting point, several advertising agencies provide extimating guides, e.g., J. Walter Thompson Company's Media Department, 420 Lexington Avenue, New York, New York 10017, 212-867-1000, annually published a brochure, *Media Information United States*. A similar digest is also available for European media. *Media Decisions* annually publishes in its August issue a "Media Cost Survey" and "Cost Trends" for nine media estimated by J. Walter Thompson's Media Department. *Advertising Age* annually publishes estimates of media costs and price trends by J. Coen of McCann-Erickson, Inc. The Association of National Advertisers (ANA), 155 E. 44th Street, New York, New York publishes two reports: *Magazine Circulation and Rate Trends* ($35) is an annual compilation of trends since 1940 covering circulation, rates and costs-per-thousand of leading consumer magazines and *ANA Newspaper Local Rate Card Service* ($200) is issued annually with supplements and is a compilation of over 1,500 daily and Sunday newspaper local rate cards.

The *Media Market Guide* published by Conceptual Dynamics Inc., 322 East 50th Street, New York, New York 10022,212-0832-7170 is divided into two volumes: *Top 100 Marketing Areas* (Spring, Summer, Fall) and *Markets 101 Down* (annual) for $55 each. Market areas are described and analyzed providing data on television set counts, color television penetration, CATV penetration, distributions of households by income, average daily temperature, listings of television and radio stations, newspapers, outdoor plants, national magazines with locally available editions, and selected city magazines. Detailed analysis indicates cost for typical ad units, average audience levels and amount of money required to attain a percentage point of coverage (cost per rating point) for each media type and selected dayparts for broadcast media.

Advertising circulation and rates are regularly compiled by Standard Rate and Data Service, Inc. (SRDS), 5201 Old Orchard Road, Skokie, Illinois 6077, 312-966-8500. The various volumes listed below include such information as publisher's statement of editorial purpose, ad rates, contract and copy regulations, mechanical requirements, issuance and closing dates, circulation statements, personnel, discounts, and other specifications.

Business Publications Rates and Data (weekly, monthly) $89.
Consumer Magazine and Farm Publication Rates and Data (weekly, monthly) $76.
Direct Mail List Rates and Data (semiannually) $65.
Newspaper Rates and Data and *Newspaper Circulation Analysis* (August

issue) (weekly, monthly) $80.
Spot Television Rates and Data (weekly, monthly) $79.
Network Rates and Data (bimonthly) $15.
Spot Radio Rates and Data (weekly, monthly) $88.
Spot Radio Small Markets Edition (semiannually) $28.
Transit Advertising Rates and Data (quarterly) $20.
Print Media Production Data (quarterly) $49.
Community Publications Rates and Data (semiannually) $12.
Canadian Advertising Rates and Data (monthly) $86.

Also available are international editions for England, France, Italy,
Mexico, West Germany, Austria, and Switzerland ranging in price from $35
to $170.

The Audit Bureau of Circulations (ABC), 123 North Wacker Drive, Chicago,
Illinois 60606, 312-236-7994, audits the circulation records of member
publishers for U.S. and Canadian magazines and newspapers. The *ABC
Publisher's Statements and Audit Reports* cover newspapers, farm publications, consumer magazines, and business publications. Summary circulation figures are reported quarterly in the *ABC FAS-FAX Reports*. Available in computer printout format is the *Newspaper Audience Report* compiled
from the ABC Data Bank, an in-house computer system which provides circulation data as well as population and household statistics. Recently
added to the reports are audience demographics (age breakouts, education,
household income, size of households, marital status, and race). Business publications are audited by Business Publications Audit of Circulation Inc., 360 Park Avenue South, New York, New York 10010, 212-532-6880.

Circulation, published annually since 1962 by American Newspaper Markets, Inc., P.O. Box 182, Northfield, Illinois 60093, 312-446-6200, is a
comprehensive print analysis shown circulation and penetration data in
every U.S. country and metro area and in television viewing areas for
every U.S. county and metro area and in television viewing areas for
every U.S. and Sunday newspaper, five national newspaper supplements and
24 leading magazines. Also useful is the annual *Ayer Directory of Publications,* Ayer Press, 210 West Washington Square, Philadelphia, Pa. 181
06, $56, which covers newspapers, magazines (consumer, farm, trade) pro-
viding both rates and circulation data.

For minority media planning the annual *Minority Group Media Guide USA*
($45) is published by Directories International, Inc., 1718 Sherman Ave-
nue, Evanston, Illinois, 312-491-0019. The directory lists foreign language, religious and black media (print, radio and television) providing
rates, circulation and other specifications. The various editions cited
earlier by Standard Rate and Data Service include special sections on
minority media. College newspaper information is published annually in
National Rate Book and College Newspaper Directory by CASS Student
Advertising, Inc., 6330 N. Pulaski Road, Chicago, Illinois 60646, 312-
286-6050 providing line rate, printing process, frequency, and enrollment
statistics.

For international media buying, Directories International also publishes *Media Guide International* annually for $210 covering advertising rates
and data for newspapers, news magazines, airline/inflight magazines, and
business/professional publications worldwide.

43

Useful for planning the placement of an ad in a consumer magazine is Hall's Magazine Editorial Reports (formerly Lloyd Hall) published by the R. Russell Hall Company, 180 West Putnam Avenue, Greenwich, Connecticut 06830, 203-661-0190. Issued monthly with year-to-date totals, it analyzes the editorial content of 55 consumer magazines, measuring editorial lineage by sixteen reader-interest areas, e.g., national affairs, beauty and grooming, food, health, building, etc.

For outdoor media, the Institute of Outdoor Advertising, the marketing division of the Outdoor Advertising Association of America, 485 Lexington Avenue, New York, New York 10017, 212-986-5920, has a computer reporting service, *Audiences Market by Market for Outdoor* which provides rates, reach and frequency, gross impressions, GRP's (gross rating points), cost per thousand, etc., by market and also annually publishes a *Buyers Guide to Outdoor Advertising,* providing rate information by city.

Audience Analysis - Measurement Services

Television audiences are measured by two services: Arbitron and A.C. Nielsen. The Arbitron Company, (formerly American Research Bureau - ARB), 1350 Avenue of the Americas, New York, New York 10019, 212-262-5032, publishes *ARBITRON Television Network Program Analysis and Syndicated Program Analysis Audience Estimates* providing for ADI (Areas of Dominant Influence) markets household audience ratings, households reached and demographic ratings. Other detailed reports that are issued include, for example, *ARBITRON Television USA - Day Part Audience Summary, ARBITRON Television - Market Summary Audience Estimates in ARBITRON Markets* (each volume covering an individual market area), *ARBITRON Television Markets and Rankings Guide (TMA),* and *ARBITRON Television CATV Coverage.* Also Available are local market television and radio reports and station county coverage reports. The A.C. Nielsen Company, 1290 Avenue of the Americas, New York, New York 10019, 212-956-2500, publishes *Nielsen Station Index (NSI)* reports, e.g., *Viewers in Profile (VIP)* measures television station audiences in over 200 local markets; *Network Programs by DMA* (Designated Market Area); *DMA Test Market Profiles, Report on Syndicated Programs, DMA CATV Audience Distribution Report, Weekly Preview Report* and other specialized reports. The *Nielsen Television Index (NTI)* provides continuing estimates of television viewing and nationally sponsored network program audiences and national ratings 52 weeks per year. Reports include the *National Audience Demographics Report, Daily Ratings, Fast National* and *Multi-Network Area Ratings, Cost/1000 Estimates* and *Program and Brand Cumulative Audiences.* A summary of television audience measurement trends are available annually in a brochure entitled, *Television..,* from A.C. Nielsen's Media Research Services Group.

Since the collapse of *Trendex* reports in 1974 and *Pulse* reports in 1977, radio audiences are currently measured by *Arbitorn's Radio Service* and *RADAR.* Arbitron measures radio network listening in its *ARBITRON Radio Nationwide Audience Estimates.* Statistical Research Inc., 111 Prospect Street, Westfield, New Jersey 70980, 201-654-4000, publishes *Radio's All Dimension Audience Research (RADAR)* reporting radio usage, demographics and estimating audiences for all AM and FM radio stations and network audiences to cleared programs including commercial exposures. Other program oriented services in the field are *Media Trends* and *Media-Stat* issued by Media Statistics, 8120 Fenton Street, Silver Spring, Maryland 20910, 301-588-4878 and *Radio Index* reports. Newer radio audience

measurements are being developed by Burke Broadcast Research, Inc., 120
E. 56th Street, New York, New York 10022, 212-371-6090 and Audits & Surveys (A&S Trac-7), 1 Park Avenue, New York, New York 10016, 212-689-9400
and *RAM (Radio Audience Measurement)*, RAM Research, P.O. Box 20107, El
Cajon, California 92021, 714-0247. Both Burke and Audits & Surveys in-
tend to offer competitive media and product usage data in addition to
basic radio audience measures. Arbitron also plans to expand its service by cross indexing radio listening with product usage, demographics
and respondents' reading and viewing patterns. A summary of radio audience data is reported annually in a brochure, *Radio Facts*, which is a-
vailable from the Radio Advertising Bureau, 485 Lexington Avenue, New
York, New York 10017, 212-599-6666.

S&MM (Sales Marketing Management), Bill Publications, 633 Third Avenue,
New York, New York 10017, has published annually since 1964 its *Annual
Survey of Newspaper and Television Markets* (usually in its September or
October issues as Part II of the *Survey of Buying Power*). For newspaper
markets and television markets *(ADI)*, it provides population and household statistics, effective buying income, and retail sales figures by
type of outlet and also ranks the 50 largest newspaper and television
markets by population.

Other useful broadcasting directories that could be used in conjunction
with audience analysis are: *Broadcasting Yearbook* ($37) and *Cable Source-
book* ($20) published annually by Broadcasting Publications Inc., 1735 De
Sales Street, N.W., Washington, D.C. 20036 and the two volume *Television
Factbook*, published annually by Television Digest, Inc. 1836 Jefferson
Place, Washington, D.C. 20036 ($85). *Statistical Trends in Broadcasting*
published annually since 1965 by Blair Television, 717 Fifth Avenue, New
York, New York 10022 ($10) is useful for statistics on television and
radio trends -- advertising expenditures, broadcast revenues, markets,
cable television data.

Intermedia Audience Studies

There have been several syndicated audience research services over
the years which provide intermedia comparisons by analyzing in depth audiences, readers, brand usage, brand loyalty and product usage. Detailed
volumes provide demographic breakouts, extensive product and brand usage
market share information, viewing, listening and reading habits, psycho-
graphic profiles, etc. For example, Axiom Market Research Bureau's *Target Group Index (TGI)* reports for 1977 consisted of 40 volumes covering
consumer products and services; demographic volumes on adults, men, women, female homemakers, managers and professionals, households; magazine
volumes on total audiences, in-home audiences, primary audiences, reader
quality report; television volumes on audiences and attention levels;
psychographics summary report; market summary report; and outdoor/transit
advertising exposure. A separate 20 volume *Major Market Index (MMI)* is
a local study of the usage of media, products and services for the top
20 market areas. All of the data is also stored on computer tape for
detailed cross-tabulation analysis.

Brand Rating Index published in the 1960's is no longer in existence
and W.R. Simmons and Associates Research Inc.'s *Selective Markets and
the Media Reaching Them* (published annually from 1963 to 1978) and Axiom
Market Research Bureau Inc.'s *Target Group Index* (published annually 1973

to 1978) merged in July, 1978 to form Simmons Market Research Bureau Inc.,
(SMRB), 219 East 42nd Street, New York, New York 10017, 212-867-1414,
using research methodologies of both AMRB and Simmons and expanding magazine coverage and adding a volume measure to product usage statistics.
Starch did publish an annual *Starch Continuing Media/Market Service* until
1972 which provided readership data, audience characteristics, product
and activity reports, and exposure to various advertising media and in
1974 published a study entitled *Reaching the Elites with Selective Publications*. A new *Starch Primary Reader Audience Report* is currently being planned for publication late 1978 by Starch INRA Hooper Inc.

Computer Media Analysis

Much of the media and marketing data today is being retrieved by means
of computer, Currently there are three major syndicated computer systems
available: *IMS* (Interactive Market Systems), 19 W. 44th Street, New York,
New York 10016, 212-949-4640, which provides agencies, advertisers, marketers and the media with various models for media planning support and
data reporting routines for information retrieval both of which currently
work in conjunction with *Target Group Index* (Axiom Market Research Bureau) and *Simmons Selective Markets and the Media Reaching Them* (W.R.
Simmons) syndicated data bases. The models are primarily aimed at estimating reach/frequency, cost per thousand, and frequency distribution
data. The data retrieval routines provide a cross-tabbing capability to
extract custom reports from the data. Each service also provides related
media analysis capability such as local market allocation of network
television schedules and magazine plan "Optimizers" which work on various
media planning strategies.

The A.C. Nielsen Company also has a set of interactive programs which
allow access to various aspects of their data sets. One of these allows
customs manipulation of their NAD (National Audience Demographics) data
and another provides access to special "overnight" national television
ratings via the user's terminal. A radio planning package working off
the ARBITRON local market radio data is available from Marketron, Inc.,
2180 Sand Hill Rd., Menlo Park, California 94025, 415-854-2767. In the
package are several sub-systems available which range from providing raw
data to the complete construction of local market plans. One of several
services of its type is Donovan Data Systems, 666 5th Avenue, New York,
New York 10017, 212-586-0055, which provides support for buying, billing,
paying, record keeping and post-evaluation of spot TV, spot radio, magazine and network television. The system is a real-time data gathering
and report distributing system for use by agencies, advertisers and
stations. Information is gathered through a national data communications
network of video terminals.

Several of the media associations also offer their members special computer runs comparing various advertising media alternatives. The Television Bureau of Advertising, 1345 Avenue of the Americas, New York, New
York 10019, 212-397-3456 offers members computer runs comparing newspaper
and television ad schedules, along with proposed mixed media schedules,
including radio data using *IMS* (Interactive Market Systems). The Radio
Advertising Bureau, Inc., 485 Lexington Avenue, New York, New York 10017,
212-688-4020 offers its members computer runs from its *ARMS II All-Radio
Marketing Study*. It measures the media mix of delivered audiences in
three media (radio, television and newspapers) among purchasers of over

100 products and services. The Magazine Publishers Association Inc., 575 Lexington Avenue, New York, New York 10022, 212-752-0055 has an *IMS* computer model, *Media Imperatives* (a W.R. Simmons study), which analyzes television vs. magazines to determine the most effective media balance based on media market potential.

Specialized Research Reports

Many of the major research companies offer specialized marketing research studies which are used in the advertising planning process. The Yankelovich Monitor issued by Yankelovich, Skelly, and White, Inc., 575 Madison Avenue, New York, New York 10022, 212-742-7500 is an annual continuing nationwide analysis of consumer and social attitudes and trends useful for tracking changing consumer values and stimulating ideas for creative and marketing areas. Some of the topics covered in the reports include analysis of trends such as physical fitness, anti-materialism, personal creativity, concern about environment, return to nature, de-focus on youth, etc.

Opinion Research Corporation, North Harrison Street, Princeton, New Jersey 08540, 609-924-5900 did a multi-volume *Youth Profile Study* in 1974 which was to be a continuing marketing/audience profile and product usage study by teens and young adults. Daniel Starch, Inc. (now Starch Inra Hooper) did a detailed analysis of the Black market in 1973 entitled *Profile of the Black Consumer* detailing specific household and personal buying habits, product usage, and spending intentions cross-tabulated by demographic characteristics.

3.
THE TRADE PRESS OF ADVERTISING: Its Content and Contribution to the Profession

Quentin J. Schultze

Few historians have seriously examined early advertising trade journals. In fact, most scholars have relied on *Printers' Ink*, the most widely-available periodical, for their primary research. This is unfortunate for two reasons. First, historians have incorrectly assumed that the articles and editorials in *Printers' Ink* were representative of the sentiments and perspectives of the entire advertising community. *Printers' Ink* was only one voice for increasingly diverse and specialized advertising trades. Second, by neglecting most advertising journals as relevant and important sources of primary information, advertising historians have seldom developed new interpretations or conclusions. Scholars typically have relied on secondary sources that were based on the assumptions of yet earlier secondary sources. The advertising press provides important information for establishing new historical interpretations of the practice, function, and significance of American advertising. This essay briefly discusses many of the more influential advertising periodicals in hopes that researchers will use them to develop innovative and provacative reinterpretations of one of the most ubiquitous aspects of America.

Between 1885 and 1910 a multitude of publishers inaugurated trade journals that cultivated mutual economic interests and promoted collective social aspirations among advertisers, agents, and publishers. The earliest journals catered to the increasingly specialized needs of advertising related occupations. *Printers' Ink*, for example, supplied newspaper agents with selling techniques, simple copywriting ideas, and newspaper circulations and rates. However, during the first decade of the 20th century advertising journals moved beyond mere trade information and became vehicles for the creations, maintenance, and transformation of professional ideals among advertising trade groups. Journals were forums for discussing ethical codes, debating professional qualifications, exchanging methods of advertising, articulating ways of improving the

The author is on the faculty of The School of Journalism, Drake University. The author's dissertation deserves mention here, because its recent completion prevented inclusion in the annotated bibliography: "Advertising, Science and Professionalism, 1885-1917." University of Illinois, Urbana-Champaign, 1978.

practitioners' public image, determining ways of using advertising to
ameliorate social ills, presenting fictional literature related to the
social aspirations of practioners, and suggesting methods of educating
novice practitioners.

After World War I, the advertising press once again showed a tendency
toward serving the increasingly specialized needs of the various members
of the industry. Professionalization became less of an important issue
among practitioners, and the press responded to this change by supplying
specialized trade information. Periodicals found that practitioners
looked to the press for advanced technical training. Indeed the advertising press after World War I became and important vehicle for exchanging
ideas about the function of advertising in modern marketing.

The increasingly professional tone of advertising journals provides
the organizing principle for this essay. Rather than simply listing
periodicals by their date of establishment, place of publication, or
occupational group, I have attempted to capture their particular social
and economic preoccupations. In the first section I discuss the role
of *Printers' Ink* in the early advertising community. Then I provide
information on many of the other early specialized journals. I next
analyze some of the early 20th century advertising journals that emphasized professionalism and social fraternity and tried to bridge across
particular advertising occupations. Finally, I review important
developments in the advertising press between World War I and the early
1950's.

Printers' Ink: Early Newspaper Agent Spokesman

One of the first and certainly the most successful pre-1900 advertising
journal was *Printers' Ink*. Founded in 1888 by George P. Rowell, a newspaper agent, *Printers' Ink* succeeded Rowell's early house organs,
Advertisers' Gazette, first published in 1867, and *Newspaper Reporter,*
begun in 1871. Rowell printed 7,600 copies of the first issue of
Printers' Ink, and by the end of 1888, only six months after initial
publication, circulation exceeded 10,000. In the first few years of the
20th century *Printers' Ink's* circulation peaked at more than 16,000.

Initially, *Printers' Ink* was little more than a scrapbook of clippings
taken from other publications. Under the direction of Rowell and the
editorship of Charles L. Benjamin, a young man with no advertising experience, the weekly journal promoted primarily the interests of newspaper advertising. Rowell remarked in 1889 that *Printers' Ink* was "in ·
fact the 'trade journal' of advertisers; the advocate of newspaper
advertising."

During the first decade of the 20th century the journal broadened its
editorial policy to include information on club activities, government
regulation, other advertising media, and the like. It encouraged readers
to submit articles of general interest to the advertising community and
established numerous successful columns. A column called "Ready-Made
Advertisements" analyzed sample newspaper advertisements sent in by
readers. Another well-liked column, "Commercial Art Criticism,"
critiqued illustrated advertisements that appeared in various media.

Rowell probably exercised strong control over *Printers' Ink's* editorial content. Through the first few years of the 20th century he led a
campaign in the pages of the journal to refute the notion that advertising could be based on scientific, psychological principles. He strongly
disliked the infusion of science into advertising practice and used
Printers' Ink to argue that the trade was primarily a craft that could
be learned through "bruised-in" experience. Early *Printers' Ink* editorials often lambasted advertising academics and professionals.

Printers' Ink's success in the late 19th century was the result of its
editorial content and early establishment. Because it was one of the
first journals published, *Printers' Ink* had an almost immediate national
circulation. There were few other journals from which newspaper
advertisers and space salesmen could acquire circulation and rate information. Rowell used *Printers' Ink* to inform advertisers and agents of
available newspaper space. Subscribers were kept abreast of changes in
or additions to Rowell's annual *Newspaper Directory*, the first comprehensive listing of American newspaper locations, circulations, and rates.
Even *Printers' Ink's* technical articles on copywriting, layout, and
advertising theory were simple, straightforward statements on common-
sense procedures. As the "Little Schoolmaster in the Art of Advertising,"
Printers' Ink was a testament of pre-professional craftmanship in late
19th century newspaper advertising.

Early Specialized Trade Journals

During *Printers' Ink's* reign in the late 19th century as the largest-
circulation advertising periodical, several dozen agents, advertisers,
and independent publishers initiated advertising journals. Since many
of these "*Printers' Ink* Babies," as Rowell called them, were short-lived,
it is difficult to determine exactly how many existed. A few, such as
Rowell's earlier publications, were primarily agency house organs
designed to attract advertising revenues from interested advertisers.
Other journals served agricultural advertisers. Several periodicals
supplied mail-order dealers with information on mail-order paper rates,
circulations, and copywriting techniques. At least three advertising
journals published information specifically on newspaper advertising.
Outdoor and railway advertisers also received their first trade publications during the turn-of-the-century period. In short, the specialization of advertising led to the rise of numerous specialized journals.

Newspaper publishers and advertisers were lucrative audiences for a
few early advertising journals besides *Printers' Ink*. The New York
agency, N.W. Ayer, began publishing a quarterly in June of 1876. Called
the *Advertiser's Guide*, it was very similar to George Rowell's early
house organs, providing newspaper circulation information. Each issue
was filled with Ayer's advertisements for its own advertising services.
Founded in 1878, *National Advertiser* published news of current happenings
in the field of newspaper advertising. It boasted a circulation of more
than 5,000 in 1907 and was read primarily by national advertisers. The
journal's editor, J.B. Eiker, was advertising manager for two successful
patent medicines, St. Jacob's Oil and Duffy's Malt Whiskey. He had an
intimate knowledge of newspaper advertising policies, since patent
medicines relied heavily on religious newspapers. Two journals supplied
newspapers with ideas for attracting advertising revenues; New York's
Fourth Estate and Chicago's *Circulation Manager*, formerly the *Milwaukee*

Circulation Manager, provided newspapers with valuable methods of self-promotion.

Mail Order Journal and *Western Monthly* published data on mail-order paper rates, circulations, and geographic coverage. Mail-order advertisers used the journals to help plan and execute campaigns. *Mail Order Journal* was begun in 1897 by Louis Guenther, formerly a mail-order advertiser. Under Guenther's leadership, the journal often editorialized that newspapers were a far better advertising medium than magazines and that Chicago was the mail-order center of the world. Guenther periodically surveyed mail-order advertisers as to their feelings about the effectiveness of various papers. He also published revealing stories by successful mail-order advertisers. Each issue of *Mail Order Journal* included a "Complete List of Magazines and Monthlies." According to Guenther, the journal's circulation exceeded 12,000 in 1907. Established in 1902, *Western Monthly* reported on the papers that reached Western Americans. Both journals provided mail-order advertisers with articles and editorials on how best to cash in on the growing rural population, which increasingly purchased manufactured goods and aspired to urban life-styles.

Chicago spawned the earliest and most successful agricultural advertising publications, *Agricultural Advertising* and *White's Class Advertising*. Both publications were started by Frank B. White, owner of White's Class Advertising Company, a Chicago agency that specialized in selling to rural Americans. White established *Agricultural Advertising* in 1893 as a house organ to increase his agency's business and enhance its reputation. The journal successfully provided manufacturers of agricultural products with information on rural markets and media. Each issue's hundred or so pages were packed with advertisements for a multitude of farm papers. White sent the monthly to manufacturers of farm-related products in hopes of winning them as clients. In 1903, the Long-Critchfield Corporation, a large general advertising agency in Chicago which also specialized in agricultural advertising, purchased White's company and controlled the journal. For a short time White published *White's Class Advertising*, which was designed to serve only manufacturers and distributors of goods of interest to farmers.

Meanwhile, Marco Morrow and R.S. Thain, two well-known Chicago advertising men, broadened the editorial policy of *Agricultural Advertising* to better reflect the general interests of Long-Critchfield. Between 1903 and its death in 1918, *Agricultural Advertising* was one of the nation's most prestigious and widely-read advertising periodicals. It published a wealth of information about the Chicago advertising community, including club happenings, short stories by staff writer Sherwood Anderson, writing techniques, and a plethora of potent pro-advertising editorials. Editorials typically reflected the beliefs expressed by *Printers' Ink:* advertising was first and foremost a business activity and artistic craft, not a scientific profession, and no amount of scientific expertise would change advertising. *Agricultural Advertising* encouraged readers to submit articles and published numerous specialized columns each month. It is an extremely valuable resource which has largely gone unnoticed by advertising historians.

Inside Information was perhaps the first advertising journal published for industry management. Subtitled "Advertising information and Ideas,

Business Facts and Figures, Methods and Possibilities," it ran articles on corporations, methods of selling stock "advertising investments," tariff and treaty regulations, and successful advertisers. *Inside Information* often reprinted articles from other advertising and business publications. Evidently the monthly was never extremely successful; it attracted few advertisers and grew increasingly thin after its initial publication by the Inside Information Publishing Company of Chicago in 1904. Nevertheless, the journal is interesting as one of the first advertising periodicals for high-level business management.

Other early specialized advertising journals included *Advertising Chat, Advisor, Current Advertising, Advertising News, Advertising World, Brains, White's Sayings, Mertz's Magazine, Rhode Island Advertiser, Western Advertiser, Bill Poster and Distributor, Ad Sense, Poster, Advertiser and Publisher, Common Sense, Plain Folk, American Advertiser, Fame, Jist,* and *King's Jester.* Established in 1892 by Outing Press of Detroit, *Brains,* sometimes called *Retailer and Advertiser,* served the needs and interests of large retailers. *Fame* was a house organ published by Artemus Ward, a legendary figure in early advertising who made a fortune creating brand demand for a soap called Sapolio. *White's Sayings* and *Mertz's Magazine* were house organs for Western practitioners; *White's Sayings* was established by C.F. White, a well-known Seattle copywriter, and published by a group called the Western Advertisers; *Mertz's Magazine* was established in 1897 under the name *Pacific Coast Advertising* as a house organ for a local agency. *Ad Sense* of Chicago discussed buying techniques for advertisers. Begun in 1896, it consolidated with *Ad Writer,* a St. Louis journal, in 1906. The Frank R. Jelleff Advertising Agency of Providence published *Rhode Island Advertiser* as a monthly forum for local advertising news of interest to retailers. *Western Advertiser,* an Omaha journal published by the Thompson Advertising Agency, discontinued in 1906 because the owners could not find experienced people for writing articles and soliciting accounts. Established in 1905, *SRA Quarterly* promoted the interests of the Street Railways Advertising Company, which sold poster space on major metropolitan railway lines. *Advertising Chat* was a house organ for S.E. Seith, a New York media representative. *Up-To-Date-Distributor,* a house organ for the Will G. Molton Distributing Agency, was devoted exclusively to the "house-to-house distribution" of advertising.

General Interest Journals of Professionalism Before World War I

Although most of the journals already discussed had relatively small circulations and served rather specific advertising trade interests, a few general interest journals emerged during the first decade of the 20th century. Whereas specialized journals focused on occupational techniques and economic interest, general interest magazines emphasized social fraternity and professionalism. They appealed to a wide array of advertising practitioners from diverse backgrounds and geographic areas and sought to elevate the social standing of all advertising practitioners by professionalizing the business.

The largest-circulation independent advertising journal was *Profitable Advertising,* begun by C.F. David of Boston in 1891. Kate F. Griswold, probably the most well-known woman in advertising during the turn-of-the century, took over the journal in 1897. Early issues resembled

Printers' Ink; they consisted of clippings from newspapers, other business journals, and magazines. Even the columns in *Profitable Advertising* were similar to those in *Printers' Ink.* "Help in Advertising," by
Henry D. Morrison, evaluated advertisements solicited from readers.

By about 1900, however, *Profitable Advertising* advocated rationalizing
the advertising business. It strongly supported advertising professionalism in both editorials and articles. It stressed the idea that
advertisers, agents, and publishers should recognize each other's
economic interests and come to professional agreements. The journal
idealized the marketing concept and encouraged all practitioners to view
themselves as servants of the public. In June of 1909 *Profitable
Advertising* merged with *Selling Magazine,* the major marketing management
magazine, and was retitled *Advertising and Selling.* *Advertising and
Selling* was particularly concerned with helping company managers to
coordinate advertising and personal selling activities.

Advertising and Selling and *Profitable Advertising* are excellent
sources of information about the activities, aspirations, and techniques
of early advertising practitioners and clubs. They reported on advertising organization meetings, evaluated plans for establishing advertising educational institutions, described successful advertising campaigns, philosophized on the nature of consumer behavior, and defined
the social and economic role of advertising. Both journals openly
admitted the conflicting economic interests that plagued the advertising
business and offered means of bringing advertisers, agents, and publishers together in a bond of professional harmony.

Another large-circulation journal that catered to the mutual professional interests of the many different advertising occupations was *Judicious
Advertising,* which absorbed *Advertising Experience* in 1903. Lord and
Thomas, the most successful turn-of-the-century Chicago advertising
agency, launched the journal as a house organ in 1902. Like *Profitable
Advertising, Judicious Advertising and Advertising Experience* had a
broad editorial policy that promoted the idea of a unified professional
group. It solicited general interest articles from all advertisers,
agents, and publishers and downplayed its role as a house organ.

Judicious Advertising and Advertising Experience rarely printed clippings from other publications; it was one of the best sources of primary
information about social and professional happenings in the advertising
community. One early column, "The Month in the Field," told of
practitioners' job changes and success stories. Another column "News
Notes About Media," reported on new and established magazines and newspapers; it reviewed publication changes, content alterations, and audience profiles. *Judicious Advertising and Advertising Experience*
published many revealing editorials about all aspects of the advertising
business. In addition, the journal examined the strategies and tactics
employed by many of the most successful early national advertisers.
Each issue of the magazine contained numerous stories by leading
company advertising managers and journal reporters. J. George Frederick,
a *Judicious Advertising and Advertising Experience* reporter and one of
the most highly-regarded advertising journalists of the period, wrote
dozens of investigations of the advertising campaigns of large-scale
advertisers.

Not surprisingly, *Judicious Advertising and Advertising Experience* portrayed the advertising agency as an indispensable part of modern business operations. It suggested that the advertising agent should be a professional man who for the betterment of mankind supplied important services to progressive businessmen. Consequently, the journal typically focused on the relationship of advertising to marketing techniques. *Judicious Advertising and Advertising Experience* published some of the most sophisticated reports on advertising effectiveness research, layout design, and magazine copywriting.

Another Chicago advertising agency initiated *Mahin's Magazine*, one of the most important advertising journals of the early 20th century. John Mahin started the journal for the expressed purpose of introducing the work of Professor Walter Dill Scott to the nation's advertising practitioners. He made Scott, who was professor of psychology at Northwestern University, editor of the journal's "psychology department." Beginning in 1902 with the first issue, *Mahin's Magazine* published each month an article by Scott on the psychology of advertising. Scott told practitioners that the merger of psychology and advertising would result in a glorious union of theory and practice. Largely through those articles, *Mahin's Magazine* acquainted advertising practitioners with social science. Only after *Mahin's magazine* introduced Scott to the advertising community did other journals begin to seriously consider the role of science in advertising.

Mahin's Magazine also first showed practitioners the value of demographic research. Although a few individual agencies and practitioners had developed their own methods of collecting statistical audience information, *Mahin's Magazine* hired George B. Waldron to formalize the relationship between demographic research and advertising markets and to report his findings to the advertising community. Using the United States census as a data base, Waldron monthly wrote provocative analyses of potential sales areas. He discussed population shifts, employment trends, income variations, and virtually all of the major demographic categories. Most importantly, Waldron indicated why such quantitative information might be of direct use to the planner of advertising campaigns.

In addition, *Mahin's Magazine* introduced the idea of professional ethics to the advertising community. The journal hired Professor Herbert L. Willett, Dean of the Disciple's Divinity House of the University of Chicago, to write a column on ethics in advertising. Willett contributed twelve articles to *Mahin's Magazine* during 1902 and 1903.

Mahin's Magazine was the journal most responsible for stimulating the development of professional ethics, psychological techniques, and formalized market research. However, the journal was often forced to defend its view of advertising professionalism; *Mahin's Magazine* and *Printers' Ink* supported opposing points of view and criticized each other's philosophy of advertising. *Printers' Ink* insisted that advertising was primarily a craft that could be learned only through indirect practical experience, whereas *Mahin's Magazine* argued that professional advertising demanded arduous scientific training.

The close editorial stances of *Judicious Advertising and Advertising*

Experience and *Mahin's Magazine* led to their merger in 1904. In 1912
Judicious Advertising and Advertising Experience changed its name back
to *Judicious Advertising* but continued to support the ideal of professionalism and to promote marketing research and scientific advertising.

The Advertising Press After World War I

World War I marked a turning point in the activities of the advertising press. First, the efforts of the advertising community toward
stimulating national loyalty, selling war bonds, and recruiting young
civilians gave tremendous impetus to the trade's professionalization.
By applying the trade's techniques on a large scale to public service
goals, practitioners helped legitimize advertising as a form of mass
persuasion by showing the American people that it was a valuable tool
for promoting American ideals. Much of the press' time during 1917 and
1918 was spent reporting on the success of war-related advertising campaigns. After World War I the trade press lost its strong preoccupation
with professionalization. Consequently, journals found that professionalization was itself no longer an adequate editorial focus. Readers
wanted specialized information about advertising techniques.

Second, the advertising press increasingly shifted in focus from
professionalization to technical specialization because of the changing
economic relationships in the advertising industry. In the years prior
to the war the industry underwent a period of rationalization. The
advertising industry triad -- advertiser, agency, publisher -- came to
at least partial agreement on advertising's function in modern mass-
marketing. Standardized commission rates, audit bureaus, and agency
recognition policies helped alleviate earlier mistrust. Consequently,
members of the triad no longer saw the need to fight for their own
economic interest. Rather, they concentrated on competing with
businesses of their own type -- advertiser with advertiser, agency with
agency, and publisher with publisher.

Not surprisingly, after World War I the advertising press increasingly
reported on the specialized techniques and economic affairs of particular phases of the industry. This shift in emphasis was evident in the
declining number of house and club journals, which could not cope with
declining circulations and rising publication costs. Whereas journals
that focused on professionalization required only meager staffs of
literate and excited writers, specialized trade journals needed a
constant supply of industry news. Although the total number of advertising journals declined after World War I, the most successful periodicals began reporting on everything from market research to regulatory
news to economic forecasts to management techniques.

The post-World War I trend toward specialization is exemplified by
Printers' Ink Monthly. Established in 1919 as an offshoot of *Printers'
Ink*, the journal reported almost exclusively on news of interest to
advertising management. Subtitled, "A Journal of Printed Salesmanship,"
it appealed to progressive advertising managers who viewed advertising as
one component of successful marketing. Publisher John Romer knew the
advertising business well. He solicited articles from such prestigious
figures as Earnest Elmo Calkins, a successful New York agency executive,
and Leo Burnett, one of the founders of the "Chicago School" of advertising. In 1921 Burnett explained to readers how to develop a product

personality, a technique which became characteristic of modern consumer goods advertising generally.

Articles in *Printers' Ink Monthly* were usually written by people in the field, not by reporters. About half of the articles in *Printers' Ink Monthly* were descriptions of successful campaigns and methods, replete with marketing information and actual advertising illustrations. Typically authored by the person who developed the project, they included discussions of such successful companies as Proctor and Gamble, Colgate, William Wrigley Company and Borden Company. In addition, knowledgeable practitioners wrote articles on the latest techniques in printing, photography, movie production, color reproduction, and engraving. Always reporting current trends in the business, the journal contained some of the earliest analyses of the relationship between advertising and marketing. It ran articles on novelty advertising, sales promotion devices, catalogue merchandising, personal salesmanship, wholesaling, retailing, and cooperative advertising programs. Romer evidently had a keen eye for the problems confronting national advertisers; his journal told advertising managers how to eliminate business risk by securing distribution and enhancing brand demand in mass markets.

Beginning in the late 1930's, *Printers' Ink Monthly* began changing its format. Paralleling the shifting interests of advertising management, it started reporting regulatory actions, public relation ideas, and media trends. Indeed, increased government regulations, public concerns about the future of free-enterprise system, and the rise of commercial radio greatly affected the management environment. The magazine's subtitle was changed to "A Magazine of Markets" in 1937, and it even more vigorously pursued a marketing orientation until it merged with *Printers' Ink* in 1942.

Because *Printers' Ink* attempted to be a general "Journal for Advertisers," its news and events orientation was sprinkled with a wide variety of valuable articles during the early 1940's. For example, the journal managed to secure some of the earliest reports by C.E. Hooper on radio audience sampling. It also inaugurated a "Jury of Marketing Opinion" which described and analyzed advertising practices of agencies and advertisers.

The merger of *Printers' Ink* and *Printers' Ink Monthly* attempted to meet the needs and interests of the audiences of both publications. The new *Printers' Ink* was called "The Weekly Magazine of Advertising, Marketing, and Sales," and took up the marketing management orientation of *Printers' Ink Monthly* while maintaining the news and column format of the old *Printers' Ink*. New columns included "News Roundup," "Inside Washington," and "People Make News." During the 1940's *Printers' Ink* slowly discontinued its discussions and analyses of particular campaigns and instead focused on advertising techniques generally. In addition, the journal tried to cater to the increasingly diverse needs of marketing management by including a wide variety of articles on sales promotion techniques, including contests, packaging, premiums, and the like. Absent from the journal's pages were articles or reports on the "science" of marketing that was evolving in major business schools.

While *Printers' Ink Monthly* catered to the increasingly specialized needs of communication-oriented marketing management, *Printers' Ink* continued to rely on the format which made it a success in the late years of the 19th century. Seemingly undaunted by World War I, *Printers' Ink* weekly published short, concisely-written editorials, feature articles, and columns. It reported on club activites, briefly reviewed governmental actions, including decisions made by the Federal Trade Commission, commented on advertiser-agency relations, and offered new ideas on advertising techniques, particularly copywriting. Unlike *Printers' Ink Monthly, Printers' Ink* served the interests of the average practitioner who was interested in practical information about advertising rather than specialized articles or lengthy discussions of marketing strategies.

During the 1930's and 1940's *Printers' Ink* deepened its commitment to serving the average practitioner. Indeed the majority of stories in the journal were written by middle-level management, not by well-known agency men or corporate executives. *Printers' Ink* became a journal of advertising-related business news and comment. It ran columns on events and personalities in all of the major related fields: "Advertising Agencies," "Mostly Media," "Among the Advertisers," and "Advertising Federation of America." One of the more valuable of the new columns was established in 1935 and written by L.D.H. Weld, who compiled the *"Printers' Ink* Indexes," monthly charts that reflected fluctuations in newspaper, magazine, radio, outdoor, and farm paper advertising. The series was quickly adopted by the Department of Commerce and used in its monthly "Survey of Current Business."

One of the most successful post-World War I trade journals was *Advertising and Selling*. Although it went through some rough years shortly after the war, by the mid 1920's it blossomed into a highly-respected periodical. Unlike *Printers' Ink*, which often showed evidence of contradictory editorial policy, *Advertising and Selling* continued its pre-war emphasis on serving both large-scale manufacturers of consumer goods and their agencies. Most editorials content fit into two major categories: improving methods of stimulating brand demand or enhancing the effectiveness of distribution. In either type of article, the journal showed how national advertisers could cope with growing competition from the private brands of chain stores and major retailers.

In 1918 the monthly merged with *The Advertising News*, a small circulation news magazine, and was renamed *Advertising and Selling with The Advertising News*. The new biweekly initially lost much of the flavor of the old *Advertising and Selling*. It ran few lengthy features and began concentrating on short articles on copy techniques, personalities in the advertising business, conventions, business association speeches, and the like. Then, in 1923, a new journal, *Advertising Fortnightly; Markets, Merchandising and Media*, absorbed the floundering *Advertising and Selling with The Advertising News* and turned it into one of the most successful and prestigious of all advertising journals.

Named *Advertising and Selling Fortnightly* until 1926, when it dropped the "Fortnightly", the New York journal actively solicited articles from the most highly-respected agency and manufacturer executives. During the late 1920's and early 1930's the magazine's table of contents was a virtual who's who of the national advertising business. Contributing editors included Earnest Elmo Calkins and Charles Austin Bates, two of New York's best-known agency men. Authors included George Burton, John E. Kennedy, Edward L. Bernays, David Sarnoff, Paul T. Cherington,

Roy Durstine, and J. George Frederick, the former *Printers' Ink* editor who wrote dozens of investigative articles on advertising campaigns for *Judicious Advertising*. During this period *Advertising and Selling* published a series of autobiographical articles by Claude Hopkins which were published in book form under the title *My Life in Advertising*. Other regular contributors included Melvin T. Copeland, an expert on industrial advertising trends and techniques; Floyd W. Parsons, who for over a decade commented each issue on the state of business in America; H.A. Haring, who reported on the possibilities for using radio advertising in the design and implementation of consumer marketing strategies; and Henry Moffett, a specialist in improving consumer relations through offering product service.

Advertising and Selling became a major communications vehicle for national advertisers and large-scale agencies in the late 1920's and early 1930's. It published information on designing and implementing cooperative advertising campaigns, sought contributors who knew the field of industrial advertising, and served as a job clearinghouse for available positions in brand management or agency work. "The News Digest," located at the back of each issue, listed changes in agency, media and advertiser personnel, as well as accounts lost and gained by agencies. The journal's classified section told of positions available and help wanted. And in 1930 *Advertising and Selling* initiated a quarterly art supplement, *Advertising Arts*.

During the late 1930's and early 1940's *Advertising and Selling* continued to offer some of the most provocative and interesting journalism on the business of advertising. It published articles by such agency men as John Caples and Albert Lasker. It also started a column called "Trends," which briefly reported on legal news, profit outlooks, areas of increased competition, and other economic indicators that related directly to the advertising business. In the mid 1940's the journal ran some excellent discussions of national advertising, including analyses of the commission versus fee systems of agency compensation, the shift in radio from program sponsorship to spot advertising, and the growing specialization of personnel in large advertising agencies. The journal's focus was formalized in 1948, when it became *Advertising and Selling and the Advertising Agency*.

The July 1948 issue of *Advertising and Selling* introduced *The Advertising Agency*, billed as a "new magazine-within-a-magazine." Actually, the new magazine was a sixteen-page section of *Advertising and Selling* devoted exclusively to the affairs and concerns of large consumer advertising agencies. Columns in the new section included "Agency Trends," "This Month's Guest Editorial," and "Copy Clinic." The New York publisher, Moore-Robbins Publishing Company, emphasized client relations, management decision-making, creative skills development, and media planning and buying, all of which were covered, although to a lesser extent, in the old *Advertising and Selling*. Agency executives were the major contributors to the new section. They discussed alternative ways of organizing agencies, offered methods of avoiding legal pitfalls, told how to establish research departments, reported on the plight of small agencies, and lamented the lack of experienced agency personnel. They also examined how agencies could minimize taxes, increase employee productivity, and design efficient and attractive office layouts.

In May of 1949 the magazine changed its title to *Advertising Agency and Advertising and Selling: Devoted to the Professional Practice of Advertising.* By this time, the journal clearly specialized in providing information for agency management. It reflected an important trend in agency operations: the increased reliance on research at all levels of decision-making. The magazine solicited articles by top agency executives on copytesting, media planning and research, and especially market research.

During the early 1950's readers were addressed by private research companies, audience measurement services, readership investigators, consumer behavior specialists and the Advertising Research Foundation, an industry-sponsored organization. Ernst Dichter, one of the fathers of motivational research, used *Advertising Agency and Advertising and Selling* to introduce agencies to his neo-Freudian techniques. Daniel Starch began publishing dozens of articles on readership studies. The magazine also solicited analyses of financial and accounting management techniques. By 1954, when its name became *Advertising Agency: The Magazine of Agency Operations and Management,* the journal was a major vehicle for bringing the promise of social science research to the advertising community. Nevertheless, such reports were epistemologically simplistic and extremely shallow in theoretical conception. It was up to more academic journals, established by university researchers, to greatly advance the social science underpinnings of advertising research. In 1958 *Advertising Agency* was sold to Advertising Publications, Inc., Chicago, publishers of *Advertising Age, Industrial Marketing,* and *Advertising Requirements.*

As the aforementioned journals indicate, one of the central trends in advertising trade press publications after World War I, and particularly after World War II, was the reporting of industry news. Virtually all periodicals began publishing some news columns, and a few journals, most notably *Advertising Highlights, Advertising Age, The Advertiser,* and *Tide* were devoted almost exclusively to industry news. *Advertising Highlights* was begun in the mid 1930's by George L. Kinter of Pittsburgh, Pennsylvania. The monthly reported on new advertising campaigns, sales achievements, slogans, industry profits, and the like. All of its articles were taken from other publications, particularly advertising journals. *Advertising Age,* the most successful post World War II advertising newsmagazine, began in 1929 as the "national newspaper of marketing." In the early 1950's its circulation skyrocketed and it became the major weekly source of industry news. *The Advertiser* existed from 1930 to the late 1950's. Originally called *The Artist and Advertiser,* it covered club activities, briefly described successful campaigns, published short articles submitted by advertisers and agency practitioners, and reported on new production techniques in both print and broadcast media. It died in the late 1950's as *Advertising Age* rose to a dominant position in the field. *Tide* was one of the more successful news journals during the 1940's and 50's. Billed by the publisher as the "newsmagazine for advertising executives," it ran short articles on such things as media buying trends, legal developments, billing techniques and procedures, agency changes and mergers, and general business activities. Like the other advertising newsmagazines, *Tide* informed practitioners of the rapidly changing business conditions in the decades following World War II.

The interested researcher should also consult some of the numerous trade journals that served very specialized advertising industries. For example, *The Mailbag* published a wealth of information on direct marketing after its establishment in 1917. It solicited revealing articles from both consumer and industrial mail order advertisers. In its pages were stories of how everything from pianos to clothes to automobiles were sold by mail. The journal printed elaborate discussions of copywriting styles, mail order catalogs, house organs, the Post Office, and direct mail follow-ups of salesman visits. In 1927 it merged with *Postage*, a small monthly published in New York as the "Official Magazine of the Direct-Mail Advertising Association," which was a department of the Associated Advertising Clubs of the World. Then it merged with the *Reporter of Direct Advertising* to become the *Reporter with Postage and the Mailbag*. The new publication often ran provocative editorials that revealed the particular preoccupations and interests of direct mail advertisers. Evidently one of the major concerns of readers during the 1920's and 30's was how to secure accurate and potentially profitable lists of customer names and addresses.

Specialty advertising was covered by a journal called *Novelty News*. This New York monthly began in 1905, became *Premium Practice* in 1933, *Premium Practice and Business Promotion* in 1944, and in 1953 was once again named *Premium Practice*. In addition to reporting on activities of the Advertising Specialty Association, the journal printed hundreds of descriptive articles on using premiums to increase sales of virtually every kind of product or service, including public utilities, refrigerators, vacuum cleaners, newspapers, cigarettes, and shoes. Early premiums included marbles, "profit-sharing certificates," and silk hosiery. The journal regularly published editorials that put for the views of specialty advertisers.

The Outdoor Advertising Association of America published *The Poster* from 1926 through 1930, when it became *Advertising Outdoors*. In addition to reporting on federal, stage, and municipa; regulation in the outdoor advertising industry, the monthly published articles on many of the most successful poster campaigns of the period. Written by advertisers, the stories typically included excellent on-location photographs of posters.

Established in 1928, *Advertising Abroad*, later called *Export Advertiser* might be of special interest to historians of multi-national advertising and marketing. Subtitled "A Journal Devoted to the Interests of American Companies Advertising in Foreign Countries," it published articles by advertisers, American agencies, and Department of Commerce officials. American businessmen wrote guest editorials for the journal. Articles stressed methods of achieving foreign distribution and summarized legal problems associated with filing foreign trademarks. Although it lasted less than a decade, the journal is a worthwhile source of information about the problems confronting American marketers who advertised in other countries.

Finally, this survey of the advertising press after World War I would not be complete without mention of non-consumer advertising. One journal is particularly important as a source of information: *Class, Industrial & Trade Advertising*. An early Crain publication, it was launched in the 1920's and quickly became a major communications vehicle for the industry. It absorbed *Industrial Marketing* in 1927, becoming *Class and Industrial Marketing*. In addition to publishing the "NIAA NEWS" (National Industrial Advertisers' Association), the journal ran a plethora of articles by industrial advertisers, reported on techniques of market analysis, instructed advertisers on how to coordinate industrial advertising with sales calls, and printed "The Advertising Chart," which graphed the total advertising pages in trade and industrial journals each month.

To summarize, between World War I and the mid-1950's the advertising trade press underwent increased specialization of content. Earlier concerned with professionalization, the press emphasized the application of marketing and management techniques to virtually all forms of advertising and promotion. Although the press was increasingly concerned with the application of scientific techniques, few journals actually developed close ties with the academic community. Rather, the advertising press served as a forum for the discussion of quasi-scientific methods of eliminating risk in increasingly impersonal market situations.

In addition I have come across the following short lived, regional or special interest periodicals which may be of interest:

Advertiser's Digest, San Francisco, 1935.
Advertiser's Handy Guide, New York (Lyman Morse Agency), 1893-1907.
Advertiser's Magazine, Kansas City, 1907-1910.
Advertisers' Weekly, New Rochelle, N.Y., 1924-1928.
Advertising, Cincinatti, 1896.
Advertising Advocate, New York, 1911.
Advertising Agency, Chicago, 1936-1938.
Advertising Displays, New York, 1930-1932.
Advertising Federation of America, Bulletin, New York, 1929-1931.
Advertising Manager, Wheeling, W.Va., 1927.
Advertising Outdoors, Chicago, 1930-1931.
Advertising Printer, New York, 1930.
Advertising Specialties, New York, 1929-1930.
American Advertiser, New York, 1905-1906.
Art in Advertising, New York, 1890-1899.
Ballyhoo, New York, 1931-1939, satirical.
Broadcast Merchandising, New York (N.B.C.), 1933-1939.
Independent Advertising, New York, 1913-1918.
International Adcrafter, Detroit, 1929.
Moving Picture Publicity, New York, 1913-1914.
Pacific Coast Advertising, Los Angeles, 1897-1905.
Practical Advertising, Atlanta, 1906-1909.
Practical Advertising, San Francisco, 1914.
Publicité-Publicity, Montreal, 1905-1920.
Signs of the Times, Cincinatti, 1906.
Southern Advertising and Publishing, Greensboro, N.C., 1925+.
Torch, Cleveland (Advertising Club), 1910-1931.

And, of course, the study of more contemporary advertising would require attention paid to *Madison Avenue*, New York, 1958-1970 and *Sponsor: For Buyers of Broadcast Advertising*, New York, 1946-1968, and the more academic *Journal of Advertising* and *Journal of Advertising Research*, New York (Advertising Research Foundation), 1960+. (ed.)

NUMBER ONE

He owns a lovely phonograph,
    yet he detests the things;
He has a splendid camera,
    and it no pleasure brings;

He's bought an automobile
    which he will never use;
He's got ten sets o' costly books
    he never will peruse;

He's purchased razors, wheels and clocks,
    though none of them he needs;
His woodshed's full of laundry soap
    and fancy garden seeds;

He loves not animals, and yet
    he's bought four blooded dogs;
The attic of his modest home
    is chucked with catalogues;

The kitchen's strewn with breakfast foods
    the family will not eat;
He's ordered twenty-four more shoes
    than there are family feet;

And then -- but there really is no use
    in telling all the tale;
It seems he's bought most everything
    that's advertised for sale;

He simply can't resist an ad' --
    is helpless quite, indeed;
He says they make his waiter howl
    regardless of his need;

But he has a proud distinction,
    though he may starve and freeze;
He's the first completed victim
    of the newest new disease.

D.H. TALMADGE, The Crescent and Grip,
                Vol. 4 (1905), p171.

III.

Annotated Bibliographies

1.000
REFERENCE WORKS

1.001 *An Advertiser's Guide to Scholarly Periodicals*. New York:
Association of American University Presses, 1958-.

> Provides a description of scholarly journals. Note: not a
> guide to the contents.

1.002 *Advertising, with Special Reference to Its Social and Economic
Effects*. Washington, DC: Library of Congress, Division of Bibliography, 1930, 13 pp.

> A bibliographical list of contemporary writings.

1.003 Agnew, Hugh E., and Anderson, Florence H.M. *Books on Advertising,
Business and Commercial English, Marketing, Retailing, Including Chain
Stores, Salesmanship, Sales Management*. New York: National Association
of Teachers of Marketing and Advertising, 1930, 23 pp.

> Not very thorough.

1.004 *American Newspaper Annual*. Philadelphia: Ayer, 1880-.

> A directory of newspapers with rate and circulation data
> indicated.

1.005 *Ayer Glossary of Advertising and Related Terms*. Philadelphia:
Ayer, 1972, 163 pp.

> Alphabetical arrangement of terms is followed by a classified
> arrangement of the same terms, more precisely defined. Classi-
> fied sections exist for TV and radio, printing, photography,
> graphic arts.

1.006 Bates, Charles Austin. *The Art and Literature of Business*.
(6 vols.). New York: By the Author, 1902.

> More an encyclopedia of marketing and advertising. Last
> volume is an index.

1.007 Bishop, Robert L. *Public Relations: A Comprehensive Biblio-
graphy: Articles and Books on Public Relations, Communications
Theory, Public Opinion, and Propaganda, 1964 - 1972*. Ann Arbor, MI:
University of Michigan Press, 1974, 212 pp.

> Updates Cutlip, 1.013.

1.008 Blum, Eleanor. *Basic Books in the Mass Media*. Urbana: University of Illinois Press, 1972, 252 pp.

> Subtitled *An Annotated, Selected Booklist Covering General
> Communications, Book Publishing, Broadcasting, Film, Magazines,
> Newspapers, Advertising, Indexes, and Scholarly and Professional
> Periodicals*.

1.009 *Books for the Advertising Man*. New York: Advertising Federation
of America, 1935, 36 pp.

> Revised frequently. Edition of 1957 titled: *Books for the
> Advertising and Marketing Man: A Classified Bibliography on
> Advertising, Marketing, Selling and Related Subjects,* 37 pp.
> Supplement issued in 1958.

1.010 Clarke, George Timothy. *Bibliography of Advertising and
Marketing Theses for the Doctorate in United States Colleges and
Universities, 1944 to 1959*. New York: Advertising Education Founda-
tion, 1961, 28 pp.

> A list of 393 doctoral theses from 38 educational institutions.
> Subject arrangement; entry is by title, followed by author,
> granting institution, and date.

1.011 *Comparative Advertising: A Systematic and Annotated Bibliography
of Comparative Advertising from 1972 - 1976*. New York: Kenyon &
Eckhardt, n.d.

> Not deposited in libraries.

1.012 Cowan, Francis N., ed. *Sales Executives' List of References to
Principle Articles, Books, Reports and Data Published since 1916,
Relating to Sales Management and Advertising*. Chicago: Dartnell, 1925,
108 pp.

1.013 Cutlip, Scott M. *A Public Relations Bibliography*. 2d ed.
Madison: University of Wisconsin Press, 1965, 305 pp.

> A comprehensive list. See also Bishop, 1.007.

1.014 Daniells, Lorna M., ed. *Studies in Enterprise: Selected
Bibliography of American and Canadian Company Histories and Biographies
of Businessmen*. Boston: Harvard Graduate School of Business, 1957,
169 pp.

> Includes few firms in the advertising industry, but many
> consumer goods manufacturers.

1.015 Danielson, Wayne A., and Wilhoit, G.C. *A Computerized Bibliography of Mass Communications Research, 1944 - 1964*. New York:
Magazine Publishers Association, 1967, 399 pp.

> KWIC index approach to articles on mass communications appearing
> in 48 social science journals. Alphabetical arrangement by
> author.

1.016 Gazurian, Johnny A. *The Advertising & Graphic Arts Glossary*.
Los Angeles: Los Angeles Trade-Technical College, 1966, 150 pp.

> Definitions are grouped in chapters arranged by: planning,
> preparation of artwork, composition, camera and platemaking,

printing, paper, binding and finishing. Alphabetical sequence follows.

1.017 Deleted.

1.018 Graham, Irwin. *Encyclopedia of Advertising*. 2d ed. New York: Fairchild, 1952, 606 pp.

Alphabetized working manual containing more than 1,100 entries relating to advertising, marketing, publishing, law, research, public relations, publicity and the graphic arts. Includes index and a directory of associations.

1.019 Grohmann, H. Victor. *Advertising Terminology: A Dictionary of Advertising Language: Terms in Common Use Throughout the Advertising Field, Allied Professions and Industries*. New York: By the Author, 1952, 86 pp.

Second edition (1958) published by Heedham & Grohmann.

1.020 Gunther, Edgar, and Goldstein, Frederick A. *Current Sources of Marketing Information: A Bibliography of Primary Marketing Data*. AMA Bibliography Series, no. 6. Chicago: American Marketing Association, 1960, 119 pp.

Annotated list of more than 1,200 books, journals, reports and documents. Classified.

1.021 Hall, Samuel Roland. *The Advertising Handbook: A Reference Work Covering the Principles and Practice of Advertising*. New York: McGraw-Hill, 1921, 743 pp.

Despite title, this is a textlike introduction to the trade.

1.022 Hamlin, Ina M. *A Market Research Bibliography*. Business Research Bulletin, no. 38. Urbana: University of Illinois, 1931, 75 pp.

A good source for a "state of the art" listing, as Illinois was one of the strongest academic centers in marketing studies.

1.023 *International Advertising Association World Directory of Marketing Communications Periodicals*. New York: IAA, 1968, 154 pp.

A guide to the trade press.

1.024 International Chamber of Commerce. *Dictionary of Advertising and Distribution in Eight Languages*. Basel: Verlag fur Recht und Gesellschaft, 1954, unpaged.

Terms are given in English with equivalents in French, German, Spanish, Dutch, Italian, Swedish and Portugese. Indexes to the main work from each language.

1.025 Jaffe, Rubin. *The Advertising Index*. Los Angeles: Educational
Committee of the L.A. Advertising Club, 1918, 141 pp.

> Suggestions for organizing a clipping file.

1.026 *Journalism Quarterly*. Iowa City, IA, 1924 -. V. 1-.

> Since its inception in 1924, each issue provides a comprehensive
> bibliography of periodical and newspaper articles on advertising.

1.027 Larson, Henrietta M. *Guide to Business History: Materials for
the Study of American Business History and Suggestions for their Use*.
Harvard Studies in Business History, vol. 12. Cambridge: Harvard
University Press, 1948, 1181 pp.

> Includes sections on the historical background and setting of
> American business; biographical works of business administrators;
> the history of individual business units; history of industries;
> general topics in business history; and research and reference
> materials. More than 4,900 annotations. See Lovett, 1.032 and
> Daniells, 1.014 for updates.

1.028 Lasswell, Harold D.; Casey, Ralph D.; and Smith, Bruce L.
*Propaganda, Communication and Public Opinion: A Comprehensive Reference
Guide*. Princeton: Princeton University Press, 1935, 435 pp.

> An excellent bibliography with advertising covered on pages 129 -
> 143 and 358 - 362.

1.029 Library of Congress. Division of Bibliography. "Selected List of
Recent References on Advertising, May 1940."

> A list of 400 items, including periodical items published since
> 1931.

1.030 *A List of Periodicals Bound Complete with Advertising Pages in
New England and New York City Libraries*. Hanover, NH: Conference of
Eastern College Librarians, NH: 1935, 15 pp.

> Valuable since many early libraries removed advertising pages
> before binding periodicals.

1.031 Lockwood, Thornton C., and Ramond, Charles K. *Sources of Published
Advertising Research*. New York: Advertising Research Foundation, 1960,
65 pp.

1.032 Lovett, Robert W. *American Economic Business History Information
Sources*. Detroit: Gale, 1971, 323 pp.

> Subtitled *An Annotated Bibliography of Recent Works Pertaining to
> Economic, Business, Agricultural, and Labor History and the History
> of Science and Technology for the United States and Canada*.
> Updates Larson, 1.027.

1.033 *McKittrick Directory of Advertisers*. New York, 1900-.

Annual since 1900 with varying titles: *Advertiser Index, McKit-trick's Directory of Advertisers, Their Managers and Agents,* etc. United with *Standard Advertising Register* to become *Standard Directory of Advertising*.

1.034 Mayer, Martin P. *The Intelligent Man's Guide to Sales Measures of Advertising*. New York: Advertising Research Foundation, 1965, 72 pp.

Primarily bibliography, pp. 29 - 71.

1.035 Millican, Richard D. *Advertising Volume and Expenditures*. Washington: Small Business Administration, 1958, 4 pp.

A bibliography originally published by Department of Commerce as *Business Service Bulletin* no. 175.

1.036 Morgan, Robert S., ed. *Who's Who in Advertising*. 2d ed. Rye, NY: Redfield, 1972, 764 pp.

Includes biographical sketches of the Advertising Hall of Fame created by the American Advertising Federation and located in the Advertising Club of New York.

1.037 *National List of Advertisers*. Toronto: MacLean Hunter, 1951-.

Annual since 1951, citing Canadian advertisers and their agencies.

1.038 Noble, Valerie. *The Effective Echo: A Dictionary of Advertising Slogans*. New York: Special Library Association, 1970, 165 pp.

A reference book listing slogans, nothing more.

1.039 Pennington, Allan L. and Peterson, Robert A. *Reference Guide to Marketing Literature*. Braintree, MA: D.H. Mark, 1970, 109 pp.

Alphabetical author listing of more than 3,000 articles from 12 journals, published since 1960.

1.040 Price, Warren. *The Literature of Journalism: An Annotated Bibliography*. Minneapolis: University of Minnesota Press, 1959, 489 pp.

Updated by *An Annotated Journalism Bibliography, 1958 - 1968,* with Calder M. Pickett in 1970.

1.041 *Public Relations, Edward L. Bernays, and the American Scene*. Boston: F.W. Faxon, 1951, 86 pp.

Annotated bibliography and reference guide to writings by and about Edward L. Bernays from 1917 to 1951.

1.042   Richard, John M. *A Guide to Advertising Information Sources*.
Scottsdale, AZ: MacDougal, 1969, 59 pp.

> An annotated list of directories, yearbooks, bibliographies and
> other information sources. 277 entries.

1.043   Rogers, J.L., ed. *Who's Who in Advertising*. New York: Harper,
1931, 284 pp.

> Biographical, with accounts managed and professional experience.

1.044   Romaine, Lawrence B. *A Guide to American Trade Catalogs, 1744 -
1900*. New York: Bowker, 1960, 422 pp.

1.045   Smith, Bruce L.; Lasswell, Harold D.; and Casey, Ralph D. *Propaganda and Promotional Activities: An Annotated Bibliography*. Minneapolis: University of Minnesota Press, 1935, 450 pp.

> Harder to find Lasswell, *et al*. A version of 1.028.

1.046   *Standard Directory of Advertising*. 1964-. New York: National
Register, 1964-.

> Frequency varies. A "Classified Edition" is issued annually,
> with 9 monthly supplements. The "Geographical Index" is annual.
> Supercedes in part the *Standard Advertising Register* (1915 - 63),
> and incorporates *McKittrick Directory of Advertisers* (1899 -
> 1960).

1.047   *Standard Rate and Data Service*. Skokie, IL: Standard Rate and
Data Service, 1919 - 50. Vol. 1 - 34.

> Title and frequency vary. Gives information on rates and adver-
> tising media. Includes newspapers, magazines, radio and televi-
> sion, films, transportation. Canadian, Mexican and United States
> rates are given.

1.048   Steilen, Charles F., and Altizer, Roley. *A Guide to Marketing/
Advertising Information: An Annotated Bibliography Covering General
As Well As Specific Secondary Sources of Marketing and Advertising
Information*. Atlanta: Adman Books, 1972, 46 pp.

1.049   *Topicator*. Denver. January 1965-.

> A classified article guide to the advertising-broadcasting trade
> press; 8 monthly issues, 3 quarterly cumulations and annual
> cumulations.

1.050   Townsend, Derek. *Advertising and Public Relations: A Four Language Dictionary and Glossary of Terms*. London: A. Redman, 1964, 152 pp.

> English, French, Italian and German, for the common market.

1.051 United States. Department of Commerce. Bureau of Foreign and Domestic Commerce. *Market Research Agencies*. Domestic Commerce Series, no. 6. Washington, DC: Government Printing Office, 1926 and annually.

> "A list of publications on domestic market research by the federal government, state government, colleges, publishers, advertising agencies, business services, chambers of commerce, individuals, business magazines, newspapers and trade associations."

1.052 Urdang, Laurence, ed. *Dictionary of Advertising Terms*. Chicago: Tatham-Laird & Kudner, 1977, 209 pp.

> Over 4,000 entries and very comprehensive.

1.053 Vigrolio, Tom, and Zahler, Jack. *Marketing and Communications Media Dictionary*. Norfolk, MA: NBS, 1969, 425 pp.

1.054 *Who's Who in Advertising*. Detroit: Business Service Corp., 1916.

See also 6.035, 8.108, 8.505, 9.103, 10.014, 10.038, 10.095.

> "Thus the advertising of the last quarter of the last century, both newspaper and magazine, is a revealing record of social history -- as it is today, for that matter. The changing habits of a people can be learned from what it buys as surely as the history of the earth can be learned from the fossils buried in its strata. Kipling knew that and complained when magazines were sent him stripped of the advertising pages to save postage. Librarians, too, have begun to bind magazines with advertising intact, and these humble adjuncts to literature may prove more valuable to the future historian than the editorial contents. In them we may trace our sociological history, the rise and fall of fads and crazes, changing interests and tastes, in foods, clothes, amusements and vices, a panorama of life as it was lived, more informing than old diaries or crumbling tombstones."

> Earnest Elmo Calkins
> (3.024, p 229-30)

2.000
HISTORIES

2.001 Abrams, Ann U. "From Simplicity to Sensation: Art in American Advertising, 1904 - 1929." *Journal of Popular Culture* 10 (Winter 1976): 620 - 28.

On the conflict between art and the selling function.

2.002 *Advertising: Yesterday, Today and Tomorrow.* Special Issue of *Printers' Ink* 283 (14 June 1963), 475 pp.

Giant special issue, but mostly a description of "today" with plugs for various media, agencies, services, etc.

2.003 Annenberg, Maurice. *Advertising, 3000 B.C. - 1900 A.D.: A Not Too Serious Compilation.* Baltimore: Maran Print, 1969, 102 pp.

Mostly facsimilies, but some text with a focus on printing.

2.004 Atherton, Lewis E. "Early Western Mercantile Advertising." *Bulletin of the Business Historical Society* 12 (September 1938): 52 - 57.

Describes mercantile advertising as dreary, in the absence of standard brands.

2.005 Barnouw, Erik. *The Sponsor: Notes on a Modern Potentate.* Cambridge: Oxford University Press, 1978, 220 pp.

A discussion of the sponsor's influence on television programming. Done by a foremost Columbia University scholar whose specialty is the history of broadcasting.

2.006 Barrow, Robert M. "Newspaper Advertising in Colonial America, 1704 - 1775." Ph.D. dissertation, University of Virginia, 1967.

Focuses on such topics as development, audience, methods and techniques, uses, and economics.

2.007 Batten, Jack. "Hey! That's Me in the Anaconda Ad." *Saturday Night* 92 (December 1977): 63 - 80.

Personal notes on advertising as it mirrors our history.

2.008 Becker, Carl M. "Advertising Ink of Yore." *Cincinnati Historical Society Bulletin* 23 (1) (1965): 29 - 38.

Reproduces nine advertisements from Cincinnati newspapers of the 1860's. Stresses the lack of sophistication of the copy.

2.009 Belkaoui, Ahmed, and Belkaoui, Janice M. "A Comparative Analysis of the Roles Played By Women in Print Advertisements." *Journal of Marketing Research* 13 (May 1976): 168 - 72.

Finds a persistance of traditional family roles.

2.010   Bernays, Edward L.   *Public Relations*.   Norman, OK: University of Oklahoma Press, 1952, 374 pp.

First half describes the historical evolution of the profession.

2.011   Boorstin, Daniel J.   *The Image: A Guide to Pseudo-Events in America*.   New York: Harper, 1964, 315 pp.

A stimulating excursion into the social impact of media, with a list of references and suggestions for further reading and writing.

2.012   Boorstin, Daniel J.   "Welcome to the Consumption Community." *Fortune* 76 (1 September 1967):   118+.

An excerpt from the third volume of *The Americans* in which he briefly reviews some marketing history to support the introduction of the concept of "consumption communities."

2.013   Borden, Neil H.   "The Role of Advertising in the Various Stages of Corporate and Economic Growth."   In *Marketing and Economic Development,* pp. 476 - 95.   Chicago: American Marketing Association, 1965.

2.014   Boss, Henry Rush.   *A Brief History of Advertising, with Some Curious Specimens of Advertisements*.   Boston: T.H. Cahill, 1886, 36 pp.

Even numbered pages are ads for publisher.

2.015   Boyce, Howard H.   "Advertising and Publishing in Colonial America." *American Heritage* 5 (Spring 1954):   6 - 10.

Several facsimilies.

2.016   Boyce, Howard H.   "American Advertising."   *American Heritage* 5 (Summer 1954):   10 - 13.

A little colonial information, a little on Barnum.

2.017   Brooks, Henry M.   *Quaint and Curious Advertisements*.   Boston: Tickner, 1886, 153 pp.

Eighteenth century ads from Boston newspapers with brief comments.

2.018   Carter, David E.   "The Changing Face of *Life*'s Advertisements, 1950 - 1966."   *Journalism Quarterly* 46 (Spring 1969):- 87.- 93.

The advertisements were studied to determine trends and whether actual practice coincides with research findings concerning effectiveness.   A sample of 36 issues from 1950 to 1966 resulted in 1, 659 full-page or larger advertisements.   Based on primary sources.

2.019 Coleman, Edgar W. *Advertising Development*. Milwaukee: Germania, 1909, 449 pp.

"A brief review and commentary upon various phases of advertising development as influenced by the advertising manager and advertising agent ... with 250 portraits of the publicity generals who are in continual rivalry for commercial conquest." Most valuable for the biographical information.

2.020 Coolsen, Frank G. "Pioneers in the Development of Advertising." *Journal of Marketing* 12 (July 1947): 80 - 86.

A thorough review of books on advertising written before 1910.

2.021 Cowan, Ruth S. "The Industrial Revolution in the Home: Household Technology and Social Change in the 20th Century." *Technology and Culture* 17 (January 1976): 1 - 23.

Uses advertising as its evidence to such an extent that the result is as much part of the history of advertising as it is the history of women.

2.022 Cowan, Ruth S. "Two Washes in the Morning and a Bridge Party at Night: The American Housewife Between the Wars." *Women's Studies* 3 (1976): 147 - 72.

Explores her study using advertising as part of her data.

2.023 Cox, Keith K. "Changes in Stereotyping of Negroes and Whites in Magazine Advertising." *Public Opinion Quarterly* 33 (1969/70): 603 - 06.

Discusses occupational role of blacks in general magazine advertisements since 1948.

2.024 Crane, Burton. *A Century of Financial Advertising in the New York Times*. New York: New York Times, 1957, 127 pp.

Mostly reproductions, but an interesting companion text primarily relating the news of the day to put the ads in perspective.

2.025 Curti, Merle. "The Changing Concept of Human Nature in the Literature of American Advertising." *Business History Review* 41 (Winter 1967): 335 - 57.

An excellent paper covering 1888 - 1954. Drawn primarily from an analysis of the content of *Printers' Ink*. The description is most satisfying for the period before 1910 and least for the post war era.

2.026 DeVries, Leonard, and Van Amstel, Ilonka. *The Wonderful World of American Advertisements, 1865 - 1900*. London: J. Murray, 1972, 143 pp.

Little text, but well illustrated. Victorian black and white engravings reproduced. See also a companion volume on English Victorian advertising.

2.027 Diamant, Lincoln. *Television's Classic Commercial: The Golden Years, 1948 - 1958*. New York: Hastings House, 1971, 305 pp.

   Thirty pages of introduction and sixty-nine of storyboards and stills.

2.028 Dornbush, Sanford, and Hickman, L. "Other-Directedness in Consumer Goods Advertising: A Test of Riesman's Historical Theory." *Social Forces* 38 (December 1959): 99 - 102.

   Ads drawn from 1890 - 1956 *Ladies Home Journals,* showing an increase in use of endorsements and interpersonal satisfaction appeals after 1921 (but a decline after 1940?).

2.029 Dundes, Alan. "Advertising and Folklore." *New York Folklore Quarterly* 19 (2) (1963): 143 - 51.

   The alteration of brand names or advertising slogans into puns and jokes with illustrative examples.

2.030 Ehrenreich, Barbara, and English, Deidre. "The Manufacture of Housework." *Socialist Revolution* 5 (October-December 1975): 5 - 40.

   "Labor saving devices" and other advertising ploys create higher expectations and work.

2.031 Elkin, Frederick. *Rebels and Colleagues: Advertising and Social Change in French Canada*. Montreal: McGill-Queen's University Press, 1973, 227 pp.

   Descriptive wealth of material on advertising before and after the "quiet revolution."

2.032 *Fifty Years of the Pioneer Spirit*. New York: Livermore & Knight, 1925, 59 pp.

   "A retrospect of a half-century of endeavour which has produced a present day organization equipped to render a very useful and complete service in advertising." Corporate commemorative.

2.033 Foster, G. Allen. *Advertising: Ancient Marketplace to Television*. New York: Criterion Books, 1967, 224 pp.

   Superficial, inaccurate, with paltry illustrations.

2.034 Fowles, Jib. *Mass Advertising as Social Forecast: A Method of Futures Research*. Westport, CT: Greenwood Press, 1976, 153 pp.

   A content analysis of *Life* Magazine ads of 1950, '60 and '70, and an attempt to relate changes in these ads to changes in the content of news stories.

2.035 Fox, Frank W.   "Advertising and the Second World War: A Study in Private Propaganda."   Ph.D. dissertation, Stanford University, 1973.

    An investigation into the institutional history of war advertising, and an analysis of war advertising content.

2.036 Fox, Frank W. *Madison Avenue Goes to War: The Strange Military Career of American Advertising, 1941 - 1945*.   Provo, UT: Brigham Young University Press, 1975, 98 pp.

    Drawn from Stanford Ph.D. dissertation, 1973.

2.037 Friedhaim, William Paul.   "Mass Advertising and Social Control: An Analysis of Advertising as an Organ of Social Conditioning, 1888 - 1918."   M.A. thesis, University of Wisconsin, 1961.

2.038 Friedrich, Carl J., and Sayre, Jeanette.   *The Development of the Control of Advertising on the Air*.   Harvard Studies in the Control of Radio, no. 1.   Cambridge, MA: Harvard University Press, 1940, 39 pp.

    History of regulation.

2.039 Geizer, Ronald.   "Advertising in *Ebony*:   1960 and 1969." *Journalism Quarterly* 48 (Spring 1971): 131 - 34.

    Finds an increase in black models and integration.

2.040 Grow, Michael.   "Bruce Barton: First Ad Man to Advise a Presidential Candidate." *Wisconsin Then and Now* 13 (4) (1966): 1 - 3.

    Barton's role in Coolidge's 1924 campaign.

2.041 Harder, Virgil E.   "A History of Direct Mail Advertising." Ph.D. dissertation, University of Illinois, 1958.

    A broad scale review of information from secondary sources.

2.042 Hedges, James B.   "Advertising the West."   In *Building the Canadian West: Land and Colonialization Policies of the C.P.R.*, pp. 94 - 125.   New York: Macmillan, 1939.

    Study of the promotional strategy of the Canadian Pacific Railway in encouraging immigration and settlement.

2.043 Hettinger, Herman S.   *A Decade of Radio Advertising*.   Chicago: University of Chicago Press, 1933, 354 pp.

    A wealth of detailed information on the first decade; based on much original data.

2.044 Holland, Donald R.   "The Origin and Development of the Advertising Agency in the United States."   M.A. thesis, Pennsylvania State University, 1970.

    Some of this can be seen in a popularized account on Volney Palmer

which appears as the cover story in *Advertising Age,* 23 April
1973.

2.045 Hornung, Clarence P., and Johnson, Fridolf. *200 Years of American
Graphic Art: A Retrospective Survey of the Printing Arts and Advertising
Since the Colonial Period*. New York: G. Braziller, 1976, 211 pp.

Many facsimilies. Some text with emphasis on changes in printing
technology as manifested in advertising ephemera.

2.046 Houck, Hohn W., ed. *Outdoor Advertising: History and Regulation*.
Notre Dame, IN: University of Notre Dame Press, 1969, 250 pp.

Includes a few interesting black and white illustrations of early
electric signs, but generally disappointing.

2.047 "How It Was in Advertising, 1776 - 1976." *Advertising Age* 147
(19 April 1976): 1+.

This and related articles form a special bicentennial issue which
includes an article by Daniel Boorstin calling advertising the
"rhetoric of democracy", brief profiles of ten men who shaped
advertising, women in advertising, a history of Colgate advertising
and a bicentennial collection of "Best Ads."

2.048 Hudson, Frederic. *Journalism in the United States, from 1690 to
1872*. New York: Harper, 1873, 789 pp.

Chapter 25 to the end discusses the author's thirty year association with James Bennett. Advertising is discussed throughout.

2.049 Hynes, Terry. "Media Manipulation and Political Campaigns: Bruce
Barton and the Presidential Elections of the Jazz Age." *Journalism
History* 4 (3) (1977): 93 - 98.

2.050 Johnson, Bobby H. "Singing Oklahoma's Praises: Boosterism in
the Soonerland." *Great Plains Journal* 11 (1) (1971): 57 - 65.

Summarizes promotional sentiment and techniques in Oklahoma
Territory, 1890 - 1907.

2.051 Jones, Edgar R., ed. *Those were the Good Old Days: A Happy Look
at American Advertising, 1880 - 1930*. New York: Simon & Schuster, 1959,
447 pp.

Entirely facsimiles.

2.052 Karolevitz, Robert F. *Old Time Agriculture in the Ads*. Aberdeen,
SD: North Plains Press, 1970, 120 pp.

As mostly reproductions, but provides a good view of the changing
farm life from 1875 - 1910.

2.053 Kassarjian, H.H. "The Negro and American Advertising, 1946 -
1965." *Journal of Marketing Research* 6 (February 1969): 29 - 39.

A study of the content of magazine advertising and the use of models.

2.054 Kitson, Harry D. *Scientific Advertising*. New York: Codex, 1926, 73 pp.

A collection of technical papers "using the historical method" reporting primitive content analysis of ads, 1895 - 1920, for changes in size, layout, art forms and positioning.

2.055 Landauer, Bella C. "Literary Allusions in American Advertising as Sources of Social History." *New York Historical Society Quarterly* 31 (July 1947): 148 - 59.

2.056 Lewis, Lawrence. *The Advertisements of the Spectator*. Boston: Houghton Mifflin, 1909, 307 pp.

"Being a story ... of Queen Anne's England as reflected in, as well as an illustration of, the origins of the art of advertising."

2.057 Leymore, Varda Langholz. *Hidden Myth: Structure and Symbolism in Advertising*. New York: Basic Books, 1975, 208 pp.

Disappointing application of structuralism. See review in the *Journal of Marketing Research* 14 (August 1977): 424 - 25.

2.058 Mackle, Elliott. "Two-Way Stretch: Some Dichotomies in the Advertising of Florida as the Boom Collapsed." *Tequesta* 33 (1973): 17 - 29.

Based on primary sources.

2.059 McMahon, A. Michael. "An American Courtship: Psychologists and Advertising Theory in the Progressive Era." *American Studies* 13 (1972): 5 - 18.

Reports on the co-opting of academics by the persuasion industry.

2.059a Mayer, Martin. *Madison Avenue, U.S.A*. New York: Harper & Row, 1958, 337 pp.

A thorough journalistic discussion of the advertising industry of the fifties.

2.060 Mika, Nick and Mika, Helen. *Friendly Persuasion: Canadian Advertising of Yesteryear*. Belleville, ON: Mika, 1974, 104 pp.

Miscellaneous 19th Century ads, but reprinting of minimal quality.

2.061 Morton, Patricia R. "Riesman's Theory of Social Character Applied to Consumer Goods Advertising." *Journalism Quarterly* 44 (Summer 1967): 337 - 40.

Updates and elaborates on Dornbush and Hickman, 2.028, with 13 product categories and 5 time periods.

2.062 Nixon, H.K. "Wartime Advertising and the Consumer." In *Consumer Problems in Wartime,* pp. 243 - 253. Edited by Kenneth Dameron. New York: McGraw-Hill, 1944.

Does not present many examples, but has a nice list of types of wartime appeals and purposes of advertising in World War II.

2.063 Nonken, Harold A. "Trends in American Magazine Advertising." M.A. thesis, University of Wisconsin, 1966.

Includes information on the career of Harry Dexter Kitson.

2.064 Pancoast, Chalmers L. *Trail Blazers of Advertising: Stories of the Romance and Adventure of the Old-Time Advertising Game.* New York: Grafton Press, 1926, 269 pp.

The stories of adventure and misadventure from the late nineteenth century: the era of P.T. Barnum, Buffalo Bill, patent medicine shows, hymn book solicitors and miscellaneous ballyhoo artists.

2.065 Pease, Otis. *The Responsibilities of American Advertising.* New Haven: Yale University Press, 1958, 232 pp.

A thorough scholarly discussion of American advertising from 1920 to 1940. Good material on the criticisms of the thirties and the industry's responses. Interesting also because the arguments pro and con are still voiced and are still valid.

2.066 Pollay, Richard W. "Lydiametrics: Applications of Econometrics to the History of Advertising." *Journal of Advertising History,* in review.

Historiography reviewing two decades of econometric analysis finding the results disappointing.

2.067 Pope, Daniel A. "The Development of National Advertising, 1865 - 1920." Ph.D. dissertation, Columbia University, 1973.

Well written presentation, which covers a range of topics including some not well described elsewhere: evolution of journals (e.g. *Printers' Ink*), associations and services (e.g. Audit Bureau of Circulation).

2.068 Porter, Patrick G. "Advertising in the Early Cigarette Industry: W. Duke, Sons & Company of Durham." *North Carolina Historical Review* 48 (1) (1971): 31 - 43.

Examines the kinds of advertising used by W. Duke, Sons and Co. of Durham in the 1880's and suggests some reasons for its apparent effectiveness.

2.069 Presbrey, Frank. *History and Development of Advertising.* Garden City, NY: Doubleday, 1929, 642 pp.

A "court history" but lots of illustrations show the changing styles of advertising. The author becomes increasingly rhapsodic

as the material he deals with approaches the twenties. The
history begins in 1860 and concerns itself exclusively with the
United States.

2.070 Printers' Ink. *Fifty Years, 1888 - 1938*. New York: Printers'
Ink, 1938, 472 pp.

A history of advertising, not *Printers' Ink*. Issued also as vol.
184, no. 4, sec. 2 (28 July 1938). An indexed massive special
issue.

2.071 Printers' Ink. *100 Years of American Advertising: 100 Years of
the J. Walter Thompson Co*. Chicago: Advertising Publications, 1964,
202 pp.

Special issue of *Advertising Age* 35 (7 December 1964).

2.072 Radin, Max. *The Lawful Pursuit of Gain*. Boston: Houghton
Mifflin, 1931, 144 pp.

Radin "examines the relation between law and its changes with the
hard creditor, the rapacious creditor, the dishonest vendor, and
the unfair competitor, and assesses the future of business."

2.073 Rosenberg, Rita S. "An Investigation of the Nature, Utilization
and Accuracy of Nutritional Claims in Magazine Food Advertisements: An
Analysis and Evaluation of the Nutritional Statements Made in Food
Advertisements Over a Fifty Year Period." M.A. Thesis, New York University, 1955, 317 pp.

2.074 Rowsome, Frank. *They Laughed When I Sat Down: An Informal History of Advertising in Words and Pictures*. New York: McGraw-Hill, 1959,
181 pp.

Better than the title suggests. Good reading and well illustrated.

2.075 Sampson, Henry. *A History of Advertising from the Earliest Times*.
London: Chatto & Windus, 1874, 616 pp.

The first history of advertising and still cited. Covers England
and good on signs, trade cards and other early forms of advertising.

2.076 Seldin, Joseph. *The Golden Fleece: Selling the Good Life to
Americans*. New York: Macmillan, 1963, 305 pp.

Written by the head of an ad agency. Very readably written,
informative and uses an historical structure. Until something
else comes along, this must be considered the best single source
on post WWII marketing history. Covers many topics: packaging,
salespromotion, premiums, public relations, media, rating services, etc. Indexed but not documented, which is a shame because
the author "quotes" many citable statements and data.

2.077 Sexton, D.E., and Haberman, P. "Women in Magazine Advertisements."
Journal of Advertising Research 14 (August 1974): 41 - 46.

An historical perspective covering the years 1950 - 1971, but
"thin" results.

2.078 Shapiro, Stephen R. "The Big Sell: Attitudes of Advertising
Writers About Their Craft in the 1920's and 1930's." Ph.D. dissertation,
University of Wisconsin, 1969.

Also includes a chapter on Bruce Barton.

2.079 Shaw, Steven J. "Colonial Newspaper Advertising: A Step Toward
Freedom of the Press." *Business History Review* 33 (1959): 409 - 20.

Describes colonial journalists taking goods in exchange for sub-
scriptions and then advertising to sell the goods, thereby
helping to overcome the skepticism of other businessmen toward
advertising.

2.080 Sherman, Sidney A. "Advertising in the United States." *Journal
of the American Statistical Association* 7 (1900): 119 - 62.

Lots of information on expenditures by firms in various industries
(all unnamed), but no aggregate statistics. Best as a source of
the miscellany of the times. Provides such diverse information as
the size of the billposter's union, the number of trade magazines
and how many window dressers existed at the turn of the century.

2.081 Sherman, Sidney A. "Advertising: Its History and Present Forms
with Special Reference to Its Economic and Social Bearings." Ph.D.
dissertation, Brown University, 1900.

2.082 Simon, Julian L., and Golembo, Leslie. "The Spread of a Cost-
Free Business Innovation." *Journal of Business* 40 (October 1967): 385 -
88.

Diffusion of "January White Sale" showing earlier use in large
cities.

2.083 Sitter, A. George; O'Connell, Stephen M.; and Mustofsky, David.
"Trends in Appearance of Models in *Ebony* Ads over 17 Years." *Journalism
Quarterly* 49 (Autumn 1972): 547 - 50.

Finds increase in black male but not black female models.

2.084 Stephenson, H.E., and McNaught, Carlton. *The Story of Advertising
in Canada: A Chronicle of Fifty Years*. Toronto: Ryerson, 1940, 364 pp.

Not very authoritatively researched and poorly written. A number
of chapters are thinly disguised pitches for using Canadian ad
agencies, Canadian media and especially the McKim ad agency.

2.085 Stephenson, William. "The Infantile Vs. the Sublime in Advertisements." *Journalism Quarterly* 40 (Summer 1963): 181 - 86.

Finds more infantile mechanisms in current full page ads than 30
years ago.

2.086 Storer, Louise K. "Military and Nationalistic Themes in War-Time American Consumer Advertising." Ph.D. dissertation, New York University, 1971.

> The periods of World War II, the Korean War and the War in Vietnam are compared. The sample is made up of all the commercial advertisements one quarter column or larger in size appearing in all the issues of *Life, Time, National Geographic, Good Housekeeping* and *Esquire.* No clear relationship between public approval of U.S. participation in the wars and the frequency of military or nationalistic themes could be demonstrated.

2.087 Sutphen, Dick. *The Mad Old Ads.* Toronto: McGraw-Hill, 1966, 127 pp.

> Quaint ads of the 19th century and some 18th century examples. Includes "material produced by some of the greatest quacks, imposters and swindlers the world has ever known."

2.088 Tull, Donald S. "An Examination of the Hypothesis that Advertising Has a Lagged Effect on Sales." Ph.D. dissertation, University of Chicago, 1956.

> A study of Packer's Tar Soap advertising and sales data.

2.089 Tull, Donald S. "A Re-examination of the Causes of the Decline in Sales of Sapolio." *Journal of Business* 28 (April 1955): 128 - 37.

> Uses econometrics to challenge conventional wisdom.

2.090 Turner, Ernest S. *The Shocking History of Advertising.* New York: E.P. Dutton, 1953, 351 pp.

> Anecdotal account of the history of advertising malpractices, fraud, misrepresentations, use of ads for quackery, etc. Better than the title suggests.

2.091 Ulanoff, Stanley M. "Comparison Advertising: An Historical Retrospective." *Working Paper,* Marketing Science Institute, February 1975, 48 pp.

> Not really historical at all.

2.092 Van Til, Roy. "The Content of U.S. Automobile Advertising, 1949 - 1973: Impact on the Shaping of Wants and Product Development." Ph.D. dissertation, Boston College, 1975.

> A sample of 750 automobile advertisements from *Life* magazine spanning the 25 year test period were classified on a number of dimensions of content. The data was broken down by year, corporation, make and price class for a number of characteristics in order to capture the richness of the competitive struggle. The conclusions include among other things that advertising has acted to limit consumer choice on many areas of potential product variation.

2.093 Wagner, Charles L.H. *The Story of Signs: An Outline History of the Sign Arts from the Earliest Recorded Times to the Present "Atomic Age."* Boston: A. MacGibbon, 1954, 123 pp.

Pretentious verbiage drawn "from the author's peregrinations."

2.094 Watkins, Julian L. *The 100 Greatest Advertisements: Who Wrote Them and What They Did.* New York: Moore, 1949, 201 pp.

A good collection of print ads from 1900 to the 1930's. Includes many famous ads, each presented as a mini case study.

2.095 Watkins, T.H. "The Boom of the Sunset Land, Southern California, 1887." *American West* 9 (6) (1972): 10 - 19.

"The Southern Pacific Railroad conducted one of the most intensive advertising campaigns in American history in the early 1880's to proclaim southern California as a yet undeveloped Eden."

2.096 Wood, James P. *The Story of Advertising.* New York: Ronald, 1958, 512 pp.

Well written, but limited as a history of advertising. The index is, unfortunately, not up to the quality of the text.

2.097 Yodelis, Mary A. "Genteel Rooms, Umbrilloes and Velvet Corks: Advertising in the Boston Press, 1763 - 1775." *Journalism History* 3 (Summer 1976): 40 - 47.

Notes shift in advertisers from loyalist to patriot papers.

See also 6.035, 6.072, 8.108, 8.505, 9.103, 10.014, 10.038, 10.095.

"I am sure that no man has gained more from life than I have -- more of true happiness and content. I trace that to the love of simple things, of common people, which made my success in advertising.
    Here at our week-end parties I meet many successful men in a most intimate way. I envy none of them. The happiest are those who live closest to nature, an essential to advertising success. So I conclude that this vocation, depending as it does on love and knowledge of the masses, offers many rewards beyond money."

                                        Claude C. Hopkins
                                        (3.058, p 205-6)

3.000
BIOGRAPHIES AND CAREER
REFLECTIONS

3.001 Abrams, George J. *How I Made A Million Dollars With Ideas*. Chicago: Playboy Press, 1972, 216 pp.

Biographical reflections aimed at stimulating creativity in copy premises.

3.002 Adams, James R. *More Power to Advertising*. New York: Harper, 1937, 179 pp.

A collection of essays on diverse topics, like "advertising needs older men," "women are just people," etc.

3.003 Adams, James R. *Sparks Off My Anvil: From Thirty Years in Advertising*. New York: Harper, 1958, 171 pp.

Mini-memos of advice and reflection.

3.004 Appel, Joseph H. *The Business Biography of John Wanamaker, Founder and Builder: America's Merchant Pioneer from 1861 to 1922*. New York: Macmillan, 1930, 471 pp.

The author profits more than the reader from his position as advertising director of the store.

3.005 Appel, Joseph H. *Growing Up With Advertising*. New York: Business Bourse, 1940, 301 pp.

Covers author's career with John Wanamaker Stores from 1899 - 1936. Has a section on pioneers in advertising, but overstates Wanamaker's importance, naturally.

3.006 Appel, Joseph H. "Reminiscences in Retailing." *Bulletin of the Business Historical Society* 12 (December 1938): 81 - 90.

Reminiscences about John Wanamaker.

3.007 Arnold, Stanley. *Tale of the Blue Horse and Other Million Dollar Adventures*. Englewood Cliffs, NJ: Prentice-Hall, 1968, 202 pp.

Subtitled as "being an account of how the author roused the forces of American Business Ingenuity." Tales of success, mostly in public relations and sales promotion, by an ex-Young & Rubicam executive. Clients include Pick-N-Pay, Ford, American Tobacco, Remington Rand, General Foods, Macy's, National Cash Register, Goodyear, and United Airlines.

3.008 Assael, Henry, ed. *The Collected Works of C.C. Parlin*. New York: Arno, 1978.

Parlin pioneered orderly fact-finding applied to advertising for Curtis Publishing.

3.009 Baker, Samm S. *Casebook of Successful Ideas for Advertising and Selling*. Garden City, NY: Hanover House, 1959, 258 pp.

Capsulized case histories from 28 years of experience.

3.010 Barnum, P.T. *Struggles and Triumphs: Or Forty Years' Recollections of P.T. Barnum*. Buffalo, NY: Warren, Johnson, 1873, 840 pp.

Lengthy and self-flattering autobiography, but full of amusing anecdotes from the life of a most unforgettable character.

3.011 Bartos, Rena, and Pearson, Arthur S. "The Founding Fathers of Advertising Research." *Journal of Advertising Research* 17 (June 1977): 1 - 32.

Transcripts of interviews with Ernest Dichter, George Gallup, Alfred Politz, Henry Brenner, A.V. Nielsen, Sr. Hans Ziesel, Frank Stanton and Archibald Crossley. Also available on 16mm film (29 min.) from the Advertising Research Foundation.

3.012 Belknap, John. *Management and Creative Advertising: Some Highly Personal Reflections on Management's Relationship (or Lack of it) with Creative People in Advertising*. Toronto: Burns & MacEachern, 1960, 45 pp.

Thin, probable purpose to attract business.

3.013 Bernays, Edward L. *Biography of an Idea: Memoirs of a Public Relation Counsel*. New York: Simon & Schuster, 1965, 849 pp.

Well written memoir by Freud's nephew, a great PR man during 1920 - 1960's. Includes notes on his experiences with Proctor and Gamble, George Washington Hill, E.A. Filene, Philco, and the United Fruit Co.

3.014 Bernays, Edward L. *Public Relations*. Norman, OK: University of Oklahoma Press, 1952, 374 pp.

History of public relations and case histories from the author's distinguished career.

3.015 Bernstein, Sid. *This Makes Sense to Me: An Opinionated Editor Speaks Out*. Chicago: Crain, 1976, 263 pp.

Columns from *Advertising Age*, 1972 - 75. Discusses sundry current topics.

3.016 Bigelow, Burton. *Elbert Hubbard: Pioneer Advertising Man*. East Aurora, NY: Roycrofters, 1931, 18 pp.

Biographical praise from his disciples.

3.017 Biow, Milton H. *Butting In: An Adman Speaks Out*. Garden City, NY: Doubleday, 1964, 250 pp.

Author's agency was for a while the largest individually owned agency. Clients include Bulova, P&G, Pepsi-Cola, Anacin.

3.018 Bogart, Leo. *Strategy in Advertising*. New York: Harcourt & Brace, 1967, 336 pp.

Reflections of a successful adman, and probably the best such book ever done. Intelligent and analytical, this serves better as a text to advertising practice than as a history of Bogart's experience.

3.019 Bowles, Chester, *Promises to Keep: My Years in Public Life, 1941 - 1969*. New York: Harper & Row, 1971, 651 pp.

Note: covers career after founding of Benton & Bowles. See Hyman, 3.061.

3.020 Brower, Charlie. *Me and Other Advertising Geniuses*. Garden City, NY: Doubleday, 1974. 230 pp.

Entertainingly written recollections by a principal in Batten, Barten, Durstine and Osborne. Covers a wide time span, as Brower was with BBDO for forty years.

3.021 Burnett, Leo. *Communications of an Advertising Man*. Chicago: By the Author, 1961, 350 pp.

Selections from the speeches, articles, memoranda and miscellaneous writings of Burnett.

3.022 Burnett, Leo. *A Tribute to Leo Burnett Through a Selection of the Inspiring Words That He Wrote or Spoke*. Chicago: By the Author, 1971, 92 pp.

3.023 Buxton, Edward. *Promise Them Anything: The Inside Story of the Madison Avenue Power Struggle*. New York: Stein & Day, 1972, 302 pp.

Current book by the publisher of *Ad Daily,* street wise and gossipy.

3.024 Calkins, Earnest Elmo. *And Hearing Not: Annals of an Ad Man*. New York: Scribner, 1946, 387 pp.

Autobiography of a successful man whose career spanned the decades of 1890 - 1940.

3.025 Calkins, Earnest Elmo. *Louder Please: The Autobiography of a Deaf Man*. Boston: Atlantic Monthly Press, 1924, 260 pp.

His distinguished career is more thoroughly retold in his other autobiography, *And Hearing Not*.

3.026 Campbell, J.M. "Advertising Recollections of a Quarter Century."
Printers' Ink Monthly (December 1919 - March 1920): 4 installments.

    Reminiscences of experiences in the railroad and Procter &
    Gamble.

3.027 Coleman, Edgar W. *Advertising Development*. Milwaukee: Germania,
1909, 449 pp.

    "A brief review and commentary upon various phases of advertising
    development as influenced by the advertising manager and adver-
    tising agent ... with 250 portraits of the publicity generals who
    are in continual rivalry for commercial conquest."

3.028 Colwell, Robert T., ed. *The One World of Sam Meek*. New York: By
the Editor, 1964, 75 pp.

    Experiences with J. Walter Thompson, primarily overseas or with
    government accounts.

3.029 Cone, Fairfax M. *The Blue Streak: Some Observations, Mostly About
Advertising*. Chicago: Crain, 1973, 200 pp.

    A selection of memos from a steady stream which Cone directed to
    the staff of Foote, Cone and Belding, from 1948 - 1969. Edited
    for brevity, but otherwise these are original source materials.

3.030 Cone, Fairfax M. *With All Its Faults: A Candid Account of Forty
Years in Advertising*. Toronto: Little, Brown, 1969, 335 pp.

    A reflective narrative by one of the more thoughtful of adver-
    tising men, the successor to Albert Lasker. Includes discussion
    of accounts like Dial Soap, Toni home permanents, the Edsel,
    Hallmark Cards, Kool-Aid and Clairol. General focus on post WWII
    advertising.

3.031 *Confessions of a Copywriter*. Chicago: Dartnell, 1930, 238 pp.

    Subtitled: *By a Widely Known New York Advertising Man Who Chooses
    to Conceal His Identity in Order to Give Unhampered Play to His
    Pen*.

3.032 Constantine, C.P. *Advertising in Action*. Seattle: Superior
Publishing, 1962, 128 pp.

    Historical vignettes of primarily west coast firms.

3.033 Cossman, E. Joseph. *How I Made $1,000,000 in Mail Order*. Engle-
wood Cliffs, NJ: Prentice-Hall, 1963, 239 pp.

    More how-to advice than reflections on the nature of the business.

3.034 Cowley, Charles. *Reminiscences of James C. Ayers and the Town of
Ayer*. Lowell, MA: Penhallow Printers, 1879, 156 pp.

    Very self-serving biographical notes of a patent medicine giant paid for by family and published by them privately; very limited circulation.

3.035 Crowther, Samuel. *John H. Patterson: Pioneer in Industrial Welfare*. Garden City, NY: Doubleday, 1924, 364 pp.

Largely a glorification of Patterson and the paternalistic National Cash Register Co. he created, this is also the story of the creation of professional salesmen and its integration with promotional efforts.

3.036 Daniels, Draper. *Giants, Pigmies and Other Advertising People*. Chicago: Crain, 1974, 257 pp.

Recollections of 30 years experience with a focus on those Daniels worked with, including Raymond Rubicam, Hartison McCann, Marion Harper and Leo Burnett.

3.037 Della Femina, Jerry. *From Those Wonderful Folks Who Gave You Pearl Harbour: Front Line Dispatches From the Advertising War*. New York: Simon & Schuster, 1970, 253 pp.

Anecdotal.

3.038 Dickinson, Howard W. *Crying Our Wares*. New York: J. Day, 1929, 308 pp.

Much biographical information, but the reader is cautioned not to look for "too much continuity." (p. xi)

3.039 Ellis, Jim. *Billboards to Buicks: Advertising as I Lived It*. New York: Abelard-Schuman, 1968, 240 pp.

Experiences with A.W. Shaw, Firestone, Erwin Wasey (for both the rise and the dramatic fall) and finally the Kudner Agency. Later published as *The Jumping Frog from Jasper County. A Hoosier Boy Lands on Madison Avenue*.

3.040 Fitz-Gibbon, Bernice. *Macy's, Gimbel's and Me: How to Earn $50,000 a Year in Retail Advertising*. New York: Simon & Schuster, 1967, 380 pp.

Nobody but nobody underates Fitz-Gibbon. Department store experiences, much drawn from earlier diverse publication. Skeptical of agencies and research.

3.041 Foreman, Robert L. *An Ad Man Ad-Libs on TV*. New York: Hastings House, 1957, 173 pp.

Miscellaneous observations by VP of production for BBD&O, from the pages of *Sponsor*.

3.042 Goldman, Eric F. *Two Way Street: The Emergence of the Public Relations Counsel*. Boston: Bellman, 1948, 23 pp.

A brief exploratory essay on the career of Edward Bernays and other pioneers.

3.043 Groucho. (pseud.). *What Groucho Says: The Almost Amiable Growls
of a Hard Working Advertising Man.* New York: Harper, 1930, 266 pp.

> Anecdotes, facts and satire, some of which has also been published
> in *Printers' Ink.*

3.044 Gundlach, Ernest T. *Facts and Fetishes in Advertising.* Chicago:
Consolidated Book Publishers, 1931, 672 pp.

> Reflections about a lengthy Chicago career with discussion of A.D.
> Lasker, "the mess of 1890 - 1910" and a plea for more tests and
> advertising research.

3.045 Gundlach, Ernest T. *Old Sox on Trumpeting.* Chicago: Consolidated
Book Publishers, 1927, 362 pp.

> A serious satire, attacking the 'bunk' in advertising, by one of
> the best known publicity men in the U.S. Farcically set in ancient
> Greece.

3.046 Gunther, John. *Taken at the Flood: The Story of Albert D. Lasker.*
New York: Harper, 1960, 368 pp.

> Biography of the man who was responsible for the continuing success
> of Lord and Thomas, an early ad agency, which was started in 1873
> (Lasker joined in 1900's), and was later reincorporated as Foote,
> Cone and Belding in 1942.

> Includes material on George Washington Hill and American Tobacco,
> John Kennedy, Claude Hopkins, the Kleenex-Kotex case history.

3.047 Hamburger, Estelle. *It's a Woman's Business.* New York: Vanguard,
1939, 300 pp.

> Advertising in the garment trade.

3.048 Hanlon, Walter. *Breaking into Advertising: The Beginner Lands a
Job.* New York: National Library Press, 1935, 124 pp.

> "Breaking-in" stories of many well known advertising men and women
> are covered on pp. 78 - 112.

3.049 Harrington, Alan. *Life in the Crystal Palace.* New York: Knopf,
1959, 263 pp.

> Organizational life viewed from the public relations department of
> a manufacturer. (General Electric?).

3.050 Harris, Neil. *Humbug: The Art of P.T. Barnum.* Boston: Little,
Brown, 1973, 337 pp.

> Academic treatment complete with bibliographic essay.

3.051 Hiebert, Ray E. *Courtier to the Crowd: The Story of Ivy Lee and
the Development of Public Relations.* Ames, IA: Iowa State University
Press, 1966, 351 pp.

A thorough academic biography of a pioneer PR man (1877 - 1934) whose clients included a who's who of persons, corporations and charitable organizations. Drawn from the Ivy Lee papers at Princeton which include drafts of some seven incomplete and unpublished books.

3.052 Higgins, Dennis. *The Art of Writing Advertising*. Chicago: Advertising Publications, 1965, 125 pp.

Interviews with Ogilvy, Reeves, Burnett, Bernbach and George Gribbin.

3.053 Hill, John A. *Some of the Writings of John A. Hill*. New York: By the Author, 1916, 155 pp.

Biography of the publisher which includes some 40 pages on advertising.

3.054 Hill, John W. *The Making of a Public Relations Man*. New York: David McKay, 1963, 273 pp.

Autobiographical reflections of a steel industry PR man.

3.055 Hirsch, Abby, and Burg, Dave. *The Great Carmen Miranda Look-Alike Contest and Other Bold-Faced Lies*. New York: St. Martin's Press, 1974, 224 pp.

Public relations where the "crass in always greener."

3.056 Holland, Donald R. "The Story of Volney Palmer: The Nation's First Agency Man." *Advertising Age* 44 (23 April 1973): 107 - 12.

Undocumented and sloppy in facts and/or proofreading (internally inconsistent birthdates, etc.), this article needs editing badly.

3.057 Holland, Donald R. "Volney B. Palmer (1799 - 1864): The Nation's First Advertising Agency Man." *Journalism Monographs* 54 (May 1976): 1 - 40.

Extracted from his M.A. thesis, "The Origin and Development of the Advertising Agency in the United States." A more popularized form appears as the cover story in *Advertising Age*, 23 April 1973.

3.058 Hopkins, Claude. *My Life in Advertising*. New York: Harper, 1927, 206 pp.

This is the autobiography of one of the great copywriters, still talked about with respect in an industry noted for its disrespect. The book is written in the same straight talk advertising style of "salesmanship in print" that make Hopkins famous.

3.059 Hotchkin, William R. "Early Advertising Adventures." *Printers' Ink Monthly* 1 (June 1920 - November 1920): various pages.

Reminiscences, primarily of time spent in retail with Wanamaker's.

3.060 Hubbard, Elbert. *Advertising and Advertisements*. East Aurora, NY: Roycrofters, 1929, 276 pp.

>   "Publicity preachments from the pen of the FRA."

3.061 Hyman, Sidney. *The Lives of William Benton*. Chicago: University of Chicago Press, 1969, 625 pp.

>   A work in keeping with the breadth of the man's life, this includes four chapters on the creation and development of Benton and Bowles until Benton's departure in 1936 for another of his many careers.

3.062 Jacobson, Jacob Zavel. *Scott of Northwestern: The Life Story of a Pioneer in Psychology and Education*. Chicago: Louis Marino, 1951, 198 pp.

>   The biography of Walter Dill Scott, author of the first *Psychology of Advertising* and later President of Northwestern University.

3.063 Jones, Howard A. *50 Years Behind the Scenes in Advertising*. Philadelphia: n.p., 1975, 235 pp.

>   Includes reflections on the experience of working for A.D. Lasker at Lord & Thomas and at Blackett, Sample, Hummert.

3.064 Jordan, Edward S. *The Inside Story of Adam and Eve*. Utica: H. Coggeshall, 1945, 94 pp.

>   Written in "seven consecutive rainy Sundays."

3.065 Kimbrough, Emily. *Through Charley's Door*. New York: Harper, 1952, 273 pp.

>   Author's experiences in the advertising department of Chicago's Marshall Field & Co. in the 1920's.

3.066 Knoble, Cliff. *Call to Market*. New York: Frederick Fell, 1963, 304 pp.

>   Reflections notable for being from a manufacturers' point of view, not an agencies', and for author's role in the ill-fated Tucker car business, for which he was prosecuted. Also makes reference to National Cash Register, Eureka Vacuum cleaners and two years of middle age unemployment.

3.067 Kynott, Harold H. *The Age of the Income Tax: Rambles with Retrospection*. Philadelphia: Kynett, 1952, 234 pp.

>   Covers advertising career 1912 to date and includes reflection of ARF and ABC.

3.068 Lambert, Gerald B. *All Out of Step: A Personal Chronicle*. New York: Doubleday, 1956, 316 pp.

>   Reflections of the man who gave America "halitosis" and Listerine, but includes only a scant 30 pages on the advertising business.

3.069 Lambert, Gerald B. "How I Sold Listerine." *Fortune* 54 (September 1956): 111+.

> Inspirational story of 1920's ads like "Always a Bridesmaid," "Even Your Friends Won't Tell You," and the creation of "Halitosis."

3.070 Lasker, Albert D. *The Lasker Story as He Told It*. Chicago: Advertising Publications, 1963, 126 pp.

> These are the edited stenographically recorded notes of an informal 6 hour talk Lasker gave his executives in 1925. Also published in 26 installments in *Advertising Age*. A fascinating document.

3.071 Lasker, Albert D. "The Personal Reminiscences of Albert Lasker." *American Heritage* 6 (December 1954): 74 - 84.

> Edited from transcripts of Columbia Oral History tapes.

3.072 Leachman, Harden B. *The Early Advertising Scene*. Wooddale, IL: By the Author, 1949, 253 pp.

> Self-published notes on the experience of small agencies in the American cities of Dallas, Kansas City, New Orleans, etc. from 1900 - 1920.

3.073 Lee, James. *Twenty-Five Years in the Mail Order Business: Or the Experiences of a Mail Order Man*. Chicago: A.E. Swett, 1902, 176 pp.

> Includes material on others in the business as well.

3.074 Littell, Robert. "The Great American Salesman." *Fortune* 5 (February 1932): 43 - 47; 123 - 28.

> Brief history of Sears, both the individual and the store.

3.075 Lois, George. *The Art of Advertising: George Lois on Mass Communication*. New York: Harry N. Abrams, 1977, 325 pp.

> The first book to establish commercial art as an art. Presents the maverick ways of communicating by one of the most successful admen/artists in the last twenty years.

3.076 Lois, George. *George, Be Careful: A Greek Florist's Kid in the Roughhouse World of Advertising*. New York: Saturday Review Press, 1972, 245 pp.

> Anecdotes by one of the contemporary advertising world's most colourful creative personalities, known for his candidness.

3.077 Lowen, Walter A., and Watson, Lillian E. *How to Get a Job and Win Success in Advertising*. New York: Prentice-Hall, 1941, 382 pp.

> Appendices include a collection of famous people writing on what qualities are most important for success, and recollecting how they got their start.

3.078 Lynch, Edmund C. "Walter Dill Scott: Pioneer Industrial Psychologist." *Business History Review* 42 (Summer 1968): 149 - 70.

>   A history of the author of the first major works on the psychology
>   of advertising. See also 3.062.

3.079 Lyon, David G. *Off Madison Avenue*. New York, Putnam, 1966,
246 pp.

>   Reflections of a man whose Madison Avenue agency collapsed, and
>   who restarted an agency from his home in Connecticut, so, this is
>   the story of cottage industry advertising consulting.

3.080 Lyon, Marguerite. *And So to Bedlam: A Worms Eye View of the
Advertising Business*. New York: Bobs-Merrill, 1943, 302 pp.

>   Anecdotes more entertaining than informative. A chapter on women
>   in the business.

3.081 McMahan, Harry W. *McMahan's New Dynamics in Advertising*. Nyack,
NY: n.p., 1969, 223 pp.

>   Insights by a widely read consultant and columnist.

3.082 Manchee, Fred. *The Huckster's Revenge: The Truth About Life on
Madison Avenue*. New York: Thomas Nelson & Sons, 1959, 308 pp.

>   Reflections by another BBD&O executive.

3.083 Marsteller, Bill. *The Wonderful World of Words: Memoranda and
Speeches of Bill Marsteller, 1951 - 1972*. New York: By the Author.

>   "Confessions of a reformed cliche addict" whose firm grew very
>   rapidly during this era.

3.084 Merwin, Samuel. *Rise and Fight Again: The Story of a Life-Long
Friend*. New York: Albert & Charles Boni, 1935, 257 pp.

>   Biography of Louis Liggett, founder of United Drugs and promoter
>   of the Rexall brand name.

3.085 Miller, George L. *Aesop Glim, Advertising Fundamentalist*. New
York: Prentice-Hall, 1930, 237 pp.

>   Articles reproduced from *Printers' Ink* and more of a guide to
>   advertising practice than the idiosyncratic title suggests.

3.086 Moore, Sidney. *So This is the Ad Biz!* New York: Pageant, 1966,
118 pp.

>   A veneer of humour, a core of concern over the stressful roles in
>   the industry. Author's experience was with magazines and then as
>   copy chief in an agency. Author is a woman.

3.087 Moses, Lionel B. *Adventures in Merchandising*. New York: Pillsbury, 1951, 209 pp.

> Adapted from *Sales Management* articles. Adventures helping the
> salesmen who sell retailers advertised products.

3.088 Ogilvy, David. *Blood, Brains and Beer: The Autobiography of
David Ogilvy*. New York: Athenuem, 1978, 181 pp.

> "Publicity for his most complex and delightful client - himself."
> (*Time,* February 13, 1978)

3.089 Ogilvy, David. *Confessions of an Advertising Man*. New York:
Athenuem, 1963, 162 pp.

> Primarily how-to advice, but very well written and personal.

3.090 Phelps, George H. *Tomorrow's Advertisers and Their Advertising
Agencies*. New York: Harper, 1929, 256 pp.

> "A crystallization of advertising trends and a picture of the
> broadening scope and power of advertising." A panegyric by the
> head of an agency, but interesting period reading.

3.091 Polykoff, Shirley. *Does She or Doesn't She?: And How She Did It!*
Garden City, NY: Doubleday, 1975, 131 pp.

> Biographical reflections by the creative copywriter/executive for
> Foote, Cone & Belding on the Clairol account, 1955 - 1975.

3.092 Printers' Ink *After Business Hours: Practical Suggestions and
Intimate Reflections of America's Leaders in Business and Industry*.
New York: Funk & Wagnalls, 1949, 366 pp.

> From the column "After Hours" in *Printers' Ink*.

3.093 Quatsoe, Frank L. *How I Made $50,000*. Pittsburgh: R.T. Lewis,
1912, 45 pp.

> Unexamined.

3.094 Rebaza, Jorge C. *Suggesting Through Advertising: How to Use the
Power of Suggestion to Increase the Power of Advertising*. New York:
Vantage, 1967, 272 pp.

> Original theorizing by Colgate-Palmolive executive based on 38
> years experience primarily in foreign markets.

3.095 Reeves, Rosser. *Reality in Advertising*. New York: Knopf, 1961,
154 pp.

> Mostly advice on copywriting from a veteran who rose to the Chair-
> man of the Board.

3.096 Reichenbach, Harry. *Phantom Fame: The Anatomy of Ballyhoo*. New York: Simon & Schuster, 1931, 258 pp.

Experiences doing motion picture publicity.

3.097 Rice, Elmer C. *How to Live on $1 a Week*. Melrose, MA: Howard Street House, 1943, 512 pp.

Fifteenth edition entitled only *How* (1957, 640 pp.). Reflections of a Yankee businessman with a lot on advertising. Penny wise.

3.098 Rollka, Arthur W. *Archibald Whootle on Advertising*. Tenafly, NJ: A.W. Publishers, 1962, 127 pp.

Satirical on biographical reflections of ad men.

3.099 Rorty, James. "I Was an Ad-Man Once." *New Republic* 73 (25 January 1933): 290 - 93.

Candid but disenchanted recollections. See his book as well.

3.100 Rorty, James. *Our Master's Voice: Advertising*. New York, J. Day, 1934, 394 pp.

The most critical of the reflections by advertising men, this draws its critical analysis from Veblen, but is for the most part naive depression socialism and tends too often to use derogatory lables without having built a case for their validity. Has some informative value, though, including a chapter on the Psychological Corporation.

3.101 Rosenbloom, Jack. *Ballyhoo, Bargains and Banners*. New York: Empire, 1934, 249 pp.

Department store experiences.

3.102 Rowell, George P. *Forty Years an Advertising Agent*. New York: Printers' Ink, 1906, 517 pp.

An autobiography full of stories of the early days of modern advertising, but no table of contents and very awkwardly indexed. Lots of tales about patent medicines.

3.103 Sackheim, Maxwell. *My First Sixty Years in Advertising*. Englewood Cliffs, NJ: Prentice-Hall, 1970, 224 pp.

A fascinating set of reflections by a little known adman, who started the Book-of-the-Month Club and in general proved to be a master of direct mail advertising.

3.104 Schofield, Perry, ed. *100 Top Copy Writers and Their Favorite Ads*. New York: Printers' Ink, 1954, 223 pp.

Mostly facsimilie reproductions, with a couple of paragraphs giving career information on each.

3.105 Schwimmer, Walter. *What Have You Done for Me Lately?* New York: Citadel Press, 1957, 256 pp.

Reflections of a partner in Schwimmer & Scott, Chicago.

3.106 Seiden, 'Hank. *Advertising Pure and Simple*. New York: n.p., 1977, 197 pp.

Although anecdotal and reflective, it is instructional on creating good TV ads.

3.107 *Sherwood Dodge: He Spoke for All of Us*. New York: Advertising Research Foundation, 1971, unpaged.

A tribute, offering quotable quotes.

3.108 Sullivan, Paul W. "G.D. Crain, Jr. and the Founding of *Advertising Age*." *Journalism History* 1 (Autumn 1974): 94 - 95.

Very brief.

3.109 Sumner, Guy L. *How I Learned the Secrets of Success in Advertising*. New York: Prentice-Hall, 1952, 246 pp.

Information on career including: Audit Bureau of Circulation, A.W. Shaw's *System*, International Correspondence School, Woman's Institute, presidency of the Association of National Advertisers, and his own agency. Covers 1907 - 52. Has a chapter on fashions in advertising over 50 years. Best for case histories of advertising strategy.

3.110 Taubeneck, George F. *One Foot in the Door: All About Specialty Merchandising - Including the Laughs*. Detroit: Conjure House, 1947, 386 pp.

3.111 Taubeneck, George F. *One Foot in the Door (The Specialty Selling Formula)*. Detroit: Conjure House, 1949, 386 pp.

Recollections, many of the legendary John H. Patterson, sales manager for NCR and direct mail advertising.

3.112 Thayer, John A. *Astir: A Publisher's Life Story*. Boston: Small, Maynard, 1910, 302 pp.

Autobiography of the advertising manager of *Ladies Home Journal* and *Delineator*. Revised as *Out of the Rut*.

3.113 Thomajan, P.K. "Edward L. Bernays and the American Mind." *Design and Paper* 23 (1947): 1 - 13.

Minor paper briefly recapturing career highlights.

3.114 Thompson, T. Harry, ed. *Wilbur Waffle, Sloganeer: An Autobiography*. Philadelphia: Ayer, 1931, 83 pp.

"A grin tale" -- mock biography and "who's whooey."

3.115 Tierney, Patricia E. *Ladies of the Avenue*. New York: Bartho-
lomew, 1971, 247 pp.

        "The advertising agency jungle ... defoliated by an insider, a
        successful woman copywriter."

3.116 Tinsman, Robert. *Advertising People and Copy Slants*. New York:
Business Bourse, 1936, 192 pp.

        By the head of the Federal Agency.

3.117 Undegraff, Robert R. *Obvious Adams: The Story of a Successful
Businessman*. New York: Harper, 1916, 56 pp.

        Inspirational success story of Oliver B. Adams.

3.118 Updegraff, Robert R. *Old Specification*. New York: McGraw-Hill,
1929, 78 pp.

        From his "little library of self starters."

3.119 Washburn, Robert C. *The Life and Times of Lydia E. Pinkham*. New
York: Putnam, 221 pp.

        "In the time of her family's most desperate poverty, she provided
        a nostrum for feminine ills which became a boon for millions and
        the bane of pure food and drug crusaders. Her company made
        millions."

3.120 Weir, Walter. *On the Writing of Advertisements*. New York:
McGraw-Hill, 1960, 206 pp.

        Personal and literate notes.

3.121 Weir, Walter. *Truth in Advertising and Other Heresies*. New York:
McGraw-Hill, 1963, 224 pp.

        A plea to fellow advertising executives for truthfulness as a
        basic attitude by a 35 year veteran.

3.122 White, Gordon E. "John Caples and His Contributions to Advertising
and Communications Research." Ph.D. dissertation, University of Illinois,
1971, 284 pp.

        Caples has been an articulate crusader for the scientific approach
        to advertising communication. This study focuses chiefly on the
        professional career of Caples, which became intertwined with the
        developing "career" of advertising research itself.

3.123 White, Lee M., and Williams, Brent. *Walter Gregory Bryan, Advertising's Advertiser*. Bulletin vol. 57 no. 33. Columbia: University
of Missouri, 1956, 16 pp.

        Biographical sketch of publisher of *New York American*. Bryan
        lived 1877 - 1941.

3.124 Wineburgh, Abraham. *The Bull on the Bus*. New York: G. Stewart, 1941, 208 pp.

> Humorous, pithy recollections by an old school ad man who sold street car advertising space to Percival Hill, father of the infamous George Washington, Campbell Soups, Wrigley Gum, etc.

3.125 Woodward, Helen. *Through Many Windows*. New York: Harper, 1932, 370 pp.

> Autobiography covering copywriting career.

3.126 Woolf, James D. *Advertising to the Mass Market*. New York: Ronald, 1946, 133 pp.

> Vice-president of J. Walter Thompson, reflecting on years of experience.

3.127 Wooley, Edward M. *Writing for Real Money: Adventures of an Author in Advertising*. Passak, NJ: By the Author, 1928, 144 pp.

> In Chicago and Detroit.

3.128 Young, James W. *Diary of an Ad Man: The War Years, June 1, 1942 - Dec. 31, 1943*. Chicago: Advertising Publications, 1944, 256 pp.

> A personal journal record of activities.

3.129 Young, James W. *Pills for the Angels*. Coapa, NM: Pinon Press, 1952, unpaged.

> Reprint of a paper presented at ANA and AAAA joint meeting, 1941.

3.130 Young, John O. *Adventures in Advertising*. New York: Harper, 1949, 207 pp.

> Related Chicago experiences with Claude Hopkins at Lord and Thomas and the early days at Young and Rubicam (1923+) Informative story telling. Indexed.

See also 1.036, 1.043, 1.054, 2.019, 2.047, 2.063, 4.002, 4.025, 8.045, 8.051, 8.150, 8.359, 8.363, 8.367, 8.374, 8.554, 10.002, 10.016, 10.111, 9.014, 9.022, 9.032, 9.071, 9.084, 9.218, 9.312, and 9.318. The last two are satirical of self serving biographies.

"What have you gentlemen done with my child? . . . You have sent him out in the streets in rags of ragtime, tatters of jive and boogie woogie, to collect money from all and sundry for hubba hubba and audio jitterbug. You have made of him a laughing stock to intelligence, surely a stench in the nostrils of the gods of the ionosphere; you have cut time into tiny segments called spots (more rightly stains) wherewith the occasional fine program is periodically smeared with impudent insistence to buy and try."

Lee de Forest - "father of radio"
as quoted in 10.013, Vol. II, p 234

4.000
ORGANIZATIONS:
Institutions, Associations
and Agency Operations

4.001 "An Abbreviated History of the Advertising Agency's Origin and Development." *Printers' Ink* 125 (4 October 1923): 25 - 28.

Truly abbreviated, but some 19th century retail information provided.

4.002 *The Advertising Man of Detroit: A Study of 500 Men Engaged in Advertising Work in Detroit, Michigan, 1928.* New York: Advertising Foundation of America, 1930, 77 pp.

Research done with the aid of the University of Detroit, and Detroit's Adcraft Club.

4.003 Agnew, Hugh E. *Cooperative Advertising by Competitors.* New York: Harper, 1926, 246 pp.

"Promoting a whole industry by combining efforts in advertising."

4.004 Agnew, Hugh E. "The History of the American Marketing Association." *Journal of Marketing* 5 (April 1941): 374 - 79.

Brief antiquarian review of the antecedents to the AMA and its *Journal of Marketing*.

4.005 *The Amazing Advertising Business.* New York: Simon & Schuster, 1957, 178 pp.

Reprinting of various articles from *Fortune* of the 50's, including articles on Listerine's history, motivation research, inter-agency rivalry for the Rival dog food account, the story of the selection of the Edsel agency and discussion of the profit and loss economics of agencies.

4.006 American Association of Advertising Agencies. *A Handbook for the Advertising Agency Account Executive.* Reading, MA: Addison-Wesley, 1969, 524 pp.

A reader.

4.007 *American Association of Advertising Agencies: Its Aims, Accomplishments and Organization.* New York: Currier Press, 1932, 63 pp.

4.008 Appel, Joseph. "A Case Study of an Advertising Agency and Some Observations on Advertising in General." *Bulletin of the Business Historical Society* 13 (October 1939): 49 - 57.

A praising review of Hower's study of N.W. Ayer.

4.009 Applebaum, William. "The *Journal of Marketing:* The First Ten Years." *Journal of Marketing* 9 (July 1947): 355 - 63.

Detailed data on articles and market research activities reported in the *Journal* from 1936 to 1946.

4.010 Association of National Advertisers. *Advertising Agency Contracts*.
New York: ANA, 1926, 63 pp.

4.011 Association of National Advertisers. *Current Advertiser Practices
in Compensating Their Advertising Agencies*. New York: ANA, 1976, 117 pp.

    Report based on survey of 2,700 advertisers.

4.012 Association of National Advertisers. *Management and Advertising
Problems in the Advertiser-Agency Relationship*. New York: ANA, 1965,
138 pp.

    Results of a commissioned survey of advertisers.

4.013 *Ayer & Son's Manual For Advertisers*. Philadelphia: Ayer, 1878,
83 pp.

    A detailed description of the "advertising agency business as
    systematized by N.W. Ayer & Son" (pp. 7 - 14), with line drawings
    of the Philadelphia offices, mail rooms, registries, etc.

4.014 *BBD&O Newsletter* (February 1966): 64 pp.

    This seventy-fifth anniversary issue is nearly all dedicated to
    the history of BBD&O and includes reprints of some famous ads,
    copy, speeches, etc. Issued by the PR department of the ad agency.

4.015 Barton, Roger A. *Advertising Agency Operations and Management*.
New York: McGraw-Hill, 1955, 434 pp.

    A practical guide to creating and operating an agency based on
    lectures given at Columbia. In addition to frequent examples,
    it includes profiles of eight agencies and a lengthy discussion
    of the agency handling of the Canada Dry Ginger Ale account in
    the U.S. reprinted from the pages of *Advertising Agency*.

4.016 Baur, Edward J. "Voluntary Control in the Advertising Industry."
Ph.D. dissertation, University of Chicago, 1942.

    Covers development of Audit Bureau of Circulation, Association of
    American Advertisers and the problem of commission structures.

4.017 Bennett, Charles O. *Facts Without Opinion: The First Fifty Years
of the Audit Bureau of Circulations*. Chicago: Audit Bureau of Circulation, 1965, 277 pp.

    Includes material from the early years of ABC to 1960. The best
    contribution is the few pages describing audit activities from
    1900 until ABC formed in 1914. Based on board minutes and features
    pictures of previous executive office holders. Myers' article is
    a better source. See 4.016 and 4.061.

4.018 Bensman, Joseph. *Dollars and Sense: Ideology, Ethics and the
Meaning of Work in Profit and Non-Profit Organizations*. New York:
Macmillan, 1967, 208 pp.

A descriptive study of the advertising man and his work can be found on pp. 9 - 68.

4.019 *The Book of the Golden Celebration*. Philadelphia: Ayer, 1913, 50 pp.

50 year commemorative for this pioneer firm.

4.020 Booz, Allen & Hamilton. *Management and Advertising Problems in the Advertiser-Agency Relationship*. New York: Association of National Advertisers, 1965, 138 pp.

Commissioned consultants' reports.

4.021 Bridge, Donald V. *Men and Methods of Newspaper Advertising*. New York: Arco, 1947, 198 pp.

History of the Newspaper Advertising Executives' Association (NAEA).

4.022 Britt, Stuart H. *Do Advertising Agencies Train Trainees?* New York: American Association of Advertising Agencies, 1968, 82 pp.

"An investigation and interpretation of training procedures in the 100 largest advertising agencies."

4.023 Buell, Victor P. *Changing Practices in Advertising Decision Making and Control*. New York: Association of National Advertisers, 1973, 114 pp.

Includes a section on historical development leading to current forms, and reproduction of Pillsbury's policy statements as illustrative.

4.024 Burt, Frank A. *American Advertising Agencies: An Inquiry into their Origin, Growth, Functions and Future*. New York: Harper, 1940, 282 pp.

Includes selected readings, and a chapter on the history of agencies, but this is drawn primarily from Rowell.

4.025 Buxton, Edward. *Creative People at Work*. New York: Executive Communications, 1975, 292 pp.

Behind the scenes. Also reports survey results of "creative people of note."

4.026 Buxton, Edward. *Promise Them Anything: The Inside Story of the Madison Avenue Power Struggle*. New York: Stein & Day, 1972, 302 pp.

Current book by the publisher of *Ad Daily*, street wise and gossipy.

4.027 Chirurg, James Thomas. *So You're Going to Choose an Advertising Agency: What to Look For and Where to Find It*. New York: Funk & Wagnalls and Printers' Ink, 1950, 107 pp.

Characterized by a "let's back up and look at this thing" attitude.

4.028 *Coupon Returns: One Advertiser's Experience*. New York: Newell-Emmett, 1932, 62 pp.

The ad campaign and records of the Cleanliness Institute.

4.029 Creel, George. *How We Advertise America*. New York: Harper, 1920, 466 pp.

A detailed record and chronicle of the Committee of Public Information.

4.030 Davis, Edwin W. *A Functional Pattern Technique for Classification of Jobs*. Contributions to Education, no. 844. New York: Columbia University Teachers College, 1942, 128 pp.

Data from a survey of 5,000 advertising persons performing 1 - 25 functions.

4.031 Ellis, Lynn W. *Why Too Many Agencies Die Young, and Too Many Older Ones Lose Money*. Westpoint, CT: Ellis Plan Foundation, 1950, 43 pp.

Many answers suggested.

4.032 Erwin, Thomas. *Solicitation and Presentation Techniques: A Case-History Manual of Successful Advertising Agency Promotion Methods for Acquiring New Accounts*. Chicago: Business Books, 1968, 513 pp.

4.033 Emery, Edwin. *History of the American Newspaper Publishers Association*. Minneapolis: University of Minnesota Press, 1950, 263 pp.

"A well researched account of a leading trade organization important to the advertising industry, but the account is virtually bare of interpretation." (Pease, p. 213)

4.034 Evans, Franklin B. *Two Men in a Pullman*. New York: A.H. Vela, 1931, 20 pp.

A vignette plugging the services of the G.M. Basford advertising agency in New York. The work also appears under the author's pseudonym, Walter F. Mulhall.

4.035 *Forty Years of Advertising*. Boston: Ayer, 1909, 60 pp.

"A collection of somewhat intimate talks, by the largest and leading agency."

4.036 Frey, Albert W., and Davis, K.R. *The Advertising Industry: Agency Services, Working Relationships, Compensation Methods*. New York: Association of National Advertisers, 1958, 424 pp.

"Commissioned by the Association of National Advertisers to provide a comprehensive and objective analysis."

4.037 Graham, Irwin. *Advertising Agency Practice*. New York: Harper, 1952, 303 pp.

> Text for students.

4.038 Gras, N.S.B., and Larson, Henrietta. "N.W. Ayer & Son, Advertising Agency, 1869 - 1939." In *Casebook in American Business History*, pp. 460 - 79. New York: F.S. Crofts, 1939.

> Extracts and condensation of Hower's books, but unsigned.

4.039 Groesbeck, Kenneth. *The Advertising Agency Business: How to Enjoy It and Make It Pay*. Chicago: Advertising Publications, 1964, 390 pp.

> As discussed in the "Agencies Ask Us" column of *Advertising Age*.

4.040 Groesbeck, Kenneth. *Advertising Agency Success: Principles, Management, Functions, Performance*. New York: Harper, 1958, 259 pp.

> Text.

4.041 Haase, Albert E. *Advertising Agency Compensation: Theory, Law, Practice*. New York: National Process, 1934, 215 pp.

> Subsidized by the Association of National Advertisers, it is naturally less satisfied with the status quo than agencies and publishers and capably presents the need for self regulation.

4.042 Haase, Albert E. *The Advertising Appropriation: How to Determine It and How to Administer It*. New York and London: Harper, 1931, 181 pp.

> Written for a professional executive audience by the managing director of the Association of National Advertisers.

4.043 Hanan, Mack. *The Critical Partnership: Standards of Advertising Agency Selection and Performance*. New York: American Marketing Association, 1966, 165 pp.

> Sees business as retaining marketing responsibility and the agency as supplier of creativity.

4.044 Hileman, Donald G., and Rose, Billy I. *Toward Professionalism in Advertising: The Story of Alpha Delta Sigma's Aid to Professionalize Advertising Through Advertising Education, 1913 - 1969*. Dallas: Taylor, 1969, 259 pp.

> Histories of local chapters as well as the national organization.

4.045 Holland, Donald R. "The Origin and Development of the Advertising Agency in the United States." M.A. thesis, Pennsylvania State University, 1970.

> Some of this can be seen in a popularized account on Volney Palmer which appears as the cover story in *Advertising Age*, 23 April 1973.

4.046 *How to Select an Advertising Agency*. New York: Printers' Ink,
1957, 54 pp.

    15 articles, including 11 specific case histories, from the pages
of the magazine.

4.047 Hower, Ralph M. *History of an Advertising Agency: N.W. Ayer &*
Son at Work, 1869 - 1939. Cambridge: Harvard University Press, 1939,
652 pp.

    Excellent detailed history written chronologically (Part I) and
also topically (Part II). The author has avoided the so-called
"romance of business" approach to business history and focuses
attention on policy, management and economic functions -- the three
fundamental aspects of a firm's development. As well as being an
excellent source for corporate history, the work includes a short
biography of Wayland Ayer and discusses early advertising techniques.

4.048 Hurwood, David L., and Bailey, Earl L. *Advertising, Sales Promo-*
tion, and Public Relations - Organizational Alternatives: A Survey.
Experiences in Marketing Management, no. 16. New York: National Industrial Conference Board, 1969, 166 pp.

4.049 Hurwood, David L., and Brown, James K. *Some Guidelines for*
Advertising Budgeting. New York: National Industrial Conference Board,
1972, 65 pp.

4.050 "J. Walter Thompson Company." *Fortune* 36 (November 1947): 94 -
101.

    The largest advertising agency in the world; who runs it and how
it works.

4.051 Keeler, Floyd Y., and Haase, Albert E. *The Advertising Agency,*
Procedure and Practice. New York: Harper, 1927, 292 pp.

    Includes reproductions of the forms to be filled out for recogni-
tion as a legitimate agency by the American Newspaper Publishers
Association. Forward by Durstine.

4.052 Kitchen, V.C. *Waste Places in Advertising*. New York: Doyle,
Kitchen & McCormick, 1929, 61 pp.

    A lengthy list of 40 "waste places" in agency work that this firm
makes a business of correcting.

4.053 Lockley, Lawrence C. *Vertical Cooperative Advertising*. New York:
McGraw-Hill, 1931, 267 pp.

    "A study undertaken of and in conjunction with the Association of
National Advertisers." (Bibliog. 257 - 259)

4.054 Lyon, Leverett S. *Advertising Allowances: A Phase of the Price-*
Making Process. Washington, DC: Brooking Institute, 1932, 125 pp.

    A study of actual practices.

4.055 McKinsey & Co. *Study on Organization of the Advertising Function.*
New York: Association of National Advertisers, 1946, 173 pp.

  Results of mail survey. Provides organizational detail for 28
  firms.

4.055a McNiven, Malcolm A., ed. *How Much to Spend for Advertising?
Methods for Determining Advertising Expenditure Levels.* New York:
Association of National Advertisers, 1969, 122 pp.

4.056 *Manual of the Outdoor Advertising Association of America.* Chicago: Outdoor Advertising Association, 1926, 229 pp.

  "Containing useful information, rules and regulations, constitu-
  tion and code of ethics."

4.057 Midgley, Ned. *The Advertising and Business Side of Radio.* New
York: Prentice-Hall, 1948, 363 pp.

  Detail of information on four networks by a CBS sales executive.
  Also discusses Hooper rating procedure in general.

4.058 Miracle, Gordon E. "An Historical Analysis to Explain the Evolution of Advertising Agency Services." *Journal of Advertising* 6 (3)
(1977): 24 - 28.

  Recapitulates the evolution from secondary sources.

4.059 Mock, James R., and Larson, Cedric. *Words that Won the War: The
Story of the Committee on Public Information, 1917 - 1919.* Princeton,
NJ: Princeton University Press, 1939, 372 pp.

  A thorough and, as a result, often dull description of George
  Creel's CPI and America's adaptation of advertising and PR
  techniques to their propaganda needs both at home and abroad.
  See especially pages 96 - 101 for the role of professional
  advertising men.

4.060 Murphy, E.J. *The Movement West: Advertising's Impact on the
Building of the West and the Years Ahead.* Denver: Sage, 1958, 178 pp.

  Primarily a history of the Advertising Association of the West.

4.061 Myers, Kenneth H., Jr. "ABC and SRDS: The Evolution of Two
Specialized Advertising Services." *Business History Review* 34 (1960):
302 - 326.

  A good discussion of the Audit Bureau of Circulation and the
  Standard Rate and Data Service. Includes background histories
  of newspaper directories.

4.062 Myers, Kenneth H., Jr. *SRDS, the National Authority Serving the
Media Buying Function.* Evanston, IL: Northwestern University Press,
1968, 335 pp.

  Published to coincide with the fiftieth anniversary of the firm

and is better than its glossy appearance would suggest. As an
alternative (since this book is hard to find) see the author's
article in the *Business History Review* 34 (1960): 302 - 326.

4.063 Paletz, David L.; Pearson, Roberta E.; and Willis, Donald L.
Politics in Public Service Advertising on Television. New York:
Praeger, 1977, 123 pp.

Academic study by political scientists focused on the Advertising
Council and the political impact of the public service ads.

4.064 Parsons, Kenneth H. *The Advertising "Game" and Some of Its
Players*. New York: Pageant, 1963, 55 pp.

66 poems, many previously published in diverse trade publications,
amusing and sometimes poignant insight into agency life.

4.065 Politz, Alfred. *Is Progress in Advertising Research Endangered
by the Advertising Research Foundation?* New York: By the Author, 1961,
19 pp.

Attacks ARF as contributing to mediocrity.

4.066 Pope, Daniel A. "The Development of National Advertising, 1865 -
1920." Ph.D. dissertation, Columbia University, 1973.

Covers a range of topics including evolution of journals (e.g.
Printers' Ink) and associations and services (e.g. Audit Bureau
of Circulation).

4.067 *Presenting and Justifying Your Advertising Budget*. New York:
Printers' Ink, 1957, 78 pp.

4.068 Printers' Ink. *100 Years of American Advertising: 100 Years of
the J. Walter Thompson Co*. Chicago: Advertising Publications, 1964,
202 pp.

Special issue of *Advertising Age* 35 (7 December 1964).

4.069 Reilly, William J. *Effects of the Advertising Agency Commission
System*. New York: By the Author, 1931, 35 pp.

Against the status quo. See Haase and Young.

4.070 Riso, Ovid. *Advertising Cost Control Handbook*. New York: Van
Nostrand Reinhold, 1973, 387 pp.

Well researched with most methods attributed to specific firms.

4.071 Roberts, Edward, ed. "Beggars, Peddlers and Advertising Men:
An Informal Anecdotal Journal of BBD&O, 1861 - 1966." (Mimeograph)
New York, BBD&O, 797 pp.

Includes excerpts from *The Improbable Robley,* a draft of a book
by Charles Brower. Written in flowery prose.

4.072 Robinson, Patrick J., ed. *Advertising Measurement and Decision Making*. Boston: Allyn & Bacon, 1968, 103 pp.

Descriptive study sponsored by Marketing Science Institute.

4.072a Robinson, Patrick J., and Luck, David J. *Promotional Decision Making, Practice and Theory: A Study in Marketing Management*. New York: McGraw-Hill, 1964, 254 pp.

In part a descriptive study of actual decision making patterns, although the identity of the firms has been masked.

4.073 Rubel, Ira W. *Advertising Agency Financial Management and Accounting*. New York: Funk & Wagnalls, 1948, 342 pp.

Internal management.

4.074 Ryan, Catherine E., ed. *Golden Salute to Advertising*. New York: Advertising Women of New York, 1962, 102 pp.

Commemorating their fiftieth year, contains an informal history of AWNY.

4.075 Samstag, Nicholas. *How Business is Bamboozled by the Ad-Boys*. New York: Heinemann, 1966, 161 pp.

A challenge to advertising agencies in a provocative book exposing nine delusions about the function of agencies. By an experienced author who "says terrible things in a soft ... voice."

4.076 Sandage, Charles H. *The Promise of Advertising*. Homewood, IL: Irwin, 1961, 207 pp.

A reader in honor of James Webb Young which includes "footnotes to history" on the Advertising Council and the Committee on Public Information.

4.077 Sands, Saul S. *Setting Advertising Objectives*. Studies in Business Policy, no. 118. New York: National Industrial Conference Board, 1966, 92 pp.

4.078 Shuman, Raphael R. *Maximum Efficiency in Advertising*. Chicago: Trade Press Association, 1912.

"The Chicago Trade Press Association and What it Accomplishes."

4.079 Slomanson, Albert J. *Publication and Advertising Agency Problems (With Constructive Answers)*. New York: Lloyd, 1931, 142 pp.

37 sundry trade articles.

4.080 Smith, Ralph Lee. *Self-regulation in Action: Story of the Better Business Bureau, 1912 - 1962*. New York: Association of Better Business Bureaus, 1961, 28 pp.

Can this be the same man who wrote *Health Hucksters* and *Bargain Hucksters?*

4.081 Thomas, Harold B. "The Background and Beginning of the Advertising Council." In *The Promise of Advertising,* pp. 15 - 58. Edited by C.H. Sandage. Homewood, IL: Irwin, 1961.

   Includes reproductions of many original documents including James Webb Young's speech and various memos that lead to the creation, in the early forties, of the Advertising Council.

4.081a Thompson, William A. *High Adventure in Advertising.* New York: North River Press, 1952, 228 pp.

   A history of the Bureau of Advertising of the American Newspaper Publishers Association by its first director, (1913 - 1948). Full of names and dates and indexed, but of dubious value as the tone is self-serving in a strangely poetic way.

4.082 Webster, Richard. *Setting Advertising Appropriations: A Critical Summary of the Existing Information on the Subject and an Analytical and Topical Reading Guide.* New York: Association of National Advertisers, 1949, 72 pp.

4.083 Wharton, Don. "The Story Back of the War Ads." *The Reader's Digest* 45 (July 1944): 103 - 05.

   On War Advertising Council, condensed from *Advertising and Selling.*

4.084 Young, James W. *Advertising Agency Compensation in Relation to the Total Cost of Advertising.* Chicago: University of Chicago Press, 1933, 186 pp.

   Upholding status quo which advertisers thought too much, sparked much discussion and rebuttal. See Haase.

4.085 Young, Robert B. *Methods of Securing and Holding Clients.* San Francisco: By the Author, 1953, 116 pp.

   A lengthy marketing audit suggested.

See also 2.044, 2.071, 3.072, 3.079, 3.090, 6.053, 6.073, 8.051, 8.399, 8.542, 10.026, 10.047, 10.102.

"The term 'agent' as applied to the profession I followed for forty years is inaccurate and misleading. It is a survival from a more primitive era. Originally advertising agents were simply represen- tatives of newspapers who secured advertising and were paid a commission -- and that was about all they did. For the magazines they performed a similar service as soon as the early periodicals condescended, as old Fletcher Harper put it, 'to degrade literature with the announcements of trades people.' "

                                        Ernest Elmo Calkins
                                        (3.024, p 228)

5.000
PSYCHOLOGY AND SOCIOLOGY
OF ADVERTISING

5.001 Aaron, Dorothy. *About Face: Towards A Positive Image of Women in Advertising*. Toronto: Ontario Status of Women Council, 1975, 30 pp.

5.002 Adams, Henry F. *Advertising and Its Mental Laws*. New York: Macmillan, 1916, 333 pp.

   An early text, notable for reports of some data on brand recognition and recall.

5.003 Barnard, W.F. *Mind Over Mind*. Cleveland: By the Author, 1919, 29 pp.

   "The soul of advertising is the pressure of mind upon mind." Very superficial.

5.004 Bayles, Samuel H., and O'Mara, Walter. *Modern Man's Quest for Identity: Its Power to Involve and Motivate People*. New York: n.p., 1968, 96 pp.

5.005 Bogart, Leo, ed. *Psychology in Media Strategy*. Chicago: American Marketing Association, 1966, 104 pp.

   Proceedings of a conference. Five pages of bibliography.

5.006 Britt, Stuart H. *The Spenders*. New York: McGraw-Hill, 1960, 293 pp.

   An early book on consumer behavior written for the "spending public" by an academic author of note.

5.007 Burtt, Harold E. *Psychology of Advertising*. New York: Houghton Mifflin, 1938, 473 pp.

   Academic text for course of same name.

5.008 Buzzi, Giancarlo. *Advertising: Its Cultural and Political Effects*. Minneapolis: University of Minnesota Press, 1968, 147 pp.

   Translated from the Italian by B. David Garmize.

5.009 Calkins, Earnest E. "The Emancipation of the Housewife." *Woman's Home Companion* 56 (February - May 1929): various pages.

   First of a series of 4 articles discussing advertising's role in packaged goods and labor saving devices. See also Ruth S. Cowan for contrast.

5.010 Cantril, Hadley, and Allport, Gordon. *The Psychology of Radio*. New York: Harper, 1935, 276 pp.

   An analysis of psychological and cultural factors shaping radio programs and listener response.

5.011 Cheskin, Louis. *Basis for Marketing Decision Through Controlled Motivation Research*. New York: Liveright, 1961, 282 pp.

    Success stories and plugs for Cheskin's research firms, but reports in relative detail several motivation research studies.

5.012 Cheskin, Louis. *How to Predict What People Will Buy*. New York: Liveright, 1957, 241 pp.

    Answer: Hire the Color Research Institute, headed by Cheskin, and learn the "Key to Motivation Research."

5.013 Cheskin, Louis. *Why People Buy: Motivation Research and its Successful Application*. New York: Liveright, 1959, 319 pp.

    A lengthy plug for his services.

5.014 Cohn, David L. *The Good Old Days: A History of American Morals and Manners as Seen Through the Sears Roebuck Catalog*. New York: Simon & Schuster, 1940, 597 pp. (Republished in 1976 by Arno Press)

    An interesting journalistic discussion. More text than illustration.

5.015 Cowan, Ruth S. "The Industrial Revolution in the Home: Household Technology and Social Change in the 20th Century." *Technology and Culture* 17 (January 1976): 1 - 23.

    Uses advertising as its evidence to such an extent that the result is as much part of the history of advertising as it is the history of women.

5.016 Cowan, Ruth S. "Two Washes in the Morning and a Bridge Party at Night: The American Housewife Between the Wars." *Women's Studies* 3 (1976): 147 - 72.

    Explores her study using advertising as part of her data.

5.017 Crow, Carl. *The Great American Customer*. New York: Harper, 1943, 252 pp.

    A journalistic treatment from secondary sources. This sketchy book does have a focus on consumer goods and their marketings.

5.018 Dichter, Ernest. *The Handbook of Consumer Motivation: The Psychology of the World of Objects*. New York: McGraw-Hill, 1964, 486 pp.

    A promotional for the Institute for Motivational Research of which Dichter was the founder and president. Encyclopedic in format.

5.019 Dichter, Ernest. *The Strategy of Desire*. Garden City, NY: Doubleday, 1960, 314 pp.

    Of most use are the appendices in which he outlines the methodology of motivation research and includes excerpts from the 1939 pioneering study he did for Plymouth while working for J. Sterling Getchell, Inc.

5.020 Dispenza, Joseph E. *Advertising the American Woman*. Dayton, OH:
Pflaum, 1975, 181 pp.

A fascinating collection of 285 advertisements directed toward
women from the 20th century, with detailed discussion. Not
unlike McLuhan's *Mechanical Bride* but covering a more diverse
sample. Unfortunately the author purposely avoids dating the
advertisements, so this source must be used more for the ideas it
contains than for any raw data.

5.021 Dockrell, Thomas E. *The Law of Mental Domination, as Proved by
History and Applied to Selling and Advertising*. New York: Commercial
Publishing, 1914, 34 pp.

5.022 Doob, Leonard. *Public Opinion and Propaganda*. New York: Holt,
1948, 600 pp.

An influential book. It analyzes the American advertising industry
to great effect as primarily an institution of propaganda.

5.023 *The Effect of Advertising on Purchase Decisions: A Preliminary
Analysis*. Peeksill, NY: Center for Research in Marketing, 1959, 152 pp.

Motivation research ideology, comparable to Dichter.

5.024 Ehrenreich, Barbara, and English, Deidre. "The Manufacture of
Housework." *Socialist Revolution* 5 (October - December 1975): 5 - 40.

"Labour saving devices" and other advertising ploys create expect-
ation and work.

5.025 Elliott, Frank Reel. *Memory for Visual, Auditory and Visual-
Auditory Material*. Archives of Psychology, no. 199. New York: n.p.,
1936, 59 pp.

Also a Ph.D. dissertation, Columbia University, 1936. Test, using
ads as stimuli, finds recall higher for radio.

5.026 Ewen, Stuart. "Advertising as Social Production." *Radical America*
3 (May - June 1969): 42 - 56.

Reprinted as "Advertising: Selling the System," in *The Poverty
of Progress: The Political Economy of American Social Problems*, ed. by
Milton Mankoff. New York: Holt, Rinehart & Winston, 1972, 524 pp.

5.027 Ewen, Stuart. *Captains of Consciousness: Advertising and the
Social Roots of the Consumer Culture*. New York: McGraw-Hill, 1976,
261 pp.

A study of advertising and the roots of consumer culture, with an
informal content analysis of 1920's ads.

5.028 Ferber, Robert, and Wales, Hugh G. *Motivation and Market Behaviour*. Homewood, IL: Irwin, 1958, 437 pp.

An anthology of experts' advice drawn together by the American
Marketing Association.

5.029 Fogg-Meade, Emily. "The Place of Advertising in Modern Business."
Journal of Political Economy 9 (1901): 218 - 42.

> Identifies the middle classes as the important audience for adver-
> tising.

5.030 Frederick, Christine M. *Selling Mrs. Consumer*. New York: Business Bourse, 1929, 405 pp.

> Written by the wife of the president of Business Bourse, J. George
> Frederick, who also authored *Masters of Advertising Copy* and edited
> *Printers' Ink*. This source is useful for an 1920's view of the
> vulnerability of women to advertising.

5.031 Frederick, J. George. *Introduction to Motivation Research*. New
York: Business Bourse, 1957, 230 pp.

> Basic, but includes a chapter on criticisms and rebuttals and
> three chapters on case histories.

5.032 Friedhaim, William P. "Mass Advertising and Social Control: An
Analysis of Advertising as an Organ of Social Conditioning, 1888 - 1918."
M.A. thesis, University of Wisconsin, 1961.

5.033 Gale, Harlow. *On the Psychology of Advertising*. Psychological
Studies, no. 1. Minneapolis: By the Author, 1900.

> This monograph, by a University of Minnesota professor, predates
> Scott's more influential work, despite Scott's recognition as *the*
> pioneer.

5.034 Gibson, Walker. "Sweet Talk: The Rhetoric of Advertising." In
Tough, Sweet and Stuffy: An Essay on Modern American Prose Styles, pp.
71 - 89. Bloomington, IN: Indiana University Press, 1966, 179 pp.

> Some content analysis.

5.035 Gilbert, Eugene. *Advertising and Marketing to Young People*.
Pleasantville, NY: Printers' Ink, 1957, 378 pp.

> From the founder of the Gilbert Youth Organization, "a firm
> researching and merchandising among youth." Rich in examples
> of both research and promotions.

5.036 Gill, Leslie E. *Advertising and Psychology*. New York: Hutchinson, 1954, 192 pp.

> Originally published in England.

5.037 Glazebrook, G. de T.; Brett, Katharine B.; and McErvel, Judith,
eds. *A Shoppers View of Canada's Past: Pages from Eaton's Catalogues,
1886 - 1930*. Toronto: University of Toronto Press, 1969, 286 pp.

> Mostly facsimiles.

5.038   Goffman, Erving. "Gender Advertisements." *Studies in the Anthropology of Visual Communication* 3 (Fall 1976): 65 - 154.

   Distinguished social scientist examines pictorial content of print advertisements for role portrayals. See review in *Journal of Marketing Research* 15 (May 1978): 313.

5.039   Greenley, A.J. *Psychology as a Sales Factor*. New York: Pitman, 1927, 214 pp.

   Originally published in England.

5.040   Hanan, Mark. *The Pacifiers: The Six Symbols We Live By*. Boston: Little, Brown, 1960, 306 pp.

   Uses advertising examples extensively in this exploration of symbols of sex, success, security, sociability and sophistication.

5.041   Hancock, G.B. "Commercial Advertisement and Social Pathology." *Social Forces* 4 (June 1926): 812 - 19.

   Argues that advertising is an imbalanced power struggle between the scientific advertiser and the defenseless consumer and sees crime as the result of advertising to the poor. Presents some data on advertising, more on crime, but fails to make the link between them convincingly.

5.042   Hattwick, M.S. *How to Use Psychology for Better Advertising*. New York: Prentice-Hall, 1950, 376 pp.

   Text, more traditional than title suggests.

5.043   Heller, Walter S. "Analysis of Package Labels." *University of California Publication in Psychology* 3 (1) (1919): 61 - 72.

   "All factors so closely related, it is impossible to separate them."

5.044   Heller, Walter S., and Brown W. "Memory and Association in the Case of Street-Car Advertising Cards." *University of California Publication in Psychology* 2 (4) (1916): 267 - 75.

   Free associations to real stimuli.

5.045   Henry, Harry. *Motivation Research: Its Practice and Uses for Advertising, Marketing and Other Business Purposes*. New York: F. Ungar, 1958, 240 pp.

   Authored by a staff member of McCann-Erickson and perhaps the best single source on the topic.

5.046   *How to Get People Excited: A Human Interest Textbook Especially Prepared ... for Others Whose Occupation is Arousing People to Buy*. New York: True Story, 1937, 46 pp.

   Sixty psychological situations ranked by their ability to get people excited, with advertising examples, pp. 37 - 46.

5.047 Jacobson, J.Z. *Scott of Northwestern: The Life Story of a Pioneer in Psychology and Education*. Chicago: L. Mariano, 1951, 198 pp.

    The biography of Walter Dill Scott, author of the first *Psychology of Advertising* and later president of Northwestern University.

5.048 Jenkins, M. "Human Nature and Advertising." *Atlantic Monthly* 94 (September 1904): 393 - 401.

    Sees human nature as synonymous with human vanity and weakness.

5.049 Kaiserman, Julius J. "Historical Trends in the Psychology of Advertising." M.A. thesis, Ohio State University, 1932.

    Follows the career of Harry D. Kitson.

5.050 Key, Wilson Bryan. *Media Sexploitation*. Englewood Cliffs, NJ: Prentice-Hall, 1976, 234 pp.

_____. *Subliminal Seduction: Ad Media's Manipulation of Not So Innocent America*. Englewood Cliffs, NJ: Prentice-Hall, 1973, 205 pp.

    Capitalizing on the public's credulousness, both books put forth the incredible thesis that advertisers employ dirty words and pornographic symbolism. "Dirty" is in the eye of the beholder and these works stand as evidence that hucksterism is still possible.

5.051 Kitson, Harry D. *Manual for the Study of the Psychology of Advertising and Selling*. Philadelphia: Lippincott, 1920, 116 pp.

    A lab manual for beginning students in a course in experimentation in advertising. Kitson was on the faculties of Indiana and the University of Chicago.

5.052 Kitson, Harry D. *The Mind of the Buyer: A Psychology of Selling*. New York: Macmillan, 1921, 211 pp.

    A salesmanship manual.

5.053 Kuhns, William. *Waysteps to Eden: Ads and Commercials*. New York: Herder & Herder, 1970, 32 pp.

    Discussion of advertising and culture with contemporary examples. McLuhan inspired.

5.054 Levy, J.M. "Experiments on Attention and Memory, with Special Reference to the Psychology of Advertising." *University of California Publication in Psychology* 2 (2) (1916): 157 - 97.

    Psychophysics of billboard positioning.

5.055 Link, Henry C. *The New Psychology of Selling and Advertising*. New York: Macmillan, 1932, 293 pp.

    By "a psychologist of international reputation and an experienced merchandising and advertising man."

5.056 Link, Henry C. *Psychology of Advertising*. Scranton: International Correspondence Schools, 1937, 42 pp.

5.057 Lohof, Bruce A. "The Higher Meaning of Marlboro Cigarettes." *Journal of Popular Culture* 3 (1969): 441 - 450.

Analyzes the commercial advertisements for Marlboro brand cigarettes as culture objects.

5.058 Lucas, Darrell B., and Benson, C.E. "Historical Trend of Negative Appeals in Advertising." *Journal of Applied Psychology* 13 (August 1929): 346 - 356.

Ads from 3 popular magazines, 1912 - 1917. Finds increasing usage.

5.059 Lucas, Darrell B., and Benson, C.E. *Psychology for Advertisers*. New York: Harper, 1930, 351 pp.

A section on measurement of effectiveness.

5.060 Lucas, Darrell B., and Britt, Stuart H. *Advertising Psychology and Research: An Introductory Book*. New York: McGraw-Hill, 1950, 765 pp.

Detailed text by psychologists who have long worked on advertising.

5.061 Lynch, Edmund C. "Walter Dill Scott: Pioneer Industrial Psychologist." *Business History Review* 42 (Summer 1968): 149 - 70.

History of the author of the first major work on the psychology of advertising and later president of Northwestern. Includes a discussion of Scott's role as the first psychologist who applied his talents to advertising.

5.062 McCann, Charles B. *Women and Department Store Newspaper Advertising*. New York: Social Research, 1957, 125 pp.

"A motivation study of attitudes toward ..."

5.063 McLuhan, Marshall. *The Mechanical Bride: Folklore of Industrial Man*. Boston: Beacon, 1951, 157 pp.

This early work of McLuhan is a fascinating discussion of the cultural content of media and advertising of the late forties and is well illustrated.

5.064 McLuhan, Marshall, and Fiore, Quentin. *The Medium is the Massage: An Inventory of Effects*. New York: Random, 1967, 160 pp.

The book, illustrative of the title's thesis, stimulated and mystified Madison Avenue. Print is not the best medium, however; listen to a record of the same title.

5.065 McMahon, A. Michael. "An American Courtship: Psychologists and Advertising Theory in the Progressive Era." *American Studies* 13 (1972): 5 - 18.

On the co-opting of academics.

5.066 Martineau, Pierre. *Motivation in Advertising: Motives That Make People Buy.* New York: McGraw-Hill, 1957, 210 pp.

Relatively informal and anecdotal.

5.067 Morton, Patricia Roe. "Riesman's Theory of Social Character Applied to Consumer Goods Advertising." *Journalism Quarterly* 44 (Summer 1967): 337 - 40.

Updates and elaborates on Dornbush and Hickman with 13 product categories and 5 time periods.

5.068 Newman, Joseph W. *Motivation Research and Marketing Management.* Boston: Harvard Graduate School of Business, 1957, 525 pp.

This Harvard work sees motivation research as "destined to be a major landmark in marketing's history" (abstract). Six selected case histories (pp. 69 - 382) present a wealth of information on methods and interpretations in their appendices.

5.069 Nixon, Howard K. "Attention and Interest in Advertising." *Archives of Psychology* 72 (1924): 68 pp.

Also Ph.D. thesis, Columbia, 1924 and published by Columbia University Press in 1926 as *An Investigation of ...* (36 pp.).

5.070 Nunes, Maxine, and White, Deanna. *The Lace Ghetto.* Toronto: New Press, 1972, 152 pp.

An articulation of the new femininism using advertising and other forms of popular media culture as evidence.

5.071 Parker, Paul. "Iconography of Advertising Art." *Harpers* 177 (June 1938): 80 - 84.

Analogy to the "new religion" of America.

5.072 Payne, Richard J., and Heyer, Robert. *Discovery in Advertising.* Paramus, NJ: Paulist Press, 1969, 188 pp.

Advertising and culture, discussion provoked by sample ads. Cf. McLuhan's *Mechanical Bride*.

5.073 Poffenberger, Albert T. "Psychological Tests in Advertising." *Journal of Experimental Psychology* 72 (August 1924): 312 - 20.

Discussion of discrepancy between recall and purchase behaviour.

5.074 Poffenberger, Albert T. *Psychology in Advertising*. Chicago: Shaw, 1925, 632 pp.

   Text by Columbia professor. Bibliography, pp. 617 - 23.

5.075 Potter, David M. *People of Plenty: Economic Abundance and the American Character*. Chicago: University of Chicago Press, 1954, 217 pp.

   A seminal work by a prominent historian. Includes a good chapter specifically on advertising with the thesis that the principle effects of advertising are not economic but "upon the values of our society."

5.076 *Psychological Impact of Newspaper and Radio Advertisements*. New York: Columbia Bureau of Applied Social Research, 1949.

   Also measures public attitudes toward the media.

5.077 Rebaza, Jorge C. *Suggesting Through Advertising: How to Use the Power of Suggestion to Increase the Power of Advertising*. New York: Vantage, 1967, 272 pp.

   Original theorizing by Colgate-Palmolive executive based on 38 years experience primarily in foreign markets.

5.078 Rheinstrom, Carroll. *Psyching the Ads: The Case Book of Advertising; the Methods and Results of 180 Advertisements*. New York: Covici, Friede, 1929, 362 pp.

   Author gives account of product or service, costs, copy analysis, results.

5.079 Rudolph, Harold J. *Attention and Interest Factors in Advertising: Survey, Analysis, Interpretation*. New York: Funk & Wagnalls, 1947, 119 pp.

   Results of systematic analysis of 2,500 advertisements.

5.080 Schultze, Quentin J. "Walter Dill Scott and Scientific Advertising." *Advertising Working Paper* 4 (November 1977): 28 pp. Urbana, IL: University of Illinois.

   Outlines the application of the academics of psychology to advertising in the early years of the 20th Century. Includes reference to Thorndike, Gale, Hollingworth and Cherington. Includes a condensation of a chapter from a forthcoming dissertation.

5.081 Scitovsky, Tibor. *The Joyless Economy: An Inquiry into Human Satisfaction and Consumer Dissatisfaction*. New York: Oxford, 1976, 310 pp.

   Sees consumer behaviour as an attempt to deal simultaneously with the conflicts of seeking both comfort and stimulation.

5.082 Scott, Walter D. *Influencing Men in Business: The Psychology of Argument and Suggestion*. New York: Ronald, 1911, 168 pp. (2d ed. 1916, 3d ed. 1928).

       Res ipsa locquitur.

5.083 Scott, Walter D. "The Psychology of Advertising." *Atlantic Monthly* 93 (1903): 29 - 36.

       First of an irregular series by various authors, this includes data
       on the growth of advertising in the 19th century.

5.084 Scott, Walter D. *The Psychology of Advertising: A Simple Exposition of the Principles of Psychology in Their Relation to Successful Advertising*. Boston: Small, Maynard, 1908, 269 pp.

       Includes bibliography, pp. 249 - 69. New editions in 1910, 1913,
       1917, 1921; and "completely revised" by D.T. Howard in 1931,
       300 pp. New York Public Library has all editions.

5.085 Scott, Walter D. *The Psychology of Advertising in Theory and Practice*. Boston: Small, Maynard, 1903, 437 pp.

       The first of the applied psychology books, written by a highly
       qualified psychologist who went on to become president of North-
       western University.

5.086 Scott, Walter D. *The Theory and Practice of Advertising*. Boston: Small, Maynard, 1903, 240 pp.

       Nearly all the chapters in this volume were first published
       serially in *Mahin's Magazine* under the title, "The Psychology
       of Advertising" -- a topic of which Scott was a pioneer. Later
       he became the President of Northwestern University and was the
       head of the university's psychological laboratory at the time of
       this work.

5.087 Scott, Walter Dill. *The Theory of Advertising: A Simple Exposition of the Principles of Psychology in Their Relation to Successful Advertising*. Boston: Small, Maynard, 1903, 240 pp.

       Alternative edition of *Theory and Practice*.

5.088 Sheldon, Roy, and Arens, Egmont. *Consumer Engineering: A New Technique for Prosperity*. New York: Harper, 1932, 259 pp.

       Showing how to stimulate consumption as a depression cure by
       manipulating taste, fashion and obsolescence. Introduction by
       Earnest Elmo Calkins, who is also credited with being the source
       of the concept, and many suggestions on this work.

5.089 Smith, George Horsley. *Motivation Research in Advertising and Marketing*. New York: McGraw-Hill, 1954, 242 pp.

       Published for the Advertising Research Foundation, this is one of
       the better reference books on the topic, describing the actual

research methods of motivation research. Improved by Henry's book four years later.

5.090 Starch, Daniel. "Fifty Years of Consumer Psychology." *American Psychological Association Meeting Proceedings*. Chicago: n.p., 7 September 1965.

Naturally with a focus on advertising effectiveness measures. Also published as an appendix (pp. 253 - 63) of Starch's *Measurement of Advertising Readership and Results*.

5.091 Stephenson, William. "The Infantile Vs. the Sublime in Advertisements." *Journalism Quarterly* 40 (Summer 1963): 181 - 86.

Finds more infantile mechanisms in current full page ads than 30 years ago.

5.092 Sterba, Richard F. "On Some Psychological Factors in Pictorial Advertising." *Psychoanalysis and the Social Sciences* 5 (1958): 187 - 218.

Armchair Freudian discussion.

5.093 Strong, Edward K., Jr. "Psychological Methods as Applied to Advertising." *Journal of Education Psychology* 4 (1913): 393 - 404.

An early academic psychological experiment. Some of the literature on the topic is cited. See also 6.066.

5.094 Strong, Edward K., Jr. *The Psychology of Selling and Advertising*. New York: McGraw-Hill, 1925, 468 pp.

More emphasis on personal selling by a professor of psychology at Stanford.

5.095 Strong, Edward K., Jr. *The Relative Merit of Advertisements: A Psychological and Statistical Study*. Archives of Psychology, no. 17. New York: Science Press, 1911, 81 pp.

Includes comparison testing of many Packer's Tar Soap ads. Using the "order of merit" method.

5.096 Stryker, Perrin. "Motivation Research." *Fortune* (June 1956): 144 - 232.

Relatively lengthy discussion of the types of motivation research and the growth of the "industry."

5.097 Vaile, Roland S., and Canoyer, Helen G. *Income and Consumption*. New York: Holt, 1938, 394 pp.

While an economics text, this is also an early text on consumer behavior, using consumer risk reduction as a central concept.

5.098 Van Til, Roy G. "The Content of U.S. Automobile Advertising, 1949 - 1973: Impact on the Shaping of Wants and Product Development." Ph.D. dissertation, Boston College, 1975.

See 2.092.

5.099 Wolff, Janet L. *What Makes Women Buy: A Guide to Understanding and Influencing the New Woman of Today.* New York: McGraw-Hill, 1958, 294 pp.

"A practical handbook ... with feminine guideposts ... translated into practical selling tools." (Intro.) Emphasis on middle class. Not indexed.

5.100 Wood, James P. *Advertising and the Soul's Belly: Repetition and Memory in Advertising.* Athens: University of Georgia Press, 1961, 116 pp.

Review of 20th century literature of various theoretical perspectives.

5.101 Wooding, Edmund, ed. *Advertising and the Subconscious: Advertising Conference Contributed Papers.* Michigan Advertising Paper, no. 2. Ann Arbor, MI: University of Michigan, Bureau of Business Research, 1959, 84 pp.

Motivation research seminars papers by Packard, and discussion by psychologists, McNeil and Cutler.

5.102 Yerkes, R.M. "The Class Experiment in Psychology with Advertisements as Materials." *Journal of Educational Psychology* 3 (January 1912): 1 - 17.

Early experiment in which the attention drawing power of ads is measured by suddenly exposing students to all ads and asking them to pick them up in rapid order as they appeal. Yerkes became famous for his experiments with the maternal behavior of monkeys.

5.103 Yoell, William A. *A Science of Advertising Through Behaviorism: Advertising and Research from a Behaviorist's Point of View.* New York: Behavior Research Institute, 1965, 47 pp.

One of several minor papers, but not on behaviorism so much as experimental psychology.

See also 1.002, 2.007, 2.009, 2.011, 2.021, 2.022, 2.023, 2.025, 2.037, 2.092, 8.021, 8.028, 8.043, 9.031..

"An advertisement has not accomplished its mission till it has instructed the possible consumer concerning the goods and then has caused him to forget where he received his instruction."

Walter Dill Scott, 1908
(5.084, p 221)

6.000
ADVERTISING
AND COPY RESEARCH

6.001 Adler (John) Associates. *The Feasibility of Establishing a CATV Advertising Laboratory*. New York: Advertising Research Foundation, 1967, 32 pp.

   Concludes that it is feasible if designed into a system as it is installed.

6.002 Advertising Research Foundation. *A Bibliography of Theory and Research Techniques in the Field of Human Motivation*. New York: Advertising Research Foundation, 1956, 117 pp.

   Would define the state of the art. Incorporates ARF's previous bibliography of motivation research.

6.003 Advertising Research Foundation. *Copy Testing: A Study Prepared by the ARF*. New York: Ronald, 1939, 131 pp.

   Thorough description and discussion of five major methods of copy testing. State of the art survey resulting from four years of committee work. Some of the analysis developed by the Psychological Corporation.

6.004 Advertising Research Foundation. *Criteria for Marketing and Advertising Research*. New York: ARF, 1953, 10 pp.

   To verify methodological validity.

6.005 Advertising Research Foundation. *Handbook of Advertising Research Foundation Technical Services*. New York: ARF, 1965, 59 pp.

6.006 Advertising Research Foundation. *Sources of Published Advertising Research*. New York: ARF, 1960, 65 pp.

6.007 American Marketing Association. *The Technique of Marketing Research*. New York: McGraw-Hill, 1937, 432 pp.

   Bibliography, pp. 403 - 422. In process during the merger of the National Association of Marketing Teachers and the American Marketing Society, it was the first publication of the new association.

6.008 Assael, Henry, ed. *The Collected Works of C.C. Parlin*. New York: Arno, 1978.

   Assael pioneered orderly fact-finding applied to advertising for Curtis Publishing.

6.009 Association of National Advertisers. *Magazine Circulation and Rate Trends, 1937 - 1955*. New York: ANA, 1956, 206 pp.

   Revised edition in 1960 covers 1940 - 1959.

6.010 Audit Bureau of Circulations. *Scientific Space Selection*. Chicago: ABC, 1921, 167 pp.

A pioneering trade manual "containing general information for advertising managers and other executives; for space buyers ... and all interested in the more intelligent selection of advertising media."

6.010a Axelrod, Joel N. *Choosing the Best Advertising Alternative: A Management Guide to Identifying the Most Effective Copy Testing Technique.* New York: Association of National Advertisers, 1971, 42 pp.

Against adhocracy.

6.011 Barkley, Key L. "Development of a New Method for Determining the Relative Efficiencies of Advertisements in Magazines." *Journal of Applied Psychology* 15 (August 1931): 390 - 410; 16 (February 1932): 74 - 90.

A formula to integrate recall and rank data into "efficiency" scores. Second installment presents experimental data.

6.012 Bartos, Rena, and Pearson, Arthur S. "Daniel Starch: The Founding-est Father." *Journal of Advertising Research* 17 (October 1977): 63 - 67.

An addendum to the "Founding Fathers" article in the June issue, consisting primarily of a photoreprint of Starch's handwritten letter reviewing his accomplishments from the vantage point of 95 years of age.

6.013 Bartos, Rena, and Pearson, Arthur S. "The Founding Fathers of Advertising Research." *Journal of Advertising Research* 17 (June 1977): 1 - 32.

Transcripts of interviews with Ernest Dichter, George Gallup, Alfred Politz, Henry Brenner, A.V. Nielsen, Sr., Hans Ziesel, Frank Stanton and Archibald Crossley. Also available on 16mm film (29 min.) from the Advertising Research Foundation.

6.014 Bergin, John. "A Half Century of Advertising Research." Address to the Annual Conference of the Advertising Research Foundation, New York, October 18, 1976. 16 pp. typescript.

Not well-titled, but some quotable quotes, mostly about the new true partnership between creative and research people, in contrast to the attitude of the early 60's, which Bergin characterizes as "deep and abiding malice."

6.015 Berridge, William A.; Winslow, Emma A.; and Finn, Richard A. *Purchasing Power of the Consumer: A Statistical Index.* Chicago: Shaw, 1925, 318 pp.

3 essays developing an index in response to prizes offered by J. Walter Thompson.

6.016 Borden, Neil H.; Lovekin, Osgood S.; Edwards, Paul K.; and Gragg, Mabel Taylor. *A Test of the Consumer Jury Method of Ranking Advertisements.* Bureau of Business Research Study, no. 11. Boston: Harvard University, Graduate School of Business, 1935, 61 pp.

Suggests methodological cautions, including the need for a sample frame for which there is product interest. Lots of data and facsimilies of tested ads.

6.017   Calkins, Earnest E., and Holden, Ralph. *Modern Advertising.* New York: Appleton, 1905, 361 pp.

Includes a discussion of national campaign strategies and procedures, and information about early market research techniques of George Waldron who worked for Mahins, an advertising agency.

6.018   Campbell, Roy H. *Measuring the Sales and Profit Results in Advertising: A Managerial Approach.* New York: Association of National Advertisers, 1969, 133 pp.

A Columbia dissertation by an experienced executive, includes 12 case studies showing alternative effectiveness measures in operation.

6.019   Caples, John. *Tested Advertising Methods: How to Profit by Removing Guesswork.* New York: Harper, 1932, 276 pp.

Primarily advice on copywriting by a man who rose to Vice President of BBD&O by writing superb copy. Forward by Bruce Barton. Includes pioneering ideas on copy testing techniques.

6.020   Carter, David E.   "The Changing Face of *Life*'s Advertisements, 1950 - 66." *Journalism Quarterly* 46 (1969):   87 - 93.

The advertisements were studied to determine trends and whether actual practice coincides with research findings concerning effectiveness.

6.021   Casson, Herbert N. *Ads and Sales: A Study of Advertising and Selling From the Standpoint of the New Principles of Scientific Management.*   Chicago: McClurg, 1911, 167 pp.

Early attempt at measuring advertising effectiveness.

6.022   Central Media Bureau, Inc. *The Computer in Advertising.* 1 vol. New York: Association of National Advertisers, 1962.

A series of papers including John C. Maloney on "The Use of Computers in Advertising Today" and a discussion of "Automation at Young & Rubicam."

6.023   Chappell, Matthew N., and Hooper, C.E. *Radio Audience Measurement.*   New York: S. Daye, 1944, 246 pp.

"Hooper ratings" write up.

6.024   Cheskin, Louis. *Secrets of Marketing Success.*   New York: Trident Press, 1967, 278 pp.

"Describes his career in market research as he shows how his work with businessmen produced some of the greatest success stories in marketing history." Clients include David Ogilvy, Lever Brothers, Philip Morris, Lincoln cars, Hires rootbeer, Eaton's, etc. A testimonial for his Color Research Institute and Louis Cheskin Associates.

6.025 Colley, Russell H. *Defining Advertising Goals For Measured Advertising Results*. New York: Association of National Advertisers, 1961, 114 pp.

Classic report which coined the acronym DAGMAR for the Association of National Advertisers which wanted ad expenditures to be made more on operational objectives and less on good faith. Includes 23 short case examples, illustrative, but clients' identities are masked.

6.026 Donovan, Howard M., and Mitchell, George. *Advertising Response: A Research into Influences that Increase Sales*. Philadelphia: Lippincott, 1924, 195 pp.

An unusual work, this reports the results of a questionnaire given to 1,000 high school students. Designed to test advertising effectiveness, the method applied was adapted from Hotchkiss and Franken's *The Leadership of Advertising Brands* - unaided brand recall.

6.027 Duncan, C.S. *Commercial Research*. New York: Macmillan, 1919.

Very early market research text, which played a seminal role, and promoted scientific methods.

6.028 Dunlap, Orrin E. *Radio in Advertising*. New York: Harper, 1931, 383 pp.

Data on 1930 NBC and CBS clients and television is discussed.

6.029 Edwards, Paul K. *The Southern Urban Negro as a Consumer*. New York: Prentice-Hall, 1932, 323 pp.

Four chapters on recognition of national brands and the selection of copy appeals.

6.030 Firth, L.E. *Testing Advertisements: A Study of Copy Testing Methods in Theory and Practice*. New York: McGraw-Hill, 1934, 282 pp.

Discussion of major techniques in a Question and Answer format; answers are extracted from writings of proponents of the technique in question.

6.031 Franken, Richard B. "Advertising Appeals Selected by the Method of Direct Impressions." *Journal of Applied Psychology* 8 (June 1924): 232 - 44.

Uses the "method of direct impression."

6.032 Franken, Richard B. *The Attention Value of Newspaper Advertise-ments*. New York: Association of National Advertisers, 1925, 55 pp.

Several empirical studies.

6.033 Franken, Richard B., and Larrabee, Carroll B. *Packages That Sell*. New York: Harper, 1928, 302 pp.

Claiming to be the first book that systemizes knowledge in the area of packaging, this reports primitive psychological experi- ments, a la Kitson, Hollingworth, Hotchkiss and Starch.

6.034 Gallup, George. *Factors of Reader Interest in 261 Advertisements*. New York: Liberty Publishing, 1932, 51 pp.

About all that is publicly published by Gallup on advertising.

6.035 Hamlin, Ina M. *A Market Research Bibliography*. Business Research Bulletin, no. 38. Urbana: University of Illinois, 1931, 75 pp.

A good source for a "state of the art" listing.

6.036 Hollingworth, H.L. "Judgements of Persuasiveness." *Psychological Review* (July 1911): 234 - 56.

Order of merit responses to copy premises.

6.037 Holmes, Joseph L. "Free Association Methods as a Measure of the Efficiency of Advertising." *Journal of Applied Psychology* 9 (March 1925): 60 - 65.

Uses a method of "controlled association."

6.038 Hotchkiss, George B. *Advertising Copy*. New York: Harper, 1924, 471 pp.

Early text which explains early copy testing techniques.

6.039 Hotchkiss, George B., and Franken, Richard B. *The Attention Value of Advertisements in a Leading Periodical*. New York: New York Univer- sity, 1920, 32 pp.

"An experiment in measuring the relative attention secured by the various advertisements printed in the Saturday Evening Post of November 8, 1919."

6.040 Hotchkiss, George B., and Franken, Richard B. *The Leadership of Advertised Brands*. Garden City, NY: Doubleday, Page, 1923, 256 pp.

Done by NYU Bureau of Business Studies, this is a study of 100 commodities showing the names and brands most familiar to the public.

6.041 Hotchkiss, George B., and Franken, Richard B. *Measurement of Advertising Effects*. New York: Harper, 1927, 248 pp.

Repeat of study published as *The Leadership of Advertised Brands*.

6.042 James, Don L. *Youth, Media and Advertising*. Study in Marketing, no. 15. Austin, TX: University of Texas, 1971, 137 pp.

Media attitudes and usages of grades 4 - 12.

6.043 Kitson, Harry D. *Scientific Advertising*. New York: Codex, 1926, 73 pp.

A collection of technical papers "using the historical method" reporting primitive content analysis of ads, 1895 - 1920, for changes in size, layout, art forms and positioning.

6.044 Lazer, William. "Market Research: Past Accomplishments and Potential Future Developments." *Journal of the Market Research Society* 16 (July 1974): 183 - 202.

The first ten pages of this article are a neatly organized retrospective on the development of research techniques. The paper was a co-winner of the Thompson Gold Medal for 1973 awarded by the English society.

6.045 Lindquest, Calvert B. *How to Tell if Your Ads Will Sell*. Chicago: Helpful Press, 1950, 97 pp.

Plug for the "Profit-Ad" system for preparing ads.

6.046 Lockley, Lawrence C. "History and Development of Marketing Research." In *Handbook of Marketing Research*, pp. I - 3 to I - 15. Edited by Robert Ferber. New York: McGraw-Hill, 1974.

A disappointing paper, but some good material on early media research activities in the 1910's and 20's.

6.047 Lockley, Lawrence C. "Notes on the History of Marketing Research." *Journal of Marketing* 14 (1950): 733 - 736.

A brief article whose content is substantially repeated in his article in Ferber's, *Handbook of Marketing Research*.

6.048 Lockwood, Thornton C., and Ramond, Charles K. *Sources of Published Advertising Research*. New York: Advertising Research Foundation, 1960, 65 pp.

6.049 Manville, Richard. *How to Create and Select Winning Advertisements: Pre-Evaluation in Advertising*. New York: Harper, 1947, 70 pp.

First published serially in *Printers' Ink,* 1941.

6.050 Mayer, Martin P. *The Intelligent Man's Guide to Sales Measures of Advertising*. New York: Advertising Research Foundation, 1965, 72 pp.

Primarily bibliography, pp. 29 - 71.

6.051   Palda, Kristian S.   *The Measurement of Cumulative Advertising Effects*.   Englewood Cliffs, NJ: Prentice-Hall, 1964, 101 pp.

A publication of his prize winning dissertation (University of Chicago, 1963) analyzing Lydia Pinkham data.   Spawned a research tradition all its own with many subsequent papers written using the same and revised Pinkham data.   See Pollay, Richard W., "Lydia-metrics: Applications of Econometrics to the History of Advertising."   An abstract of the original can also be seen in the *Journal of Business* 38 (April 1965):   162 - 79.

6.052   Ramond, Charles K.   *Advertising Research: The State of the Art*. New York: Association of National Advertisers, 1976, 148 pp.

Annotated bibliography, pp. 111 - 136.   Ramond was a long standing principal in the Advertising Research Foundation and editor of the *Journal of Advertising Research*.

6.053   Reilly, William J.   "The Place of the Research Department of the Advertising Agency in Market Research."   Ph.D. dissertation, University of Chicago, 1927, 200 pp.

Also covers activities of a large sample of research departments. Bibliography, pp. 184 - 200.

6.054   *The Repetition of Advertising*.   New York: Batten, Barton, Durstine & Osborn, 1967, 31 pp.

"A survey of 80 years of research on repetition and its effect on the consumer."

6.055   Rice, Berkeley.   "Rattlesnakes, French Fries and Pupillometric Oversell."   *Psychology Today* 7 (February 1974):   55 - 9.

A mini-history of advertising's attempt to use pupillary response as a measure of advertising effectiveness in the 1960's.

6.056   Rousseau, Lee M.   *Successful Advertising Through Evaluation*. Newark: Barten Press, 1946, 37 pp.

Pamphlet on effectiveness measures.

6.057   Rudolph, Harold J.   *Four Million Inquiries from Magazine Advertising*.   New York: Columbia University Press, 1936, 101 pp.

Foreward by George Gallup.   Results of extensive testing of ads using coupon returns as criterion.

6.058   *Sense and Nonsense in Creative Research: A Guide to Terms and Techniques*.   New York: Grey Advertising, 1962, 87 pp.

Their presentation on good research.   Alvin Achenbaum probably a principal force in creating this.

6.059   Shaw, A.W. *An Approach to Business Problems*. Cambridge, MA: Harvard University Press, 1916.

An early marketing research book.

6.060   Stanley, Thomas. *The Measurement of Advertising Effects*. Garden City, NY: Doubleday, Page, 1935.

Text of research methods.

6.061   Starch, Daniel. *An Analysis of over 3,000,000 Inquiries Received by 98 Firms from 2,339 Magazine Advertisements*. Cambridge: By the Author, 1927, 43 pp.

Analysis of coupon returns.

6.062   Starch, Daniel. *Measuring Advertising Readership and Results*. New York: McGraw-Hill, 1966, 270 pp.

Reviews history of measurement briefly and talks of advertising's role in society, but bulk of content is on Starch readership methods and results of years of research. Has an appendix of "Fifty Years of Consumer Psychology."

6.063   Starch, Daniel. *Measuring Product Sales Made by Advertising*. Mamaroneck, NY: By the Author, 1961, 97 pp.

6.064   Starch, Daniel. "Testing the Effectiveness of Advertisements." *Harvard Business Review* 1 (1923): 464 - 74.

Benchmark paper displaying still primitive attempts of advertising research. Despite primitiveness, it proved to be a foundation for fame and fortune for Starch.

6.065   Starch, Daniel. *300 Effective Advertisements, Selected on the Basis of 5,000,000 Inquiries Received From 3,500 Magazine and Newspaper Advertisements of 163 Firms*. Cambridge, MA: By the Author, 1931, 248 pp.

Almost entirely facsimilies with no data on individual ads reprinted.

6.066   Strong, Edward K., Jr. "Effect of Size of Advertisements and the Frequency of Their Presentation." *Psychological Review* 21 (March 1914): 136 - 52. See author's other work: 5.093, 5.094, 5.095.

6.067   Swan, Carroll J. *Which Ad Pulled Best? Tests, Results, Conclusions, Sales Inquiries, Readership*. New York: Funk & Wagnalls, 1951, 163 pp.

57 tests of 139 ads.

6.068   Swan, Carrol J., ed. *Tested Advertising Copy*. New York: Printers' Ink, 1955, 208 pp.

"201 tests of 480 ads, with factual results in readership, inquiries on sales, and analyses of basic success factors for ad copy as viewed by Gallup, Politz, *et al*.

6.069 Thorelli, Hans B.; Becker, Helmut; and Engledow, Jack. *The Information Seekers: An International Study of Consumer Information and Advertising Image*. Cambridge: Ballinger, 1974, 373 pp.

Primarily U.S. and Germany.

6.070 Tolley, B. Stuart. *Advertising and Market Research: A New Methodology*. Chicago: Nelson-Hall, 1977, 312 pp.

6.071 Townsend, William S., and Townsend, A.J. *Why an Advertisement Succeeds or Fails*. New York: By the Authors, 1937, 64 pp.

A plug for pretesting ads with a checklist of sales-effectiveness elements.

6.072 United States. Department of Commerce. Bureau of Foreign and Domestic Commerce. *Market Research Agencies*. Domestic Commerce Series, no. 6. Washington, DC: Government Printing Office, 1926 and annually.

"A list of publications on domestic market research by the federal government, state governments, colleges, publishers, advertising agencies, business services, chambers of commerce, individuals, business magazines, newspapers, and trade associations."

6.073 Weinberg, Robert S. *An Analytic Approach to Advertising Expenditure Strategy*. New York: Association of National Advertisers, 1960, 127 pp.

Operations research in action, by the manager of Market Research, I.B.M.

6.074 Wheatley, John J., ed. *Measuring Advertising Effectiveness: Selected Readings*. Homewood, IL: Irwin, 1969, 233 pp.

Edited for the American Marketing Association.

6.075 White, Gordon E. "John Caples and His Contributions to Advertising and Communications Research." Ph.D. dissertation, University of Illinois at Urbana-Champagne, 1971, 284 pp.

Caples has been an articulate crusader for the scientific approach to advertising communication.

6.076 White, Percival. *Advertising Research*. New York: Appleton, 1927, 597 pp.

Discusses duplication of media coverage, media selection techniques, evaluation of advertising effectiveness, consumer behavior, etc.

6.077 White, Percival. *Market Analysis: Its Principles and Methods*. New York: McGraw-Hill, 1921.

A very early market research text. See also Duncan.

6.078   Wolfe, Harry D.   *Pretesting Advertising*.   New York: National Industrial Conference Board, Study 109, 1963, 212 pp.

Includes 105 cases with methodology described.

6.079   Wolfe, Harry D.; Brown, James K.; and Thompson, G. Clark. *Measuring Advertising Results*.   Studies in Business Policy, no. 102. New York: National Industrial Conference Board, 1962, 177 pp.

Includes description of 98 cases histories and methods used.

See also 2.028, 3.008, 3.011, 3.044, 3.122, all of section 5.000 but especially 5.060, 5.090, 8.013, 8.202, 8.254 and motivation research references.

"The reason advertising itself is so vital today is that the manufacturers of our country, as we all know, have *solved* the problems of production.   The amount of production, the quality of it and the innovations in it are assured.   Where we face difficulties is in the distribution of these products.   How to get them into the hands of more and more people.   How to raise and keep raising their standard of living.   How to keep demand on the increase so that the consumer, dissatisfied with the status quo, will always be looking for the new, the improved and the better."

Bob Foreman
(3.041, p xii)

7.000
CRITICISMS AND REBUTTALS:
Ethics and Polemics

7.001 Ad Man (pseud.). "Do You Believe in Ads?" *Outlook* 143 (4 August 1926): 475 - 77.

   Cover story, with advice to protect reader against shoddy merchandise sold by retailers.

7.002 Adams, Samuel H. *The Great American Fraud*. Chicago: American Medical Association, 1908, 166 pp.

   A republication of Adam's famous series of articles for *Colliers* in which he exposes the patent medicine business. Instrumental in awakening public consciousness and precipitating the Pure Food and Drug Laws of Dr. Wiley in 1906. Good for information on narcotic drugs, the letter brokerage business and advertising contracts.

7.003 Alexander, George J. *Honesty and Competition: False Advertising Law and Policy Under FTC Administration*. Syracuse: Syracuse University Press, 1967, 315 pp.

   History of judicial interpretations for lawyers.

7.004 Appel, Joseph H. *The Master Merchant, and Other Writings*. N.p., 1909, 320 pp.

   Large print, inspirational messages.

7.005 Babson, Roger W., and Stone, C.N. *Consumer Protection: How It Can Be Secured*. New York: Harper, 1938, 207 pp.

   "Organized consumers can develop a crusading zeal more ardent than that of communism."

7.006 Backman, Jules. *Advertising and Competition*. New York: New York University Press, 1967, 239 pp.

   An often quoted economic study.

7.007 Baker, Samm S. *The Permissable Lie: The Inside Truth About Advertising*. Cleveland: World Publishing, 1968, 236 pp.

   Argues that puffery is social reality for admen. Everybody does it, even to themselves.

7.008 Barmash, Isadore. *The World Is Full of It: How We Are Oversold, Overinfluenced and Overwhelmed by the Communications Manipulators*. New York: Delacorte Press, 1974, 269 pp.

7.009 Barzun, Jacques. "Myths for Materialists." In *American Thought*, pp. 459 - 68. New York: Gresham, 1947.

   Originally appeared in *Chimera* 1946.

7.010 Batten, Henry A. "An Advertising Man Looks at Advertising."
Atlantic 150 (July 1932): 53 - 57

> Finds much truth in criticism of advertising for "blatancy,
> vulgarity and charlatanism," but puts burden on individual con-
> sumers.

7.011 Bauer, Raymond A., and Greyser, Stephen A. *Advertising in America:
The Consumer View.* Boston: Harvard Graduate School of Business, 1968,
473 pp.

> A report and interpretation of the American Association of Adver-
> tising Agencies' study on the consumer judgement of advertising.

7.012 Bensman, Joseph. "The Advertising Man." In *Dollars and Sense:
Ideology, Ethics and the Meaning of Work in Profit and Non Profit Organizations.* pp. 9 - 68. New York: Macmillan, 1967, 208 pp.

> Descriptive study of the ethics of agency personnel, manifest and
> verbalized.

7.013 Better Business Bureau. *Business-Consumer Relations Conference.*
New York: BBB, 1940, 134 pp.

> Proceedings. Advertising is defended by Raymond Rubicam. A
> similar event occurred in 1939.

7.014 Bloom, Paul N. *Advertising, Competition and Public Policy: A
Simulation Study.* Cambridge: Ballinger, 1976, 203 pp.

> Examines economic public policy, including taxation, for simulated
> impact on industry structure.

7.015 Borden, Neil H. *Advertising in Our Economy.* Chicago: Irwin,
1945, 301 pp.

> A condensed version of *The Economic Effects of Advertising.*

7.016 Borden, Neil H. *The Economic Effects of Advertising.* Chicago:
Irwin, 1942, 988 pp.

> A monumental classic, often quoted.

7.017 Borsodi, Ralph. *National Advertising Versus Prosperity: A Study
of the Economic Consequences of National Advertising.* New York: Arcadia
Press, 1923, 303 pp.

> Indicts advertising on economic grounds because it "creates waste-
> ful conflicts, demoralizes distribution, changes the basis of
> profit from greater values to greater advertising resources and
> raises the producers' profits."

7.018 Brainerd, John G., ed. *The Ultimate Consumer: A Study in Economic
Illiteracy.* Annals of the American Academy of Political and Social
Science, vol. 173. Philadelphia: n.p., 1934, 230 pp.

> 22 good articles by authors such as Means, Kallet, Warne and Lynd.

7.019 Brandt, Michael T., and Preston, Ivan L. "The Federal Trade Commission's Use of Evidence to Determine Deception." *Journal of Marketing* 41 (January 1977): 54 - 62.

> Surveys changing evidential criteria from 1916 - 1973. A better source might be Brandt's thesis from which this is adapted. See also Preston's *Great American Blowup*.

7.020 Breniser, Ross D. *The Schemes Back of the Ads*. Philadelphia: (By the Author), 1914, 36 pp.

> Small pamphlet exposing direct mail ads for their true purpose - sample offers, agency solicitation, "free" offers, etc. Includes discussion of electric belts, opium cures, asthma cures, etc.

7.021 Brigance, William N. "Wisdom While You Wait." *North American Review* 226 (December 1928): 751 - 57.

> Mocking exposé of correspondence schools.

7.022 Bristol, Lee H. *Profits in Advance*. New York: Harper, 1932, 180 pp.

> Depression discussion of "modern" business. Bristol, as in Bristol-Myers, also president of ANA.

7.023 Brozen, Yale, ed. *Advertising and Society*. New York: New York University Press, 1974, 189 pp.

> Papers from a distinguished lecture series held at the University of Chicago.

7.024 Buck, Glen. *What's the Matter with Advertising?* Chicago: By the Author, 1934, 36 pp.

> A pitch for "fine and honest craftsmanship to bring radio into a fulfillment of its splendid possibilities." Also comments on Rorty in sparkling prose which is surprisingly critical of commercial vulgarity.

7.025 Calkins, Earnest E. *Business the Civilizer*. Boston: Little, Brown, 1928, 309 pp.

> A paean to advertising and business written by an adman. A good view of the unbounded virtues selling was held to have in the 1920's. See also Barton's *The Man Nobody Knows*.

7.026 Campbell, Persia. *The Consumer Interest: A Study in Consumer Economics*. New York: Harper, 1949, 660 pp.

> Provides a rationale for the 1930's consumer movement.

7.027 Campbell, Persia. *Consumer Representation in the New Deal*. New York: Columbia University Press, 1940, 298 pp.

> Also a study in history, economics and public law.

7.028 Canada. Special Senate Committee on Mass Media. *Words, Music,*
Dollars: A Study of the Economics of Publishing and Broadcasting.
Ottawa: Information Canada, 1970, 572 pp.

> Vol. 2 of the Special Senate Committee's report, also known as the
> Davey Commission reports. Includes material on the economics of
> advertising, advertising agencies, and regulation.

7.029 Carpenter, Charles E. *Dollars and Sense*. Garden City, NY:
Doubleday, 1928, 256 pp.

> A reply to Chase's *Your Money's Worth*.

7.030 *Caveat Emptor*. New York: Arno, 1976, 344 pp.

> 12 articles trace the growth of the concept of "caveat emptor."

7.031 Chapman, Clowry. *The Law of Advertising and Sales: And Related*
Business Law with which is Combined Advertising and Sales that Develop
Good Will. 2 vols. Denver: By the Author, 1908.

> Claims to be the first work of this type.

7.032 Chapman, Clowry. *The Law on Advertising*. New York: Harper, 1929,
495 pp.

> Introduction by Earnest Elmo Calkins. Earlier (1908) edition
> privately published in Denver.

7.033 Chase, Stuart. "Putting Halitosis on the Map." *Survey* 61 (1 November 1928): 127 - 29.

> Very general treatment on the costliness of advertising.

7.034 Chase, Stuart, and Schlink, F.J. *Your Money's Worth: A Study in*
the Waste of the Consumer Dollar. New York: Macmillan, 1927, 285 pp.

> The first of the exposés which, with the following depression,
> gained popularity and lead to the creation of the Consumer
> Research Union and popular support for reform legislation. See
> other works by Schlink, Phillips, Kallett, and Rejoinder by
> Carpenter, Eskew.

7.035 Cherington, Paul T. *The Consumer Looks at Advertising*. New
York: Harper, 1928, 196 pp.

> Discussion of economic aspects. Introduction by Stanley Resor.

7.036 Christians, Clifford G.; Schultze, Quentin J.; and Sims, Norman
H. "Community, Epistemology and Mass Media Ethics." *Journalism History:*
In press.

> Examines in part, the conflict between professionalism and
> community-based ethical norms in advertising for the Progressive
> era.

7.037 Clarke, Blake. *The Advertising Smoke Screen*. New York: Harper, 1944, 228 pp.

A journalistic report on the FTC received complaints, stipulations and orders of the day, written in a muckraking style. The products covered are cigarettes, laxatives, Listerine (dandruff), headache potions, vitamins, toothpaste and cold and weight reduction remedies.

7.038 Cloyes, Corrie. *Advertising and Its Role in War and Peace*. Washington: U.S. Government Printing Office, 1943, 92 pp.

Dept. of Commerce publication reproducing favourable attitudes toward advertising expressed by various government officials.

7.039 Comanor, William S., and Wilson, Thomas A. *Advertising and Market Power*. Cambridge, MA: Harvard University Press, 1974, 257 pp.

Economic analysis of the effects of advertising based on 1947 - 64 data.

7.040 *Concerning a Literature Which Compels Action: In the Interest of Advertising as a Profession*. Chicago: Lord & Thomas, 1911, 47 pp.

Alternative title: *Altruism in Advertising*.

7.041 Cook, James. *Remedies and Rackets: The Truth About Patent Medicines Today*. New York: Norton, 1958, 252 pp.

Focuses on controversy over patent medicines versus general medicines.

7.042 Dieterich, Daniel, ed. *Teaching About Doublespeak*. Urbana: National Council of Teachers of English, 1976, 218 pp.

Papers to help teachers prepare students.

7.043 Digges, Isaac W. *The Modern Law of Advertising and Marketing: A Layman's Guidebook for Everyone Concerned with the Marketing of America's Goods and Services*. New York: Funk & Wagnalls, 1948, 310 pp.

On contracts in advertising, regulation, trademarks, cooperative advertising, copy claims, etc.

7.044 Dwight, Frederick. "The Significance of Advertising." *Yale Review* 18 (August 1909).

General discussion, but relates conflict over subway advertising in New York.

7.045 Ellison, Earl J., and Brock, Frank W. *The Run for Your Money*. New York: Dodge, 1935, 258 pp.

Exposure of swindles from Better Business Bureau files, with some reprinted from *Reader's Digest*. Makes an interesting inventory of depression survival shams.

7.046   Eskew, G.L. *Guinea Pigs and Bugbears*. Chicago: Research Press, 1938, 271 pp.

> A vigorous defence of business practice and an attack on Consumer Research Union as "radical, sensational and subversive."

7.047   *The Ethical Problems of Modern Advertising*. New York: Ronald, 1931, 134 pp.

> Lectures given at Northwestern by Earnest Elmo Calkins, L.D.H. Weld, R.S. Butler, Stuart Chase and others.

7.048   Ewen, Stuart. "Advertising as a Way of Life." *Liberation* 19 (January 1975): 17 - 34.

> An excerpt from *Captains of Consciousness*.

7.049   Ewen, Stuart. *Captains of Consciousness: Advertising and the Social Roots of the Consumer Culture*. New York: McGraw-Hill, 1976, 261 pp.

> A study of advertising and the roots of consumer culture. With an informal content analysis of 1920's ads.

7.050   Feldman, George J., and Zorn, Burton A. *Robinson-Patman Act: Advertising and Promotional Allowances*. Washington: Bureau of National Affairs, 1948, 290 pp.

7.051   Ferguson, James M. *Advertising and Competition: Theory, Measurement, Fact*. Cambridge, MA: Ballinger, 1974, 190 pp.

> Consequences of advertising on industrial structure. Bibliography, pp. 171 - 88.

7.052   Finkelhor, Francis. *Legal Phases of Advertising*. New York: McGraw-Hill, 1938, 345 pp.

> Extensive, with even a short chapter on skywriting. Well indexed and documented. Table of cases, pp. 319 - 35.

7.053   Fisher, John. *The Plot to Make You Buy*. New York: McGraw-Hill, 1968, 209 pp.

> A turncoat Toronto adman blows the whistle on his fellow conspirators on both sides of the border.

7.054   Fiske, Edward R. *Mouse-Traps and Democracy*. New York: Wardell, 1941, 154 pp.

7.055   French, George. *Advertising: The Social and Economic Problem*. New York: Ronald, 1915, 258 pp.

> Text-like discussion. Reprints 1913 "Baltimore Code" of Advertising Clubs of America, and Standards of Practice of the Associated Advertising Clubs of America.

7.056 Fritschler, A. Lee. *Smoking and Politics: Policy Making and the Federal Bureaucracy*. New York: Appleton, Century, Crofts, 1969, 165 pp.

Policy analysis of cigarette labelling, a battle joined by various advertising associations.

7.057 Gardner, Edward H. *The Economics of Advertising*. Chicago: Advertising Federation of American Educational Committee, 1931, 32 pp.

"Public education in defense of advertising by anecdotal evidence and conventional wisdom argument."

7.058 Garrett, Thomas M. *An Introduction to Some Ethical Problems of Modern American Advertising*. Rome: Gregorian University Press, 1961, 209 pp.

Author was on the faculty of University of Scranton.

7.059 Gass, Alice D. "Advertising: Read It and Chuckle." *Forum* 80 (December 1928): 955 - 57.

Suggests advertising is ludicrous, not litigatious as Stuart Chase suggested.

7.060 Geller, Max. *Advertising at the Crossroads: Federal Regulation Vs. Voluntary Controls*. New York: Ronald, 1952, 335 pp.

Well researched discussion which urges voluntary controls. Reviews of FTC and FCC cases.

7.061 Gentry, Curt. *The Vulnerable Americans*. Garden City, NY: Doubleday, 1966, 333 pp.

Discusses direct mail advertising frauds and sundry swindles and cons.

7.062 Goodman, Walter. *The Clowns of Commerce*. New York: Sagamore Press, 1957, 278 pp.

"An irreverant investigation into the motives and morals of the professional persuaders." Often satirical, rarely bitter.

7.063 Goulart, Ron. *The Assault on Childhood*. Los Angeles: Sherbourne, 1969, 278 pp.

Criticism naturally focused on food and toy advertising.

7.064 Greyser, Stephen A. "Americans and Advertising: Thirty Years of Public Opinion." *Public Opinion Quarterly* 30 (1966): 13 - 18.

"There seems to be no reason to believe that Americans are particularly more, or less, critical of advertising today than they have been in the past."

7.065 Groner, Alex. *Advertising: The Case for Competition*. New York:
Association of National Advertisers, 1967, 46 pp.

A report on Backman's *Advertising and Competition*.

7.066 Gruening, Ernst. *The Public Pays: A Study of Power Propaganda*.
New York: Vanguard, 1931, 273 pp.

A discussion of the "public relations" advertising of private
utilities fighting political battles. Based on FTC testimony.
The author was later a senator from Alaska.

7.067 Hackett, Catherine, and Sterling, John C. "The New Deal and
Advertising: Two Points of View." *Forum* 91 (Feburary 1934): 98 - 104.

The pro and con of the necessity and value/risks of the Tugwell
Bill.

7.068 Harding, T. Swann. *The Joy of Ignorance*. New York: Goodwin,
1932, 369 pp.

Critique of public ignorance, abetted by advertising, about things
such as coffee, cigarettes, patent medicines.

7.069 Harding, T. Swann. *The Popular Price of Fraud*. New York: Longmans, Green, 1935, 376 pp.

Examines excessive claims in drug and food advertising, the government's food and drug policies, and includes a plea for public
education.

7.070 Hibschmann, Harry J. *The "Verboten" Dictionary*. Chicago: Advertising Publications, 1941, 32 pp.

"Verboten" because of court decisions interpreting the Wheeler-
Lea Act.

7.071 Hill, Conrad R. *The Aberrant Image of Advertising*. School of
Journalism Paper, no. 202. Lincoln, NE: University of Nebraska Press,
1960, 57 pp.

Review of criticism and justifications by advertisers.

7.072 Holbrook, Stewart H. *The Golden Age of Quackery*. New York:
Macmillan, 1959, 302 pp.

A journalist's excursion through the world of patent medicine and
its mountebanks.

7.073 Holt, Hamilton. *Commercialism and Journalism*. New York: Houghton
Mifflin, 1909, 105 pp.

Lecture on "morals of trade" by the managing editor of *The Independent*.

7.074   Howard, John A., and Hulbert, James. *Advertising and the Public
Interest: A Staff Report to the Federal Trade Commission.* Chicago:
Crain, 1973, 96 pp.

> An analysis of the testimony given in FTC hearings on modern
> advertising practices.

7.075   Hoyt, Elizabeth E. *Consumption in Our Society.* New York: McGraw-
Hill, 1938, 420 pp.

> Discussion of economics, critical of advertising.

7.076   Hoyt, Elizabeth E. *The Consumption of Wealth.* New York: Macmillan, 1928, 344 pp.

> Focus on social and cultural problems of consumers.

7.077   Huntington, William S. *How They Swindled You: An Exposition of
Fraud Practiced Upon Businessmen By Advertising and Charity.* Chicago:
Aiken, 1896, 63 pp.

> Story of fraudulent advertising salesmen, selling worthless space
> to agentless businessmen. Names names. Also appears under
> pseudonym, A.F. Aiker.

7.078   Huse, Howard R. *The Illiteracy of the Literate: A Guide to the
Art of Intelligent Reading.* New York: Appleton-Century, 1933, 272 pp.

> Discusses advertising on pp. 128 - 61, under "Verbomania: the
> Pathology of Language."

7.079   Hutchinson, Ray. *The Gospel According to Madison Avenue.* New
York: Bruce, 1969, 161 pp.

> By an anti-academic author, intentionally "as unlike a textbook
> or thesis" as possible, the result being an uninformative polemic.

7.080   Hyman, Allen, and Johnson, M. Bruce, eds. *Advertising and Free
Speech.* Lexington, MA: Lexington Books, 1977, 108 pp.

> Conference papers, University of Miami Law School, on whether
> lawyers should advertise.

7.081   *In Behalf of Advertising: A Series of Essays Published in National
Periodicals From 1919 to 1928.* Philadelphia: Ayer, 1929, 266 pp.

> Reproduction of the forceful copy part of ads promoting advertising.

7.082   Jastrow, Joseph. *The Betrayal of Intelligence: A Preface to
Debunking.* New York: Greenberg, 1938, 170 pp.

> With a chapter specifically on advertising.

7.083 Jellinek, J. Stephen. *The Inner Editor: The Offense and Defense of Communication*. New York: Stein & Day, 1977.

Essay and ad-hoc theorizing on consumer self defense against advertising.

7.084 Johnston, Bert. *One Nation for Sale*. Cincinnati: Johnson & Hardin, 1943, 192 pp.

A polemic with a theme of the positive impact of advertising on "Joe America."

7.085 Kallen, Horace M. *The Decline and Rise of the Consumer: A Philosophy of Consumer Cooperation*. New York: Appleton-Century, 1936, 484 pp.

"An attempt ... to formulate the social philosophy of the consumer." Discusses the history of cooperation and benefits to consumers from the development of cooperative practices.

7.086 Kallet, Arthur. *Counterfeit: Not Your Money But What It Buys*. New York: Vanguard, 1935, 96 pp.

An enthusiastic attack on many products and methods. Best material is that on advertising of Zonite, Pebeco and laxatives, and Scott tissues. Includes a satire on the use of "experts and scientists" in ads.

7.087 Kallet, Arthur, and Schlink, F.J. *100,000,000 Guinea Pigs: Dangers in Everyday Foods, Drugs, and Cosmetics*. New York: Grosset & Dunlap, 1933, 312 pp.

One of the muckraking depression series that founded the Consumer Research Union.

7.088 Katz, Norman D. "Consumers Union: The Movement and the Magazine." Ph.D. dissertation, Rutgers University, 1977.

Assesses the development of the consumer ideology, the literature of the movement and the founding of Consumers' Research Union.

7.089 Kenner, Edward J. *The Fight for Truth in Advertising*. New York: Roundtable Press, 1936, 298 pp.

"A living record of the way a great profession turned to combat its own abuses" written for a 25th anniversary of the founding of the industry's vigilance committees, which evolved into today's Better Business Bureaus.

7.090 Kenyon, Bernice L. "A Housewife Looks at Advertising." *American Mercury* 29 (June 1933): 181 - 89.

A critical view of "bad" advertising; the ugly, the sentimental (silly), the extravagant, the vague and the scary. But the author is hardly a typical housewife, as her cook or maid would attest.

7.091 Kinter, Earl W. *A Primer on the Law of Deceptive Practices: A Guide for the Businessman*. New York: Macmillan, 1971, 593 pp.

Detail on the FTC and courts' explicit definitions of deceptive advertising.

7.092 Leven, Maurice; Moulton, Harold G., Warburton, Clark. *America's Capacity to Consume*. Washington: Brooking Institute, 1934, 272 pp.

Focus on the distribution of wealth.

7.093 Levy, Sidney J., and Zaltman, Gerald. *Marketing, Society, and Conflict*. Englewood Cliffs, NJ: Prentice-Hall, 1975, 134 pp.

A sophisticated conceptualization of the conflicts inherent in marketplace transactions, but only a small amount directly related to advertising.

7.094 Liston, Robert A. *Why We Think the Way We Do*. New York: Watts, 1977, 132 pp.

Examination of propaganda and advertising to innoculate a juvenile audience.

7.095 McTighe, John A. "Self-Regulation Efforts of Advertisers, Their Agents and the Media." In *Consumer Protection From Deceptive Advertising*, pp. 83 - 121. Edited by Frederic Stuart. Hempstead, NY: Hofstra University, 1974.

Reproduces AAAA Code of Ethics, the *Printers' Ink* statute, the NAB radio and television codes, and excerpts from the American Federation of Advertisers *Truth Book*.

7.096 Mahin, John L. *Advertising: Selling the Consumer*. Garden City, NY: Doubleday, Page, 1914, 298 pp.

A text, defensive in tone, in support of the Association of Advertising Clubs of the World. Annotated bibliography with each chapter.

7.097 Mannes, Marya. *But Will It Sell?* Philadelphia: Lippincott, 1964, 240 pp.

A passionate plea to guard against the "money thinkers," this is a collection of articles of social criticism with the first section of the work discussing the supermarket and advertising.

7.098 Manning-Anderson, Joanne. *Advertised Specials: A Promotional Gimmick or a Real Break for Consumers?* Washington: Public Citizen, 1974, 26 pp.

Documents and materials for a do-it-yourself survey of food advertising by supermarkets.

7.099 Matthews, Joseph B. *Guinea Pigs No More*. New York: Covici,
Friede, 1936, 311 pp.

   More depression muckraking.

7.100 Matthews, Joseph B., and Shallcross, R.E. *Partners in Plunder:
The Cost of Business Dictatorship*. Washington: Consumers' Research,
1935, 444 pp.

   Vigorous depression muckraking, with the second chapter devoted
   specifically to advertising. It quotes W.C. D'Arcy and Claude
   Hopkins in its attack that is at least carefully footnoted and
   indexed.

7.101 Merz, Charles. *The Great American Band Wagon*. New York: Literary
Guild of America, 1928, 263 pp.

   Satirical work with some material on advertising.

7.102 Mitchell, Malcolm. *Propaganda, Polls and Public Opinion: Are the
People Manipulated?* Englewood Cliffs, NJ: Prentice-Hall, 1977, 120 pp.

   Reader and questions for high school discussion, with a chapter on
   advertising.

7.103 Montague, Dr. J.F. *I Know Just the Thing for That*. New York:
Day, 1934, 265 pp.

   Exposé of patent medicines, particularly laxatives.

7.104 Moore, Frank. *Legal Protection of Goodwill: Trademarks, Trade
Emblems, Advertising, Unfair Competition*. New York:. Ronald, 1936,
218 pp.

   One chapter specifically on advertising.

7.105 Morell, Peter. *Poisons, Potions and Profits: The Antidote to
Radio Advertising*. New York: Knight, 1937, 292 pp.

   "It names names" and based on material from Consumers' Union files.
   Focuses on patent medicines and follows the tradition of
   100,000,000 Guinea Pigs as vigorous muckraking.

7.106 Moriarty, William D. *The Economics of Marketing and Advertising*.
New York: Harper, 1923, 592 pp.

7.107 Moskin, J. Robert, ed. *The Case for Advertising*. New York:
American Association of Advertising Agencies, 1973, 95 pp.

   "Highlights of the industry presentation to the FTC" by a joint
   committee of the ANA and AAAA.

7.108 Mowbray, A.Q. *The Thumb on the Scale: Or the Supermarket Shell
Game*. Philadelphia: Lippincott, 1967, 201 pp.

   Based on the congressional hearing for the unsuccessful Hart bill
   for "truth in packaging."

7.109 Nadel, Mark V. *The Politics of Consumer Protection*. New York: Bobbs-Merrill, 1971, 257 pp.

> Academic examination of the fate of the consumer interest in federal government policy-making. Primarily for the 60's but introductory chapter is historical.

7.110 National Opinion Research Center. *The People Look at Radio*. Chapel Hill, NC: University of Carolina Press, 1946, 158 pp.

> Survey results notable for their portrayal of what is wrong with commercials.

7.111 Nichols, John P. *The Chain Store Tell Its Story*. New York: Institute of Distribution, 1940, 274 pp.

> Defense of chains, has long section using question and answer format. Excellent bibliography.

7.112 Nicosia, Francesco M., ed. *Advertising Management and Society: A Business Point of View*. New York: McGraw-Hill, 1974, 386 pp.

> Based on testimony before FTC in 1971 by members of AAAA and ANA.

7.113 *Nostrums and Quackery*. Chicago: American Medical Association Press, 1912, 708 pp.

> Reproductions of articles originally appearing in a journal of AMA, citing advertisements and medical evidence for the sham and shame of patent medicine promotions.

7.114 Olson, Warren E. *The American Advertising Man: A Study of His Attitudes and Values*. Ph.D. thesis, University of Minnesota, 1955, 435 pp. See also Bensman, *Dollars and Sense*.

7.115 Orman, Felix. *A Vital Need of the Times*. New York: Orman, 1918, 148 pp.

> "A symposium of views and comments expressed by leaders of American economic thought, and a collection of letters to the author" which ends with an advertisement for the author's firm specializing in institutional advertising. Despite its obvious commercial intent, this includes the ideas of an impressive collection of people on the merit of selling Americans on big business.

7.116 *Outdoor Advertising Along Highways: A Legal Analysis: A Report of the Highway Laws Project*. Washington: National Research Council, Highway Research Board, 1958, 101 pp.

> NRC's special report, No. 41.

7.117 Packard, Vance. *The Hidden Persuaders*. New York: McKay, 1957, 275 pp.

> Perhaps the most widely read post WWII attack on advertising.

7.118 Palmer, Rachel L., and Alpher, I.M.   *40,000,000 Guinea Pig Children*. New York: Vanguard, 1937, 249 pp.

Muckraking continuation of series.

7.119 Palmer, Rachel L., and Greenberg, S.K.   *Facts and Frauds in Women's Hygiene*. New York: Vanguard, 1936, 311 pp.

"A medical guide against misleading claims and dangerous products."

7.120 Patterson, William D., ed.   *America: Miracle at Work*. New York: Prentice-Hall, 1953, 104 pp.

Optimistic self-congratulations from the advertising industry to itself for public interest campaigns of 1952 honouring the "first annual Saturday Review Awards for Distinguished Advertising in the Public Interest."

7.121 Pease, Otis. "Advertising Ethics: A Persistant Dilemma." *Arizona Review* 18 (October 1969): 1 - 5.

Adapted from his chapter in *Frontiers in Advertising Theory and Research*.

7.122 Pease, Otis. "Advertising: Its Ethics and Its Critics." *In Frontiers of Advertising Theory and Research,* pp. 19 - 28. Edited by Hugh W. Sargent. Palo Alto: Pacific Books, 1972.

Off-the-cuff observations.

7.123 Pease, Otis.   *The Responsibilities of American Advertising*. New Haven: Yale University Press, 1958, 232 pp.

A thorough scholarly discussion of American advertising from 1920 to 1940. Highly recommended because of the quality of the work and also the importance of the era. The criticisms and the industry's responses. Interesting because the arguments pro and con are still voiced and valid.

7.124 Phillips, Mary C.   *More Than Skin Deep*. New York: R.R. Smith, 1948, 200 pp.

Sequel to *Skin Deep* with more exposes.

7.125 Phillips, Mary C.   *Skin Deep: The Truth About Beauty Aids - Safe and Harmful*. New York: Vanguard, 1934, 254 pp.

One of a memorable series, this exposé is concerned with makeup and cosmetics of the 20's and early 30's.

7.126 Plummer, Arthur N.   *The Great American Swindle, Incorporated*. New York: By the Author, 1932, 318 pp.

Holds advertising as key in the "swindle" of 1929, the stock market crash.

7.127   Posner, Richard A. *Regulation of Advertising by the FTC*. Washington: American Enterprise Institute for Public Policy Research, 1973, 40 pp.

Not very detailed compared to easily obtained law texts.

7.128   Powers, John O. "Advertising." *Annals of the American Academy of Political and Social Science* 22 (1903): 470 - 74.

Defense of advertising, based on "assuring and satisfying business."

7.129   Pratt, Earl M. *Brain Ore ... A Collection for Advertisers and Educators*. Chicago: Registration League, 1897, 36 pp.

Quotes in support of advertising from various sources.

7.130   Preston, Ivan L. *The Great American Blowup: Puffery in Advertising and Selling*. Madison, WI: University of Wisconsin Press, 1975, 368 pp.

A review of puffery and deception in advertising, this work is as rich in the legal history of prosecutions and judgements. Both comprehensive and lively to read.

7.131   Quinn, Francis X., ed. *Ethics, Advertising and Responsibility*. Westminister, MD: Canterbury Press, 1963, 165 pp.

A reader from the Institute of Social Ethics, Georgetown University. Media, advertisers, and governments all reproached.

7.132   Rheinstrom, Carroll. *Psyching the Ads: The Case Book of Advertising; the Methods and Results of 180 Advertisements*. New York: Covici, Friede, 1929, 362 pp.

"This analysis ... illustrates ways in which social history, advertising inventory and design victimize the consumer."

7.133   Riegel, Edwin C., *Barnum and Bunk*. New York: Riegel Corp., 1928, 147 pp.

Attack on false advertising by Macy's.

7.134   Riegel, Edwin C., *Main Street Follies*. New York: Riegel Corp., 1928, 125 pp.

Another attack on retailing.

7.135   Riemer, Barry M. *The Great American Con Machine*. Port Washington, NY: Ashley Books, 1975, 101 pp.

Expose of boiler room telephone sales of "advertising space to small retailers."

7.136 Robinson, Charles M. "Abuses of Public Advertising." *Atlantic Monthly* 93 (1909): 289 - 99.

On the aesthetics of signs and outdoor advertising.

7.137 Roper, Burt W. *State Advertising Legislation*. New York: Printers' Ink, 1945, 302 pp.

Co-published with U.S. Department of Commerce.

7.138 Rorty, James. *Order on the Air:* New York: Day, 1934, 32 pp.

Radio advertising regulation.

7.139 Rorty, James. *Our Master's Voice: Advertising*. New York: Day, 1934, 394 pp.

The most critical of the reflections by advertising men, this draws its critical analysis from Veblen, but is for the most part naive depression socialism and tends too often to use derogatory labels without having built a case for their validity. Has some informative value, though, including a chapter on the Psychological Corporation.

7.140 Rotzoll, Kim B.; Haefner, James E.; and Sandage, Charles H. *Advertising in Contemporary Society: Perspectives Toward Understanding*. Columbus, OH: Grid, 1976, 151 pp.

A reader for students.

7.141 Sandage, Charles H., and Fryburger, Vernon, eds. *The Role of Advertising*. Homewood, IL: Irwin, 1960, 499 pp.

A book of readings on advertising's economic and social roles.

7.142 Sarazan, Bert M. *Delusions in Advertising*. Washington: Progress Press, 1947, 89 pp.

An appeal for truthfulness in advertising by one the flock.

7.143 Schemorhorn, James. *Advertising: The Light that Serves and Saves*. New York: Doubleday, Page, 1914, 30 pp.

Published for the Educational Committee of the Associated Advertising Clubs of America.

7.144 Schlink, F.J. "Bear Oil: Old Magic for New Times." *New Republic* 59 (31 July 1929): 277 - 79.

A brief discussion of advertising by "unique selling proposition," authored by one of the more articulate consumer critics of the New Deal era.

7.145   Schlink, F.J.   *Eat, Drink and Be Wary*. New York: Covici,
Friede, 1935, 322 pp.

>   Primarily on food advertising by the President of Consumers'
>   Research.

7.146   Schmalensee, R.   *The Economics of Advertising*. Amsterdam: North
Holland Press, 1972, 312 pp.

>   Economic analysis of 1950 - 1967 data for the U.S.

7.147   Schrank, Jeffrey.   *Deception Detection: An Educator's Guide to
the Art of Insight*. Boston: Beacon Press, 1975, 154 pp.

>   A reader to train students in consumer society survival skills.

7.148   Seldin, Joseph.   *The Golden Fleece: Selling the Good Life to
Americans*. New York: Macmillan, 1963, 305 pp.

>   Written by the head of an ad agency.   Readably written and uses
>   an historical structure.   Indexed but not documented.

7.149   Sethi, S. Prakash.   *Advocacy Advertising and Large Corporations:
Social Conflict, Big Business Image, the News Media, and Public Policy*.
Lexington, MA: Lexington Books, 1977, 355 pp.

>   Review of practices and issues of corporate promotional messages
>   on public issues.

7.150   Sheldon, Roy, and Arens, Egmont.   *Consumer Engineering: A New
Technique for Prosperity*. New York: Harper, 1932, 259 pp.

>   Showing how to stimulate consumption as a depression cure by
>   manipulating taste, fashion and obsolescence.   Introduction by
>   Earnest Elmo Calkins, who is also credited with being the source
>   of the concept, and many suggestions on this work.

7.151   Shimek, John L.   *Billions of False Impressions: An Anthology of
Deception*. Chicago: Concepts of Postal Economics, 1970, 256 pp.

>   This is a response to "junk mail" publicity in a media rivalry
>   between newspapers and direct mailers.   Reproduces press clippings
>   and various publications of COPE.

7.152   Simon, Julian L.   *Issues in the Economics of Advertising*. Urbana:
University of Illinois Press, 1970, 371 pp.

>   Contains a bibliographic essay (pp. 316 - 30) on sources of data
>   for the study of advertising, reprinted in the book you hold.

7.153   Simon, Morton J.   *The Advertising Truth Book*. New York: Advertising Federation of America, 1960, 56 pp.

>   Pamphlet guide to self-policing practices.

7.154 Simon, Morton J. *The Law For Advertising and Marketing*. New York: Norton, 1956, 645 pp.

Thorough, with an opening chapter on the legal history of the advertising agency based on Hower, Presbrey & Rowell.

7.155 Smith, Ralph L. *The Bargain Hucksters*. New York: Crowell, 1962, 236 pp.

Consumer issues, indexed.

7.156 Smith, Ralph L. *The Health Hucksters*. New York: Crowell, 1960, 248 pp.

Modern patent medicine advertising.

7.157 Smith, Ralph L. *Self-regulation in action: Story of the Better Business Bureau, 1912 - 1962*. New York: Association of Better Business Bureaus, 1961, 28 pp.

Commemorative, published prematurely. Can this be the same man who wrote *Health Hucksters* and *Bargain Hucksters?*

7.158 Sokolsy, George E. *The American Way of Life*. New York: Farrar & Rinehart, 1939, 180 pp.

Originally articles for *Liberty,* a vigorous defense of commercial capitalism.

7.159 Sorenson, Helen. *The Consumer Movement: What It Is and What It Means*. New York: Harper, 1941, 245 pp.

A history starting in 1899 with the Consumer's League.

7.160 Steiner, Robert L. "The Prejudice Against Marketing." *Journal of Marketing* 40 (July 1976): 2 - 9.

7.161 Stote, Amos. *Why We Live*. Garden City, NY: Doubleday, Page, 1925, 188 pp.

"For happiness, economic happiness" (p. 185). Published for the Associated Advertising Clubs of the World, includes a confusing chapter on the "new advertising."

7.162 Stridsberg, Albert. *Controversy Advertising: How Advertisers Present Points of View in Public Affairs*. New York: Hastings House, 1977.

Includes several cases, one dating from 1913. Also appears in Books in Print as from the Informational (sic-International) Advertising Association.

7.163 Tinkham, Julian. *The Debunkment of Advertising and Prosperity*. New York: Little & Ives, 1930, 131 pp.

Second section, "Advertising is Non-Essential - Tax It!," published separately in 1918.

7.164 *Truth in Advertising: A Symposium of the Toronto School of Theology, University of Toronto.* Toronto: Fitzhenry & Whiteside, 1972, 37 pp.

>   Using truth norms for various forms of logical argument in a tightly presented normative discussion.

7.165 Tuerck, David G. *Issues in Advertising: The Economics of Persuasion.* Washington: American Enterprise Institute for Public Policy Research, 1978, 284 pp.

>   Edited transcripts of a conference sponsored by the American Enterprise Institute. Although primarily the esoterica of economists, the introductory essays include one by Robert Pitofsky reviewing the FTC resurgance of the last decade.

7.166 U.S. Congress. Federal Radio Commission. *Commercial Radio Advertising.* S. Rept. 137, 72nd Cong., 1932, 201 pp.

>   Report studies the use of radio facilities for commercial advertising purposes.

7.167 U.S. Congress. Government Operations Committee. *Advertising and Promotion of Prescription Drugs (Safety and Effectiveness of New Drugs). Hearings before the Government Operations Committee,* 92nd Cong., 1971, 108 pp.

7.168 U.C. Congress. House. Interstate and Foreign Commerce Committee. *Broadcast Advertisements. Hearings before the House Interstate and Foreign Commerce Committee on H.R. 8316,* 88th Cong., 1963, 381 pp.

>   On proposed restriction of the length of commercial endorsements.

7.169 U.S. Congress. House. Interstate and Foreign Commerce Committee. *Cigarette Labelling and Advertising. Hearings before the House Interstate and Foreign Commerce Committee,* 88th Cong., 1965, 324 pp.

7.170 U.S. Congress. House. Interstate and Foreign Commerce Committee. *Cigarette Labelling and Advertising. Hearings before the House Interstate and Foreign Commerce Committee on H.R. 2248, H.R. 3014, H.R. 4007, H.R. 4244, H.R. 7051,* 89th Cong., 1965, 712 pp.

7.171 U.S. Congress. House. Interstate and Foreign Commerce Committee. *Food, Drugs and Cosmetics. Hearings before the House Interstate and Foreign Commerce Committee on H.R. 6906 and related bills,* 74th Cong., 1935, 774 pp.

7.172 U.S. Congress. House. Interstate and Foreign Commerce Committee. *Regulation of Prices. Hearings before the House Interstate and Foreign Commerce Committee on H.R. 13568,* 64th Cong., 1916, 303 pp.; pt. 2, 1917, 658 pp.

>   Discussion of bill to protect the public against dishonest advertising and false pretenses in merchandising.

7.173 U.S. Congress. House. Public Works Committee. *Highway Beautifi-cation. Hearings before the Subcommittee on Roads of the House Public Works Committee on H.R. 8487 and related bills,* 89th Cong., 1965, 500 pp.

7.174 U.S. Congress. House. Select Committee on Small Business. *Adver-tising and Small Business. Hearings before the House Subcommittee on Activities of Regulatory Agencies Relating to Small Business on H.R. 5, H.R. 19,* 92nd Cong., 1971, 660 + 350 pp.

   On a proposal to create a National Advertising Review Board.

7.175 U.S. Congress. Senate. Banking and Currency Committee. *War Bond Government Newspaper Advertising Program. Hearings before the Senate Banking and Currency Committee on S. 1457,* 78th Cong., 1943, 138 pp.

7.176 U.S. Congress. Senate. Commerce Committee. *Cigarette Labelling and Advertising. Hearings before the Senate Commerce Committee on S. 559, S. 547,* 89th Cong., 1965, 1028 + 253 pp.

7.177 U.S. Congress. Senate. Commerce Committee. *Cigarette Labelling and Advertising. Hearings before the Consumer Subcommittee of the Senate Commerce Committee on H.R. 643, H.R. 1237, H.R. 3055, H.R. 6543, and similar bills,* 91st Cong., 1969, 1420 pp.

7.178 U.S. Congress. Senate. Commerce Committee. *Food, Drugs and Cosmetics. Hearings before the Senate Commerce Committee on S. 1944,* 73rd Cong., 1934, 505 pp.

7.179 U.S. Congress. Senate. Commerce Committee. *Food, Drugs and Cosmetics. Hearings before the Senate Commerce Committee on S. 2800,* 73rd Cong., 1934, 667 pp.

7.180 U.S. Congress. Senate. Commerce Committee. *Food, Drugs and Cosmetics. Hearings before the Senate Commerce Committee on S. 5,* 74th Cong., 1935, 372 pp.

   Discussion of the move "to prevent false advertising of food, drink, drugs, and cosmetics."

7.181 U.S. Congress. Senate. Commerce Committee. *Relationship Between Drug Abuse and Advertising. Hearings before the Consumer Subcommittee of the Senate Commerce Committee on S.J. Res. 200,* 91st Cong., 1971, 128 pp.

7.182 U.S. Congress. Senate. Judiciary Committee. *Possible Anti-Competitive Efforts of Sales of Network TV Advertising. Hearings before the Subcommittee on Anti-Trust and Monopoly of the Senate Judiciary Committee on S. Res. 191,* 89th Cong., 1966, 1387 pp.

7.183 U.S. Congress. Senate. Public Works Committee. *Highway Beauti-fication and Highway Safety Programs. Hearings before the Subcommittee on Roads of the Senate Public Works Committee on S. 1467,* 1967, 462 pp.

7.184 U.S. Congress. Senate. Public Works Committee. *Highway Beauti-fication and Scenic Road Program. Hearings before the Subcommittee on Public Roads of the Senate Public Works Committee on S. 2084, S. 1974, S. 2259,* 89th Cong., 1965, 537 pp.

7.185   Vaile, Roland S.   *Economics of Advertising*.   New York: Ronald, 1927, 183 pp.

Includes lengthy discussion of California Fruit Growers Association (Sunkist).

7.186   Valenstein, Lawrence, and Weiss, E.B.   *Business Under the Recovery Act*.   New York: McGraw-Hill, 1933, 314 pp.

Authors urge the advertising industry to welcome rather than fear the act.

7.187   Vaughn, Floyd.   *Marketing and Advertising: An Economic Appraisal*. Princeton: Princeton University Press, 1928, 255 pp.

Costs and values of distribution and promotion.

7.188   Veblen, Thorstein.   *Absentee Ownership and Business Enterprise in Recent Times*.   New York: B.W. Huebsch, 1923, 445 pp.

In chapter 11 Veblen argues that advertising is "the fabrication of customers" and wails against the size of the industry in an articulate and quotable way.

7.189   Walker, S.H., and Sklar, Paul.   *Business Finds its Voice: Management Efforts to Sell the Business Idea to the Public*.   New York: Harper, 1938, 93 pp.

Reprinting of articles originally appearing in *Harpers* in January, February and March 1938, detailing the efforts of business to sell the public on the virtues of business.

7.190   Warner, John D.   "Advertising Run Mad."   *Municipal Affairs* 4 (1900):   267 - 93.

Aesthetics of New York outdoor ads with quotes and review of legislation elsewhere.

7.191   Watkins, George T.   *"Fishing for Suckers":   Advertising Schemes that Get Money from the Innocent, Gullible and Unwary*.   Boston: By the Author, 1916, 48 pp.

7.192   Weir, Walter.   *Truth in Advertising and Other Heresies*.   New York: McGraw-Hill, 1963, 224 pp.

A plea to fellow advertising executives for truthfulness as a basic attitude by a 35 year veteran.

7.193   White, William A.   "The Ethics of Advertising."   *Atlantic Monthly* 164 (November 1939):   665+.

Important because of reputation of the author, this article notes little substantive change over a fifty year period.

7.194 Whiteside, Thomas. *Selling Death: Cigarette Advertising and Public Health*. New York: Liveright, 1971, 153 pp.

Includes a lengthy discussion of the PR struggle to resist the banning of cigarette ads on TV which originally appeared in the *New Yorker*.

7.195 Whyte, William H., Jr. *Is Anybody Listening?* New York: Simon & Schuster, 1952, 239 pp.

"How and why U.S. business fumbles when it talks to human beings" with special attention to attempts to tell and sell the American business way of life.

7.196 Wight, Robin. *The Day the Pigs Refused to be Driven to Market: Advertising and the Consumer Revolution*. New York: Random, 1974, 230 pp.

First published in England, although report on the American experience.

7.197 Wiseman, Mark. "From Behind the Advertising Looking-Glass." *Survey* 61 (1 November 1928): 130 - 32.

Starts with a plug for *Your Money's Worth*.

7.198 Woodward, Helen. *It's An Art*. New York: Harcourt, Brace, 1938, 405 pp.

Discussion of social issues by a successful ad person, more sympathetic than most to consumers' plight.

7.199 Wright, John S., and Mertes, John E. *Advertising's Role in Society*. St. Paul: West Publication, 1974, 501 pp.

Reader for students.

See also 2.072, 2.081, 8.163, 8.206, 10.004, 10.102, 10.114.

"Our faults of taste, quality, and even integrity are many. Yet I console myself with the thought that, if we pour out our pleas to the many in order to influence the few, so does the church. If our failures sometimes seem more numerous than our successes, so are those of book publishers and the theater. If we sometimes influence men to live beyond their means so, sometimes does matrimony. And if we are too often dull, repetitious, and redundant, so is the United States Senate."

Bruce Barton
(3.020, p 21)

8.000
TEXTBOOKS AND
"HOW-TO" DISCUSSIONS

8.001 Aaker, David A., ed. *Advertising Management: Practical Perspectives.* Englewood Cliffs, NJ: Prentice-Hall, 1975, 399 pp.

A reader.

8.002 Aaker, David A., and Myers, John G. *Advertising Management.* Englewood Cliffs, NJ: Prentice-Hall, 1975, 612 pp.

8.003 Adams, Charles F. *Common Sense in Advertising.* New York: McGraw-Hill, 1965, 200 pp.

A simple book offering basic advice.

8.004 *Advertising: First Aid to Business.* New York: Consolidated Reporting, (1941?), 237 pp.

Typewritten copy in the Library of Congress appears to be a draft of a book, with variously authored chapters, given as lectures to the Advertising Women of New York.

8.005 Agnew, Hugh E. *Advertising Media: How to Weigh and Measure.* New York: Van Nostrand, 1932, 426 pp.

Later editions with W.B. Dygert, co-author.

8.006 Agnew, Hugh E., and Hotchkiss, George B. *Advertising Principles.* Modern Business Texts Series, no. 7. New York: Alexander Hamilton Institute, 1927, 356 pp.

A short course for executive home study by well known authors.

8.007 Amstell, I. Joel. *What You Should Know About Advertising.* Dobbs Ferry, NY: Oceana, 1969, 83 pp.

Very basic.

8.008 Aymar, Gordon C. *An Introduction to Advertising Illustration.* New York: Harper, 1929, 236 pp.

8.009 Azoy, Anastasio C.M., Jr. *A Primer of Advertising.* New York: Harper, 1930, 178 pp.

Well titled.

8.010 Bailey, I.A., and Dunn, Albert H. *Introduction to Modern Advertising.* Scranton: International Business Schools, 1962, 113 pp.

Correspondence text.

8.011 Balmer, Edwin. *The Science of Advertising.* Chicago: Wallace Press, 1909, 64 pp.

Subtitled: The Force of Advertising as a Business Influence, its Place in the National Development, and the Public Result of its

Practical Operation. Copyright by *Science Magazine* where it may
have first appeared.

8.012 Barban, Arnold M.; Jugenheimer, Donald W.; and Young, Lee F.
Advertising Media Sourcebook and Workbook. Columbus, OH: Grid, 1975,
186 pp.

8.013 Barton, Roger A. *Advertising Handbook*. New York: Prentice-Hall,
1950, 1015 pp.

A collection of advertising articles, including Daniel Starch on
the "uses of advertising research."

8.014 Barton, Roger A., ed. *Handbook of Advertising Management*. New
York: McGraw-Hill, 1970, unpaged.

For the corporate advertising manager. Specialists have contributed chapters on aspects of the organization of the advertising
department, planning, research, copy, etc. Includes a glossary.
Indexed.

8.015 Bates, Charles A. *Good Advertising*. New York: Holmes, 1890,
595 pp.

A large, early treatment which includes many chapters reprinted
from his *Printers' Ink* column. Ends with a plug.

8.016 Beardsley, William W. *The Circular Advertising Department*. New
York: Ronald, 1924, 116 pp.

"Circular" as in mailings, not as in "running in ..."

8.017 Bird, Harry L. *This Fascinating Advertising Business*. Indianapolis: Bobbs-Merrill, 1947, 405 pp.

Well researched text-like discussion. See also Mayer, *Madison
Avenue, U.S.A.*

8.018 Blanchard, Frank L. *The Essentials of Advertising*. New York:
McGraw-Hill, 1921, 322 pp.

A text by a former editor of *Printers' Ink* and *Editor and Publisher*.

8.019 Bowman, Neal B. *Advertising Principles*. Philadelphia: Birnbaum-
Jackson, 1931, 153 pp.

Thin text.

8.020 Bowman, Neal B. *Advertising Simplified*. Philadelphia: Bowman,
1927, 104 pp.

Thinner text.

8.021   Boyd, Harper W., Jr., and Levy, Sidney J. *Promotion: A Behavioral View*. Englewood Cliffs, NJ: Prentice-Hall, 1967, 115 pp.

A paperback text.

8.022   Boyd, Harper W., Jr., and Newman, Joseph W., eds. *Advertising Management: Selected Readings*. Homewood, IL: Irwin, 1965, 569 pp.

8.023   Boyenton, William H. *Let's Look at Your Advertising*. Bound Brook, NJ: Advance Publishers, 1953, 123 pp.

Basics for businessmen.

8.024   Brennan, Ed. *Advertising Media*. New York: McGraw-Hill, 1951, 410 pp.

Basic text.

8.025   Brewster, Arthur J., and Palmer, Herbert H. *Introduction to Advertising*. New York: McGraw-Hill, 1924, 476 pp.

8.026   Bridge, Harry P. *Practical Advertising: A Comprehensive Guide to the Planning and Preparation of Modern Advertising in All of its Phases*. New York: Rinehart, 1949, 842 pp.

Text which includes problems.

8.027   Bridgewater, Howard. *Advertising: Or, the Art of Making Known; a Simple Exercise on the Principles of Advertising*. New York: Pitman, 1910, 120 pp.

Part of their "Practical Primer" series.

8.028   Brink, Edward L., and Kelley, William T. *The Management of Promotion: Consumer Behavior and Demand Stimulation*. Englewood Cliffs, NJ: Prentice-Hall, 1963, 417 pp.

A text foreshadowing the emergence of consumer behavior books, courses, journals, degrees, etc.

8.029   Brown, Lyndon; Lessler, Richard S.; and Weilbacher, William M. *Advertising Media: Creative Planning in Media Selection*. New York: Ronald, 1957, 395 pp.

8.030   Bunting, Henry S. *The Elementary Laws of Advertising and How to Use Them*. Chicago: Novelty News Press, 1913, 188 pp.

8.031   Burke, John D. *Advertising in the Marketplace*. New York: McGraw-Hill, 1973, 440 pp.

8.032   Burton, Philip W. *Principles of Advertising*. New York: Prentice-Hall, 1955, 541 pp.

8.033   Burton, Philip W. *The Profitable Science of Making Media Work*. New London, CT: Printers' Ink, 1959, 448 pp.

8.034 Burton, Philip W., and Miller, J. Robert. *Advertising Fundamentals*. Columbus, OH: Grid, 1976, 688 pp.

8.035 Calkins, Earnest E. *Advertising*. Chicago: American Library Association, 1929, 32 pp.

> Part of a "reading with a purpose" series which includes a short bibliography.

8.036 Calkins, Earnest E. *The Business of Advertising*. New York: Appleton, 1915, 363 pp.

> Written in lieu of a new edition to *Modern Advertising*.

8.037 Calkins, Earnest E. *Modern Advertising*. New York: Appleton, 1907, 361 pp.

8.038 *Check List of Advertising Essentials*. 3d ed. Pleasantville, NY: Printers' Ink, 1955, 336 pp.

8.039 Cherington, Paul T. *The Advertising Book, 1916*. Garden City, NY: Doubleday, Page, 1916, 604 pp.

> Printed for the Associated Advertising Clubs of the World. Also appears as *The First Advertising Book*.

8.040 Coe, Barbara J. *Advertising Practice: Analytic and Creative Exercises*. Englewood Cliffs, NJ: Prentice-Hall, 1972, 413 pp.

8.041 Cohen, Dorothy. *Advertising*. New York: Wiley, 1972, 689 pp.

> Text by ex-FTC Commissioner.

8.042 Cover, John H. *Advertising: Its Problems and Methods*. New York: Appleton, 1926, 319 pp.

> Includes a chapter on market analysis by Percival White.

8.043 Crane, Edgar. *Marketing Communications: A Behavioral Approach to Men, Messages, and Media*. New York: Wiley, 1965, 569 pp.

8.044 Crane, Edgar. *Marketing Communications: Decision Making as a Process of Interaction Between Buyer and Seller*. 2nd ed. New York: Wiley, 1972, 499 pp.

8.045 Crawford, John W. *Advertising: Communications for Management*. Boston: Allyn & Bacon, 1960, 466 pp.

> Text by ex-vice-president of Kenyon & Eckhardt.

8.046 Crisp, Richard D., ed. *How to Increase Advertising Effectiveness*. New York: McGraw-Hill, 1958, 194 pp.

> Typescript "consultant's reports on current business problems."

8.047 Davis, Donald W. *Basic Text in Advertising*. Pleasantville, NY: Printers' Ink, 1955, 665 pp.

8.048 DeBewer, Herbert F. *Advertising Principles*. New York: Alexander Hamilton Institute, 1917, 330 pp.

   A home study course.

8.049 DeVoe, Merrill. *How to Plan Advertising Campaigns*. Los Angeles: Advertising Book Publishers, 1950, 134 pp.

   Minor textlike discussion.

8.050 DeWeese, Truman A. *Book on Advertising*. New York: The System Co., 1910, 165 pp.

   Condensed reprint of *Principles of Practical Publicity*.

8.051 DeWeese, Truman A. *The Principles Of Practical Publicity: Being a Treatise On The Art Of Advertising*. Buffalo, NY: Matthews-Norton Works, 1906, 244 pp.

   The author, ex-advertising manager of Shredded Wheat, is critical of agencies for conflict of interests in multiple clients.

8.052 Dickinson, Howard W. *Primer of Promotion*. New York: J. Day, 927, 85 pp.

   Elemental text.

8.053 Dirksen, Charles J.; Kroeger, Arthur; and Nicosia, Francesco. *Advertising Principles, Problems and Cases*. 5th ed. Homewood, IL: Irwin, 1977, 690 pp.

   First-4th ed. published under title: *Advertising Principles and Problems;* originally published in 1960.

8.054 Doremus, William L. *Advertising*. New York: Alexander Hamilton Institute, 1964, 295 pp.

8.055 Duffy, Ben. *Advertising Media and Markets*. New York: Prentice-Hall, 1939, 437 pp.

   Title changes in later editions to *Profitable Advertising in Today's Media and Markets*.

8.056 Dunn, Arthur. *Scientific Selling and Advertising*. 3rd ed. New York: Industrial Publishing, 1919, 119 pp.

   Primarily on selling.

8.057 Dunn, Samuel W. *Advertising: Its Role in Modern Marketing*. New York: Holt, 1961, 621 pp.

8.058 Durkee, Burton R. *How to Make Advertising Work*. New York: Mc-
Graw-Hill, 1967, 226 pp.

       Chatty "how to" advice.

8.059 Durstine, Roy S. *This Advertising Business*. New York: Scribner,
1928, 331 pp.

8.060 Dygert, Warren B. *Advertising Principles and Practices*. New York:
Longman, Green, 1936, 212 pp.

8.061 Eldridge, Harold F. *Making Advertisements Pay*. Columbia, SC: By
the Author, 1917, 231 pp.

       "A compilation of methods and experience records drawn from many
       sources, with comment ... by recognized authorities."

8.062 Elmore, Elba W. *How to Apply Modern Magic in Advertising*. Los
Angeles: Stationers, 1940, 85 pp.

       Basic text.

8.063 Engel, James F.; Wales, Hugh G.; and Warshaw, Martin R. *Promotional Strategy*. Homewood, IL: Irwin, 1967, 665 pp.

8.064 Fowler, Nathaniel C., Jr. *About Advertising and Printing*. Boston:
Thayer, 1889, 160 pp.

       "A concise, practical and original manual on the art of local ad-
       vertising" by the advertising manager of the manufacturer of Col-
       umbia bicycles. Reproduces press relations material not ads.

8.065 Fowler, Nathaniel C., Jr. *Building Business: An Illustrated
Manual for Aggressive Businessmen*. Boston: The Trade Co., 1893, 518 pp.

       "A treatise on advertising." A pitch for it too. A wealth of
       information, including the raw data from a survey of 177 firms,
       mostly on their media selection and scheduling preferences. Also
       includes a section on "Advertising to Women."

8.066 Fowler, Nathaniel C., Jr. *Fowler's Publicity: An Encyclopedia of
Advertising and Printing and All that Pertains to the Public-Seeing Side
of Business*. New York: Publicity Publishing, 1897, 1016 pp.

       Very early text - "a life of study in advertising revered in ink."

8.067 Freer, Cyril C. *The Inner Side of Advertising: A Practical Handbook for Advertisers, Those Engaged in Advertising, and Students*. New
York: Van Nostrand, 1921, 347 pp.

       English author. Notable for its inclusion of specific chapters on
       advertising to children and in politics.

8.068 French, George. *The Art and Science of Advertising*. Boston:
Sherman, French, 1909, 291 pp.

       Beautifully printed.

8.069 French, George. *How to Advertise: A Guide to Designing, Laying Out, and Composing Advertisements*. New York: Doubleday, Page, 1919, 279 pp.

8.070 French, George. *Twentieth Century Advertising*. New York: Van Nostrand, 1926, 588 pp.

> Wordy discussion on a wide variety of topics.

8.071 Frey, Albert W. *Advertising*. New York: Ronald, 1947, 746 pp.

> The first of many editions of a book with a heavy emphasis on national rather than retail advertising.

8.072 Frey, Albert W. *How Many Dollars for Advertising?* New York: Ronald, 1955, 164 pp.

> Simple text discussion of the budget problem.

8.073 Fryburger, Vernon, ed. *The New World of Advertising*. Chicago: Crain, 1975, 129 pp.

> Text-like reader.

8.074 Galloway, Lee, and Harmon, G. Howard. *Advertising, Selling and Credits*. New York: Alexander Hamilton Institute, 1912, 651 pp.

8.075 Gauss, Chester A.; Wightman, Lucias I. *Sales and Advertising: A Practical Treatise Covering the Psychology of Selling and Advertising, Analysis of Sales, Advertising and Its Relation to Selling, Copywriting, Typography, Mechanics of Advertising, Advertising Department Systems, and the Control of Advertising and Sales Expense*. (2 vols.) Chicago: American Technical Society, 1922.

> Vol. 2 is on advertising. A 1935 edition exists with co-author Harry Bates.

8.076 Gaw, Walter A. *Advertising: Methods and Media*. San Francisco: Woodsworth, 1961, 460 pp.

8.077 Gaw, Walter A. *An Outline of Advertising*. Totowa, NJ: Littlefield, Adams, 1966, 224 pp.

8.078 Giles, Ray. *Turn Your Imagination into Money!* New York: Harper, 1934, 205 pp.

> Some chapters adapted from *Printers' Ink* or *Advertising and Selling*, but primarily on salesmanship ideas.

8.079 Goode, Kenneth M. *Manual of Modern Advertising*. New York: Greenberg, 1932, 457 pp.

> Revised in 1937 to *Modern Advertising* and in 1941 to *Advertising*.

8.080 Goode, Kenneth M. *Modern Adverting Makes Money*. New York: Harper, 1934, 203 pp.

8.081   Goode, Kenneth M. *Ten Points for Advertisers*. New York: Harper,
1940, 299 pp.

8.082   Goode, Kenneth M., and Kaufman, Zenn. *Profitable Showmanship*.
New York: Prentice-Hall, 1939, 180 pp.

> "Two well-known sales and advertising experts bring ballyhoo down
> to earth," for getting publicity and making more effective sales
> presentations.

8.083   Goode, Kenneth M., and Kaufman, Zenn. *Showmanship in Business*.
New York: Harper, 1936, 266 pp.

> Showmanship is the "skillfully colored adaptation to ... the
> other fellow's sense of values" (p5).

8.084   Goode, Kenneth M., and Powel, Hartford, Jr. *What About Advertising?* New York: Harper, 1927, 399 pp.

8.085   Goode, Kenneth M., and Rheinstrom, Carroll. *More Profits From
Advertising: And More Advertising From Profits*. New York: Harper, 1931,
275 pp.

> Begins with a lengthy polemic on behalf of advertising, seeing a
> remedy for depression in "the astounding strength of an awakened
> Samson." Last two thirds is a thin text.

8.086   Groesbeck, Kenneth. *Invitation to Advertising: How it Works, How
to Get the Most Out of It*. New York: Simon & Schuster, 1951, 392 pp.

> A chatty work aimed at businessmen but covering much the same
> material as a text.

8.087   Hall, Samuel R. *The Advertising Handbook: A Reference Work
Covering the Principles and Practice of Advertising*. New York: McGraw-
Hill, 1921, 743 pp.

> Second edition appears in 1930.

8.088   Hall, Samuel R. *Theory and Practice of Advertising: A Textbook
Covering the Development and Fundamental Principles of Advertising and
Methods of Representative Advertisers*. New York: McGraw-Hill, 1926,
686 pp.

8.089   Harris, Theodore. *The Science and Art of Advertising*. Boston:
Ward, 1888, 17 pp.

> Pamphlets for potential advertisers for whom the consumer "world
> is his oyster, *and none too large for his mouth."* (Emphasis in
> original)

8.090   Hawley, Raymond, and Zabin, James. *Understanding Advertising*.
New York: Gregg, 1931, 150 pp.

> Basic introductory text with questions and exercises.

8.091 Hepner, Harry W. *Effective Advertising*. New York: McGraw-Hill, 1941, 584 pp.

> Later editions appear as *Modern Advertising: Practices and Principles*. 4th edition, 1964 titled *Advertising: Creative Communication with Consumers*.

8.092 Hess, Herbert W. *Advertising*. New York: Universal Business Institute, 1910, 507 pp.

8.093 Hess, Herbert W. *Advertising: Its Economics, Philosophy, and Technique*. Philadelphia: Lippincott, 1931, 516 pp.

> Major revision of *Productive Advertising*. Text by a University of Pennsylvania professor, with emphasis on consumer psychology.

8.094 Hess, Herbert W. *Productive Advertising*. Philadelphia: Lippincott, 1915, 358 pp.

8.095 Holden, Ralph. *Modern Advertising*. New York: Appleton, 1907, 361 pp.

8.096 Hollingworth, H.L. *Advertising and Selling: Principles of Appeal and Response*. New York: Appleton-Century, 1913, 313 pp.

8.097 Hotchkiss, George B. *An Outline of Advertising: Its Philosophy, Science, Art and Strategy*. New York: Macmillan, 1935, 509 pp.

> The first edition of what became a classic textbook. Very thorough, and usable as defining the state of the art.

8.098 *How to Advertise and Why*. Scranton, PA: International Textbook Press, 1927, 87 pp.

> A home study course book. Includes an amply illustrated lengthy section on the psychology of advertising, apparently reprinted from a 1918 edition.

8.099 Howard, Kenneth S. *How to Write Advertisements*. New York: McGraw-Hill, 1937, 257 pp.

> Based on 25 years experience, this is a general but basic "how to" work. Not just copywriting.

8.100 Hymers, Robert, and Sharpe, Leonard. *The Technique and Practice of Advertising Art*. New York: Pitman, 1940, 313 pp.

8.101 Johnson, Axel P., ed. *Library of Advertising*. 6 vols. Chicago: Chicago University of Commerce, 1911.

> Amply illustrated, large print readers.

8.102 Kastor, Ernest H. *Advertising*. Chicago: LaSalle Extension University, 1918, 317 pp.

> Correspondence text.

8.103 Kendall, Frederick Charles, ed. *The New American Tempo and Other Articles of Modern Advertising and Selling Practice*. New York: Advertising & Selling, 1927, 86 pp.

       Reprints of articles from the periodical, *Advertising & Selling*.

8.104 Kernan, Jerome B.; Dommermuth, William P.; and Sommers, Montrose S. *Promotion: An Introductory Analysis*. New York: McGraw-Hill, 1970, 367 pp.

8.105 King, Herbert F. *Practical Advertising: Its Principles and Its Functions in the Sales Plan*. New York: Appleton, 1933, 387 pp.

8.106 Kirkpatrick, Charles A. *Advertising: Mass Communication in Marketing*. Boston: Houghton, Mifflin, 1959, 638 pp.

       Later editions with James A. Littlefield.

8.107 Kleppner, Otto. *Advertising as a Business Force*. Scranton: International Correspondence Schools, 1937, 66 pp.

8.108 Kleppner, Otto. *Advertising Procedure*. New York: Prentice-Hall, 1925, 539 pp.

       A classic! The 1925 edition was the first of many - the sixth (1973) is current and successful, and is the 53rd printing. Includes the author's conception of advertising history, a glossary and large classified bibliography.

8.109 Kleppner, Otto, and Settle, Irving, eds. *Exploring Advertising*. Englewood Cliffs, NJ: Prentice-Hall, 1970, 328 pp.

       A reader; the authors are primarily professionals, not professors.

8.110 Larned, William L. *Illustration in Advertising*. New York: McGraw-Hill, 1925, 321 pp.

8.111 Larrabee, Carroll B., and Marks, Henry W. *Check Lists of Advertising, Selling and Merchandising Essentials*. New York: McGraw-Hill, 1937, 396 pp.

       Sixty-seven lists of dos, don'ts, tests, ways, points, etc.

8.112 Lavidge, Arthur W. *A Common Sense Guide to Professional Advertising*. Blue-Ridge Summit, PA: Tab Books, 1973, 318 pp.

8.113 *Library of Sales and Advertising*. 4 vols. Chicago: Shaw, 1914.

       Only 1 volume on advertising.

8.114 Lichtenberg, Bernard, and Barton, Bruce. *Advertising Campaigns*. New York: Alexander Hamilton Institute, 1926, 343 pp.

       Correspondence text, but includes some 1924 data on expenditures for brands.

8.115 Littlefield, James E., ed. *Readings in Advertising: Current Viewpoints on Selected Topics*. St. Paul: West Publishing, 1975, 450 pp.

8.116 Littlefield, James E., and Kirkpatrick, C.A. *Advertising: Mass Communication in Marketing*. 3d ed. Boston: Houghton Mifflin, 1970.

8.117 Longman, Kenneth A. *Advertising*. New York: Harcourt-Brace Jovanovich, 1971, 425 pp.

8.118 Lownds, William G.; Chenery, Edward D.; and Wiltshire, George J. *Advertising and Selling Digest: A Digest of Thirty-Six Lectures Given by Leading Authorities Under the Auspices of the Advertising Club of New York*. New York: Advertising Club of New York, 1926, 249 pp.

8.119 MacGaheran, Joseph. *Advertising Campaigns*. New York: Alexander Hamilton Institute, 1944, 394 pp.

8.120 McNeal, James U. *Readings in Promotion Management*. New York: Appleton, Century, Crofts, 1966, 353 pp.

8.121 Mahin, John L. *Advertising and Salesmanship*. Garden City, NY: Doubleday, Page, 1925, 302 pp.

8.122 Mahin, John L. *Advertising: Selling the Consumer*. Garden City, NY: Doubleday, Page, 1914, 260 pp. (1919 reprint, 98 pp.)

> Published for the Associated Advertising Clubs of the World. Bibliography at the end of each chapter.

8.123 Mandell, Maurice I. *Advertising*. Englewood Cliffs, NJ: Prentice-Hall, 1968, 656 pp.

8.124 Manly, John M., and Powell, John A. *Better Advertising: A Practical Manual of the Principles of Advertising, Embracing Institutional and Direct Advertising, Reason Why and Human Interest Copy, Elements of the Advertisement, and the Makeup of Advertising Circulars and Folders*. Chicago: Drake, 1921, 157 pp.

8.125 Martin, Mac. *Advertising Campaigns*. New York: Alexander Hamilton Institute, 1917, 338 pp.

> As home study course, this was well received in its day.

8.126 Maytham, Thomas E. *Introduction to Advertising Principles and Practice*. New York: Harper, 1948, 404 pp.

8.127 Melcher, Daniel, and Larrick, Nancy. *Printing and Promotion Handbook: How to Plan, Produce, and Use Printing, Advertising and Direct Mail*. 3d ed. New York: McGraw-Hill, 1966, 451 pp.

> Alphabetically arranged handbook for the beginner.

8.128 *The Men Who Advertise: An Account of Successful Advertisers, Together with Hints of the Method of Advertising*. New York: Rowell's American Newspaper Directory, 1870.

Difficult to find. Shows how advertising was advertised to
skeptical businessmen.

8.129 Michman, Ronald D., and Jugenheimer, Donald W. *Strategic Advertising Decisions: Selected Readings.* Columbus, OH: Grid, 1976, 421 pp.

8.130 Milner, Thomas S. *How to Make Money, Or the Principles of Success
in Trade.* Montreal: Nolan, 1865, 93 pp.

Chapter 12 covers advertising, making this a valuable source for
early Canadian attitudes and the earliest item in this list.
Available at the Lande Collection at McGill University.

8.131 Nesbit, Wilbur D. *First Principles of Advertising.* New York:
Gregg, 1922, 111 pp.

For the beginning student. No index.

8.132 Nixon, Howard K. *Principles of Advertising.* New York: McGraw-
Hill, 1937, 541 pp.

Text by a Columbia professor.

8.133 Nolan, Carroll A., and Warmke, Roman F. *Marketing, Sales, Promotion and Advertising.* 7th ed. Cincinnati: Southwestern, 1965, 613 pp.

8.134 Norris, James S. *Advertising.* Reston, VA: Reston, 1977, 401 pp.

8.135 Nylen, David W. *Advertising, Planning, Implementation and Control.*
Cincinnati: Southwestern, 1975, 598 pp.

8.136 Obermayer, Henry. *Successful Advertising Management.* New York:
McGraw-Hill, 1969, 241 pp.

8.137 Oliver, Robert E. *Advertising.* Toronto: McGraw-Hill, 1969,
166 pp.

Past president of the Association of Canadian Advertisers.

8.138 Opdycke, John B. *Advertising and Selling Practice.* Chicago:
Shaw, 1918, 206 pp.

8.139 Osborn, Alexander F. *Brass Tacks of Advertising.* Buffalo, NY:
Hausauer-Jones, 1915, 135 pp.

Subtitled: *An Unmysterious Analysis of the Practical Phases of the
Kind of Advertising Which Analyzes.* Text-like compilation of mini-
essays.

8.140 Osborn, Alexander F. *A Short Course in Advertising.* New York:
Scribner, 1921, 248 pp.

8.141 Oxenfeldt, Alfred R., and Swan, Carroll. *Management of the Advertising Function.* Belmont, CA: Wadsworth, 1964, 88 pp.

8.142   Parrish, Amos, and MacBride, Burt. *Advertising*. New York: Alexander Hamilton Institute, 1927, 333 pp.

8.143   Parsons, Frank A. *The Principles of Advertising Arrangement*. New York: Prang, 1912, 127 pp.

> Focus on layout, published for the Advertising Men's League of New York.

8.144   Patti, Charles H., and Murphy, John H. *Advertising Management: Cases and Concepts*. Columbus, OH: Grid, 1978, 298 pp.

8.145   Pleuthner, Williard A., ed. *460 Secrets of Advertising Exports*. New York: Nelson, 1961, 288 pp.

> "Key ideas on: copy, layout, media ...; plus a profile of successful work habits."

8.146   Powell, George H. *Powell's Practical Advertiser*. New York: By the Author, 1905, 229 pp.

> "A practical work for advertising writers and businessmen, with instructions on planning, preparing, placing and managing modern publicity. With cyclopedia of over one thousand useful advertisements."

8.147   Powell, George H. *Ten Talks on Modern Advertising*. Springfield, MA: n.p., 1893, 66 pp.

8.148   Praigg, Noble T., ed. *Advertising and Selling, by 150 Advertising and Sales Executives*. Garden City, NY: Doubleday, Page, 1923, 483 pp.

> Produced by the Associated Advertising Clubs of the World; digests of 1923 convention speeches. Much space given to promotional methods for banks, utilities, churches, communities, etc.

8.149   *Advertising Idea Book*. New York: Funk & Wagnall's 1951, 348 pp.

> "Arranged in dictionary style."

8.150   *After Business Hours: Practical Suggestions and Intimate Reflections of America's Leaders in Business and Industry*. New York: Funk & Wagnalls, 1949, 366 pp.

> From the column "After Hours" in *Printers' Ink*.

8.151   Quera, Leon. *Advertising Campaigns: Formulation and Tactics*. Columbus, OH: Grid, 1973, 378 pp.

8.152   Richards, William H. *Power in Advertising*. Kansas City: Empire, 1915, 274 pp.

> Also authored minor works: *How to Make Money by Advertising* (1913) and *Straight Tips for Advertisers* (1906).

8.153 Richardson, A.O. *The Power of Advertising*. New York: Lambert, 1913, 300 pp.

First published in Australia.

8.154 Rochester Industrial Advertisers. *Practical Advertising Procedure*. New York: McGraw-Hill, 1948, 446 pp.

8.155 Roman, Kenneth, and Maas, Jane. *How to Advertise*. New York: St. Martins Press, 1976, 159 pp.

8.156 Rowse, Edward J., and Fish, L.J. *The Fundamentals of Advertising*. Cincinnati: Southwestern, 1926, 223 pp.

Minor text. Later editions with various co-authors.

8.157 Rubin, Manning J. *Making Advertising Pay*. New York: Harnis Jordan, 1913, 89 pp.

8.158 Russell, Thomas, ed. *Advertising Methods and Mediums*. Chicago: National Institute of Business, 1910, 416 pp.

Part of the International Business Library.

8.159 Sampson, Edith. *Advertise!* Boston: D.C. Heath, 1918, 247 pp.

Simple text. Author was advertising manager for retail stores in Denver. No explicit recollections.

8.160 Samstag, Nicholas. *Persuasion for Profit*. Norman, OK: University of Oklahoma Press, 1957, 208 pp.

Hard to classify. A well written primer on advertising with an emphasis on recognizing opportunities for promotion of creative concepts in copywriting.

8.161 Sandage, Charles H. *Advertising: Theory and Practice*. Chicago: Business Publications, 1936, 618 pp.

First of many editions, later published by Irwin.

8.162 Sandage, Charles H. *The Promise of Advertising*. Homewood, IL: Irwin, 1961, 207 pp.

Readings dedicated to James Webb Young. Includes an article giving history of the Advertising Council.

8.163 Sandage, Charles H., and Fryburger, Vernon. *The Role of Advertising: A Book of Readings*. Homewood, IL: Irwin, 1960, 499 pp.

Some emphasis on advertising in society and social issues.

8.164 Sargent, Hugh W., ed. *Frontiers of Advertising Theory and Research: A Symposium Honoring C.H. Sandage*. Palo Alto: Pacific, 1972, 191 pp.

8.165 Scott, James D. *Advertising Principles and Problems*. New York: Prentice-Hall, 1953, 803 pp.

8.166 *Selling Forces*. Philadelphia: Curtis, 1913, 282 pp.

A book length discussion of advertising functions and, of course, a plug for Curtis Publications. Illustrated.

8.167 Settle, Irene, ed. *Exploring Advertising*. Englewood Cliffs, NJ: Prentice-Hall, 1969, 328 pp.

A reader.

8.168 Sheinkopf, Kenneth G., and O'Keefe, M. Timothy. *Advertising Principles and Practice: Selected Readings*. Washington: College and University Press, 1975, 171 pp.

8.169 Sheldon, George H. *Advertising: Elements and Principles*. New York: Harcourt, Brace, 1925, 443 pp.

A text for beginners by an author who feels that "Printers' Ink disseminates more constructive practical advertising fact and theory in one year than all the textbooks on these subjects ever written."

8.170 Shryer, William A. *Analytical Advertising*. Detroit: Business Service, 1912, 228 pp.

Text, but no index.

8.171 Simmons, Harry. *Successful Sales Promotion*. New York: Prentice-Hall, 1950, 441 pp.

8.172 Simon, Julian L. *The Management of Advertising*. Englewood Cliffs, NJ: Prentice-Hall, 1971, 287 pp.

Expert and extensive use of managerial economics makes this unique.

8.173 Sissors, Jack E., and Petray, E. Reynold. *Advertising Media Planning*. Chicago: Crain, 1976, 341 pp.

8.174 Slomanson, Albert J. *Selling and Buying Advertising Space*. New York: Lloyd, 1928, 157 pp.

8.175 Smith, Cynthia S. *How to Get Big Results from a Small Advertising Budget*. New York: Hawthorne, 1973, 221 pp.

8.176 Solow, Martin, and Handman, Edward. *Effective Advertising*. New York: Grossett & Dunlap, 1964, 96 pp.

Paperback text.

8.178 Stanley, Richard E. *Promotion: Advertising, Publicity, Personal Selling, Sales Promotion*. Englewood Cliffs, NJ: Prentice-Hall, 1977, 394 pp.

8.179 Stansfield, Richard H. *The Dartnell Advertising Manager's Handbook*. Chicago: Dartnell, 1969, 1503 pp.

       Massive.

8.180 Starch, Daniel. *Advertising: Its Principles, Practice and
Techniques*. Chicago: Foresman, 1914, 281 pp.

       His first text.

8.181 Starch, Daniel. *Advertising Principles*. New York: Shaw, 1927,
593 pp.

       An abridgement of *Principles of Advertising*.

8.182 Starch, Daniel. *Principles of Advertising*. New York: Shaw, 1923,
998 pp.

8.183 Stryker, A.M. *Advertiser's Hand Book, Written and Compiled According to the Latest Advertising Knowledge*. Chicago: Trade Journal Advertiser, 1909, 167 pp.

       A lot on printing problems.

8.184 Taplin, Walter. *Advertising: A New Approach*. Boston: Little,
Brown, 1960, 208 pp.

       An controversial discussion of the management issues of adver-
       tising by an academic. Not a traditional text. Little original
       research reported.

8.185 Taylor, Henry C. (pseud). *What an Advertiser Should Know: A
Handbook for Everyone Who Advertises*. Chicago: Browne & Howell, 1914,
95 pp.

       Very basic.

8.186 Terry, John J. *The Art of Advertising: Or, How to Make Advertising Pay*. Boston: By the Author, 1888, 79 pp.

       A vest pocket book "for inexperienced advertisers."

8.187 Tillman, Rollie, and Kirkpatrick, Charles A. *Promotion: Persuasive Communication in Marketing*. Homewood, IL: Irwin, 1968, 477 pp.

8.188 Tipper, Harry. *The New Business*. Garden City, NY: Doubleday,
Page, 1914, 391 pp.

       For Associated Advertising Clubs of the World, but reads like an
       "introduction to business" text with only a slight marketing
       orientation. Plugs advertising's role in affecting a firm's
       morale levels.

8.189 Tipper, Harry, and French, George. *Advertising Campaigns*. New
York: Van Nostrand, 1923, 432 pp.

8.190 Tipper, Harry, and Hotchkiss, George B. *Advertising: A Practical Presentation of the Principles Underlying the Planning of Successful Advertising Campaigns and the Preparation of Advertising Copy.* New York: Alexander Hamilton Institute, 1914, 464 pp.

8.191 Tipper, Harry; Hollingworth, Harry L.; Hotchkiss, George B., and Parsons, Frank A. *The Principles of Advertising.* New York: Ronald, 1915, 473 pp.

An early text from New York University faculty.

8.192. Townsend, William S., and Townsend, A.J. *Why An Advertisement Succeeds or Fails.* New York: By the Authors, 1937, 64 pp.

A plug for pretesting ads with a checklist of sales-effectiveness elements.

8.193 Wademan, Victor. *Risk-Free Advertising: How to Come Close to It.* New York: Wiley, 1977, 145 pp.

Promoting the company of this young Harvard MBA - a new breed of advertising entrepreneur.

8.194 Wadsworth, Gerald B. *Principles and Practices of Advertising.* New York: By the Author, 1913, 277 pp.

8.195 Wagenseller, George W. *Theory and Practice of Advertising.* Middleburgh, PA: By the Author, 1902, 64 pp.

"An elementary course ... for use in business and literary schools, commercial departments of public schools and for private study."

8.196 Wales, Hugh G.; Gentry, Dwight L.; and Wales, Max. *Advertising Copy, Layout & Typography.* New York: Ronald, 1958, 491 pp.

Introductory advertising text.

8.197 Webster, Frederick E., Jr. *Marketing Communication: Modern Promotional Strategy.* New York: Ronald, 1971, 694 pp.

8.198 Wedding, C. Nugent, and Lessler, Richard S. *Advertising Management.* New York: Ronald, 1962, 629 pp.

Text and cases.

8.199 Weiss, E.B.; Kendall, F.C.; and Larrabee, C.B. *Handbook of Advertising.* New York: McGraw-Hill, 1938, 530 pp.

Introduction by Earnest Elmo Calkins and 17 chapters by various authors.

8.200 Whittier, Charles L. *Creative Advertising.* New York: Holt, 1955, 585 pp.

8.201 Wirsig, Woodrow, ed. *Principles of Advertising*. New York: Pitman, 1963, 560 pp.

Also appears by "Committee on Advertising."

8.202 Wiseman, Mark. *The Anatomy of Advertising: An Analytical Approach to Campaign Planning and Advertisement Making*. 2 vols. New York: Harper, 1942.

The two sections bound together, but printed so that they could be published separately. The author, formerly director of the Laboratory for Advertising Analysis, places emphasis on the need for research to get ideas and to test copy.

8.203 Wolfe, Harry D. *Evaluating Media*. Studies in Business Policy, no. 121. New York: National Industrial Conference Board, 1966, 185 pp.

8.204 Woolf, James D. *Salesense in Advertising: A Selection of Articles from Advertising Age*. Chicago: Advertising Age, 1955, 383 pp.

8.205 Wright, John S., and Warner, Daniel S. *Advertising*. New York: McGraw-Hill, 1960, 590 pp.

8.206 Wright, John S., and Warner, Daniel S. ed. *Speaking of Advertising*. New York: McGraw-Hill, 1963, 484 pp.

Fifty readings, many of which are difficult to find elsewhere.

8.207 Young, Frank H. *Modern Advertising Art*. New York: Covici, Friede, 1930, 199 pp.

Foreward by Earnest Elmo Calkins.

8.208 Young, James W. *How to Become an Advertising Man*. Chicago: Advertising Publications, 1963, 95 pp.

Young, the "dean of American Advertising," retired in 1928 at the age of 42. This book is a simple text which had its origins in a course Young taught at night school for the University of Chicago, and adapted for a training program at J. Walter Thompson. (Robert Maynard Hutchins hired Young at Chicago as a Professor of Business History and Advertising.)

8.209 Young, James W. *A Technique for Producing Ideas*. Chicago: Advertising Publications, 1946, 61 pp.

Essentially a lecture given to students at the University of Chicago.

8.210 Zacher, Robert V. *Advertising Techniques and Management*. Homewood, IL: Irwin, 1961, 666 pp.

8.300 SPECIAL APPLICATIONS TEXTS

8.301 Acheson, Arthur. *Trade-Mark Advertising as an Investment*. New York: New York Evening Post, 1917, 46 pp.

8.302 Agnew, Clark M., and O'Brien, Neil. *Television Advertising*. New York: McGraw-Hill, 1958, 350 pp.

Text with some emphasis on production.

8.303 Agnew, Hugh E. *Outdoor Advertising*. New York: McGraw-Hill, 1938, 310 pp.

8.304 Arnold, Frank A. *Broadcast Advertising: The Fourth Dimension*. New York: Wiley, 1931, 275 pp.

Revised in 1933 to include a small amount on television.

8.305 Association of National Advertisers. *Advertising at the Point of Purchase*. New York: McGraw-Hill, 1957, 240 pp.

150 case histories and advice for national advertisers wanting deal display cooperation and a "handy reference guide and working manual."

8.306 Bartholemew, Ralph. *A Short Course on Direct Mail*. New York: Publishers Printing, 1928, 63 pp.

8.307 Bellaire, Arthur. *TV Advertising: A Handbook of Modern Practice*. New York: Harper, 1959, 202 pp.

8.308 Bieger, Len, and Lubin, Aileen. *Mediability: A Guide for Non-Profits*. Washington: Taft, 1975, 110 pp.

Basic advice for public service advertisers.

8.309 Book, Albert C., and Carey, Norman D. *The Television Commercial: Creativity and Craftsmanship*. New York: Decker, 1970, 79 pp.

Sees TV ads as "an American art form ... ahead of most TV programs in being in tune with the U.S."

8.310 Brewster, Arthur J. *An Introduction to Retail Advertising*. Chicago: Shaw, 1926, 319 pp.

8.311 Brown, David L. *Export Advertising*. New York: Ronald, 1923, 342 pp.

8.312 Buckley, Homer J. *The Science of Marketing by Mail*. New York: Forbes, 1924, 323 pp.

Written in the enthusiastic, straight-talk selling idiom of the 20's, it makes a "pitch" for direct mail that is over 300 pages long, but good copy all the way.

8.313 Bunting, Henry S. *Specialty Advertising: The New Way to Build Business*. Waukegan, IL: Novelty News Press, 1925, 158 pp.

8.314 Burdick, Rupert L. *Advertising to Retailers: Specialized Means and Methods for Developing Trade Distribution*. New York: Ronald, 1923, 308 pp.

8.315 Carr, Jack. *Cordially Yours: Or, How to Become a Letter Writer in One Easy Lifetime*. New York: Graphic Books, 1947, 247 pp.

       Direct mail in letter format only.

8.316 Cody, Sherwin. *How to Deal with Human Nature in Business: A Practical Book on Doing Business by Correspondence, Advertising and Salesmanship*. New York: Funk & Wagnalls, 1915, 488 pp.

8.317 Collins, Kenneth. *Retail Selling and the New Order*. New York: Greenberg, 1934, 203 pp.

       Pushing advertising as cure for retailers' depression blues.

8.318 Collins, Kenneth R. *The Road to Good Advertising*. New York: Greenberg, 1932, 217 pp.

       Emphasis on retail advertising.

8.319 Crain, Gustavus D.; Schloss, Julius B.; and Woods, C.F. *Technical and Mail-Order Advertising*. Scranton, PA: International Textbook Press, 1926.

       Home study course on mail order and streetcar advertising.

8.320 Cripton, John K. *Successful Direct Mail Methods*. New York: McGraw-Hill, 1936, 336 pp.

8.321 Day, Enid. *Radio Broadcasting for Retailers*. New York: Fairchild, 1947, 194 pp.

       One part for sponsors, one for prospective careerists.

8.322 Dench, Ernest A. *Advertising by Motion Pictures*. Cincinnati, Standard Publishing, 1916, 255 pp.

       Many short pitches for application of this medium.

8.323 Dix, Warren R. *Industrial Advertising for Profit and Prestige*. Pleasantville, NY: Printers' Ink, 1956, 321 pp.

8.324 Doremus, William L. *Advertising for Profit: A Guide for Small Business*. New York: Pitman, 1947, 130 pp.

       Superficial treatment for retailers. Introduction by G.B. Hotchkiss.

8.325 Dunlap, Orrin E. *Advertising by Radio*. New York: Ronald, 1929, 186 pp.

Includes an inventory of broadcast advertisers.

8.326 Dygert, Warren B. *Radio as an Advertising Medium*. New York: McGraw-Hill, 1939, 261 pp.

8.327 Edgar, Albert E. *How to Advertise a Retail Store*. 4th ed. Columbus, OH: Advertising World, 1913, 582 pp.

"Including mail order advertising; a complete manual for promoting publicity; illustrated with over 500 original newspaper advertisements."

8.328 Edwards, Charles M., Jr., and Howard, William H. *Retail Advertising and Sales Promotion*. New York: Prentice-Hall, 1936, 723 pp.

A best seller, authored by faculty from the New York University School of Retailing. Emphasis on research.

8.329 Egner, Frank, and Walter, L. Rohe. *Direct Mail Advertising and Selling*. New York: Harper, 1940, 215 pp.

8.330 Eldridge, Francis R. *Advertising and Selling Abroad*. New York: Harper, 1930, 202 pp.

8.331 Elliott, Ernest E. *How to Advertise a Church*. New York: G.H. Doran, 1920, 93 pp.

8.332 Farrington, Frank. *Retail Advertising - Complete*. Chicago: Byxbee, 1910, 266 pp.

Small unorganized text-like discussion.

8.333 Felix, Edgar A. *Using Radio in Sales Promotion: A Book for Advertisers, Station Managers and Broadcasting Artists*. New York: McGraw-Hill, 1927, 386 pp.

Includes material on the structure of the industry.

8.334 Flanagan, George A. *Modern Institutional Advertising Including Corporate, Corporate Image, Association, Service, and All Other Major Forms of Non-Profit Advertising*. New York: McGraw-Hill, 1967, 299 pp.

Includes writing ads and, of course, the Advertising Council.

8.335 Fochs, Arnold. *Advertising That Won Elections*. Duluth: A.J. Publishing, 1974, 272 pp.

"A collection of unusual political ads used by candidate for city, county and state offices."

8.336 Fox, Irving P. *One Thousand Ways and Schemes to Attract Trade, Gathered from Actual Experiences of Successful Merchants*. 5th ed. Boston: Spatula, 1927, 165 pp.

"Illustrated with half-tone and line cuts suitable for advertising purposes."

8.337 Freeman, William M. *The Big Name*. New York: Printers' Ink, 1957, 230 pp.

All on the use of testimonials to sell, with most of the book an informal discussion of campaigns based on testimonials. The first chapter is the best for a review of major issues and some good anecdotal examples, such as Constance Talmadge signing 400 testimonials in one day.

8.338 Garver, Robert I. *Successful Radio Advertising with Sponsor Participation Programs*. New York: Prentice-Hall, 1949, 329 pp.

Based in part on an original survey on sponsor participation programs.

8.339 Gentile, Richard J. *Retail Advertising: A Management Approach*. New York: Chain Store Publishing, 1976, 181 pp.

8.340 Gilbert, Eugene. *Advertising and Marketing to Young People*. Pleasantville, NY: Printers' Ink, 1957, 378 pp.

"Vital information on the vast pre-school to young married market" by the president of Gilbert Youth Research, relating case histories and results from over 1900 research studies.

8.341 Goode, Kenneth M. *What About Radio?* New York: Harper, 1937, 255 pp.

As an advertising medium.

8.342 Grisier, Orville J. *How to Make Sign Advertising Pay*. Philadelphia: D. McKay, 1941, 166 pp.

Outdoor signs.

8.343 Gross, Alfred, and Houghton, Dale. *Sales Promotion*. New York: Ronald, 1950, 434 pp.

Academic authors discussing the myriad activities of, and ephemera in, conventional advertising.

8.344 Gross, Michael. *Dealer Display Advertising*. New York: Ronald, 1936, 182 pp.

8.345 Grumbine, E. Evalyn. *Reaching Juvenile Markets: How to Advertise, Sell and Merchandise Through Boys and Girls*. New York: McGraw-Hill, 1938, 430 pp.

"Through" as well as the implicit "to." "Instead of being exploited children can benefit materially from their experiences (with) ... the national advertiser." Sometimes work listed under author's married name, McNally. See also, Gilbert.

8.346 Haight, William. *Retail Advertising: Management and Technique.* Morristown, NJ: General Learning, 1976, 530 pp.

8.347 Hall, Samuel R. *Mail Order and Direct Mail Selling.* New York: McGraw-Hill, 1928, 494 pp.

8.348 Hall, Samuel R. *Retail Advertising and Selling.* New York: McGraw-Hill, 1924, 590 pp.

8.349 Hanford, Mabel P. *Advertising and Selling Through Business Publications.* New York: Harper, 1938, 190 pp.

Text with foreword by Roy Durstine.

8.350 Hart, Charles S. *Foreign Advertising Methods.* New York: DeBower, 1928, 262 pp.

8.351 Heighton, Elizabeth, and Cunningham, Don R. *Advertising in the Broadcast Media.* Belmont, CA: Wadsworth, 1976, 349 pp.

8.352 Hendricks, William L., and Orr, Montgomery. *Showmanship in Advertising: The Fundmentals of Salesmanship in Print.* New York: Showman's Trade Review, 1949, 220 pp.

Primarily for theatres.

8.353 Hendricks, William L., and Waugh, Howard. *The Encyclopedia of Exploitation.* New York: Showman's Trade Review, 1937, 432 pp.

A long list of promotional ideas designed to promote show business.

8.354 Herper, George L., and Collins, Richard A. *Specialty Advertising in Marketing.* Homewood, IL: Irwin, 1972, 219 pp.

8.355 Herrold, Lloyd D. *Advertising for the Retailer.* New York: Appleton-Century, 1923, 677 pp.

Developed for correspondence course of the University of Wisconsin.

8.356 Herrold, Lloyd D. *Advertising Real Estate.* New York: McGraw-Hill, 1931, 325 pp.

8.357 Hettinger, Herman S., and Neff, W.J. *Practical Radio Advertising.* New York: Prentice-Hall, 1938, 372 pp.

Text; appendices with data on rates, usage and ratings.

8.358 Hinman, Albert A., and Dorau, H.B. *Real Estate Merchandising.* Chicago: Shaw, 1926, 363 pp.

8.359 Hotchkin, William R. *Making More Money in Advertising.* New York: By the Author, 1926, 273 pp.

Focus on retailing, based on experience with Wanamakers.

8.360 Hutchins, Mosher S. *Cooperative Advertising: The Way to Make it Pay*. New York: Ronald, 1953, 255 pp.

8.361 Ireland, H.I. *Retail Advertising*. Scranton, PA: International Textbook Press, 1926.

       Includes many examples in the home study course.

8.362 Ireland, H.I., and Schulze, Edward H. *Department Store Advertising*. Scranton, PA: International Textbook Press, 1926.

       Home study course with a section on advertising letters and examples of the Institute of Business Science's own direct mail campaign.

8.363 Jones, Duane. *Ads, Women and Boxtops*. Pleasantville, NY: Printers' Ink, 1955, 128 pp.

       How to sell packaged goods based on experience with Benton & Bowles, etc.

8.364 Knowlton, Don. *Advertising for Banks*. New York: Rand McNally, 1932, 533 pp.

8.365 Landry, Stuart O. *Harnessing the Power of the Press*. New Orleans: Upton, 1934, 48 pp.

       On newspaper advertising.

8.366 Lash, Lee. *An Analytic Sketch of General Publicity*. Philadelphia: G.H. Buchanan, 1905, 154 pp.

       Includes discussion on copy and a lot of push on theatre curtains as an effective medium.

8.367 Lewis, Elias St. Elmo. *Financial Advertising*. Indianapolis: Levey Brothers, 1908, 992 pp.

       Ex ad manager for National Cash Register and Burroughs Adding Machine offers practical suggestions.

8.368 Lewis, Norman. *Samples, Demonstrations and Packaging: Their Use in Advertising*. New York: Ronald, 1928, 250 pp.

       Principle emphasis on sampling.

8.369 Lippincott, Wilmot. *Outdoor Advertising*. New York: McGraw-Hill, 1923, 340 pp.

       32 pages of color prints. Introduction by Percival White.

8.370 Longnecker, John W. *Selling Insurance by Cooperative Advertising*. New York: F.S. Crofts, 1929, 252 pp.

8.371 Look, Al. *Advertising at Retail*. Denver: G. Bell, 1958, 274 pp.

8.372 Luccock, Halford E. "The Advertising Man Talks." *Methodist Review* 98 (1916): 407 - 17.

Author gives advice to preachers on pushing religion.

8.373 Lund, John V. *Newspaper Advertising*. New York: Prentice-Hall, 1947, 459 pp.

8.374 McCaffrey, Maurice. *Advertising Wins Election: A Handbook of Political Advertising*. Minneapolis: Gilbert, 1962, 184 pp.

Only 8 years and 24 candidates worth of experience, but candid in his disclosure of the pragmatics.

8.375 McClure, Leslie W., and Fulton, Paul C. *Advertising in the Printed Media*. New York: Macmillan, 1964, 338 pp.

For future print media salesmen.

8.376 McClure, Leslie W., and Fulton, Paul C. *Newspaper Advertising and Promotion*. New York: Macmillan, 1950, 479 pp.

8.377 MacDonald, John A. *Successful Advertising: How To Accomplish It*. Philadelphia: Lincoln, 1902, 400 pp.

"A practical work for advertisers and businessmen" with a heavy focus on retail and direct mail, with advice specific to certain trades and types of retail stores in "Sayings to Swing Trade."

8.378 MacGregor, Theodore D. *Pushing Your Business*. New York: Banker's Publishing, 1913, 202 pp.

A textbook of practical advice for banks and sundry financial institutions.

8.379 McMahan, Harry W. *The Television Commercial: How to Create and Produce Effective TV Advertising*. New York: Hastings House, 1954, 177 pp.

Landmark book by an author who became an authority on TV and a serious collector of videotaped ads.

8.380 McNaughton, Flint. *Intensive Selling*. Chicago: Selling Aid, 1918, 144 pp.

Direct advertising with a focus on wartime conditions.

8.381 Messner, Frederick R. *Industrial Advertising: Planning, Creating, Evaluating and Merchandising it More Effectively*. New York: McGraw-Hill, 1963, 314 pp.

8.382 Milton, Shirley F. *Advertising for Modern Retailers: Making it Work in a Consumer World*. New York: Fairchild, 1974, 239 pp.

8.383 Mowry, Don E. *Community Advertising: How to Advertise the Community Where You Live*. Madison, WI: Cantwell, 1924, 456 pp.

    Guide for Chambers of Commerce everywhere.

8.384 Namm, Benjamin H. *Advertising the Retail Store*. New York: U.P.C., 1924, 228 pp.

    Originally written as in-house memos. 1926 edition published by Scientific Book Corp.

8.385 O'Neill, Neville, ed. *The Advertising Agency Looks at Radio*. New York: Appleton, 1932, 232 pp.

    A reader, covering text topics.

8.386 *Outdoor Advertising: The Modern Marketing Force: A Manual for Businessmen and Others Interested in the Fundamentals of Outdoor Advertising*. Chicago: Outdoor Advertising Association of America, 1928, 227.

8.387 Parish, Chester. *Advertising Real Estate*. New York: Prentice-Hall, 1930, 380 pp.

8.388 Parrish, Amos, and MacBride, Burt. *Retail Advertising*. New York: Alexander Hamilton Institute, 1931, 323 pp.

    Volume 7 of a home study course on merchandising.

8.389 Parsons, Frank A. *The Art Appeal in Display Advertising*. New York: Harper, 1921, 132 pp.

8.390 Picken, James H. *Principles of Selling by Mail*. Chicago: Shaw, 1927, 374 pp.

    Could be titled: Business Letter Writing.

8.391 Plummer, Gail. *The Business of Show Business*. New York: Harper, 1961, 238 pp.

    Theatrical publicity.

8.392 Pratt, Veneur E. *Selling by Mail: Principles and Practice*. New York: McGraw-Hill, 1924, 428 pp.

    Text by an ex-Sears executive.

8.393 Pratt, William K. *The Advertising Manual: Being a Treatise on the Subject of Advertising and an Exposition of the Correct Methods to be Applied in the Preparation of Newspaper Advertisements from Which the Best Returns May Be Expected*. Chicago: D. Stern, 1909, 278 pp.

8.394 Preston, Harold P. *Successful Mail Selling*. New York: Ronald, 1941, 228 pp.

8.395 Propson, Carl. *Export Advertising Practice*. New York: Prentice-Hall, 1923, 271 pp.

8.396 Ramsay, Robert E. *Effective Direct Advertising: The Principles and Practice of Producing Direct Advertising for Distribution by Mail or Otherwise*. New York: Appleton, 1921, 640 pp.

8.397 Reddall, Arthur H. *Publicity Methods for Life Underwriters*. New York: F.S. Crofts, 1927, 356 pp.

"Approved by the National Association of Life Underwriters."

8.398 Reed, Vergil Daniel. *Advertising and Selling Industrial Goods*. Ronald, 1936, 287 pp.

Some representative campaigns.

8.399 Ross, Frederick J. *Some Fundamentals of Association Advertising Procedure*. New York: Fuller, Smith & Ross, 1933, 50 pp.

Advice to trade associations.

8.400 Rowen, Joseph R., and Blankertz, Donald F. *Profitable Retail Advertising*. New York: Ronald, 1951, 285 pp.

Basic text.

8.401 Rowland, Carrie M. *Advertising in Modern Retailing*. New York: Harper, 1954, 268 pp.

8.402 Sampson, J.W. *Profitable Mail Persuasion*. New York: Park Row, 1926, 389 pp.

Practical advice, "the gist of a lifetime experience in mail advertising and selling." Unindexed.

8.403 Samson, Harland E. *Advertising and Displaying Merchandise*. Cincinatti: Southwestern, 1967, 218 pp.

8.404 Sandage, Charles H. *Radio Advertising for Retailers*. Cambridge, MA: Harvard University Press, 1945, 280 pp.

A mix of empirical results and advice to retailers. Data is for retail trade only, and primarily from 1942.

8.405 Savenor, William. *610 Ideas for Show Cards, Window Signs and Advertisements*. New York: Croft, 1934, 100 pp.

Sign painting.

8.406 Sawyer, Samuel. *Secrets of the Mail-Order Trade: A Practical Manual for Those Embarking in the Business of Advertising and Selling Goods by Mail*. New York: Sawyer, 1900, 180 pp.

Text with simple formulae for 21 items merchandisable by mail.

8.407 Schiller, Robert D., ed. *Market and Media Evaluation: The AIA Handbook of Advertising to Business, Industry, Government and the Professions*. New York: Macmillan, 1969, 434 pp.

The AIA is the Association of Industrial Advertisers. A reader with various chapters authored by practitioners.

8.408 Schneller, Frederic A., and Hamilton, Raymond V. *Advertising For the High School Journalist*. Iowa City: Clio Press, 1928, 58 pp.

8.409 Seehafer, Eugene F., and Laemmar, Jack W. *Successful Radio and Television Advertising*. New York: McGraw-Hill, 1951, 574 pp.

8.410 Settle, Irving. *Effective Retail Advertising*. New York: Fairchild, 1950, 216 pp.

8.411 Settle, Irving, and Glenn, Norman. *Television Advertising and Production Handbook*. New York: Crowell, 1953, 480 pp.

Reader, much on production.

8.412 Shragor, John. *How to Make Money in Advertising: The Proven Rules for Successful Advertising*. New York: Mail Order Advertising Association, 1953, 118 pp.

Direct mail.

8.413 Sloan, Clifford, and Mooney, James D. *Advertising the Technical Product*. New York: McGraw-Hill, 1920, 365 pp.

Text, with annotated criticisms of many industrial ads.

8.414 Smith, Roland B. *Advertising to Business*. Homewood, IL: Irwin, 1957, 392 pp.

8.415 Spaulding, A.W. *Advertising Property Insurance*. Indianapolis: Rough Notes, 1927, 354 pp.

8.416 Squire, Irving, and Wilson, K.A. *Informing Your Public*. New York: Associated Press, 1924, 158 pp.

Publicity for public welfare organizations, especially Christian.

8.417 Stoecker, Herbert J. *Bookvertising: With 85 Studies and Expert Opinion on How to Prepare Successful Bookvertising*. New York: Saybrook House, 1942, 203 pp.

"A study of the advertising of books used by industries, institutions, and associations."

8.418 Stone, Robert F. *Profitable Direct Mail Methods*. New York: Prentice-Hall, 1947, 452 pp.

8.419 Taft, William N. *Retail Advertising*. Scranton, PA: International Textbook, 1929, 73 pp.

8.420 Thomson, William A. *Making Millions Read and Buy: The Influence and Use of the Newspaper in Advertising*. New York: Drey, 1934, 248 pp.

Large print text-like work, probably intended for small retailers.

8.421 Tighe, Charles R. *1001 Tested Programs and Merchandising Ideas*.
New York: Broadcast Publishing, 1936, 180 pp.

    In radio advertising.

8.422 Tobias, Marvin E. *Profitable Retail Advertising*. New York:
Harper, 1930, 276 pp.

    Large print, basic concepts.

8.423 Tompkins, Norman C. *Sales and Advertising Opportunities for the
Small Manufacturer*. New York: Funk & Wagnalls, 1950, 346 pp.

8.424 Wakeman, Delbert W. *Money Making Used Car Advertising*. San
Francisco: Gilbert Press, 1956, 160 pp.

8.425 Whitmore, Eugene. *Building Your Business with Calendar and
Specialty Advertising*. Chicago: Dartnell, 1957, 255 pp.

8.426 Wiggons, Raymond P. *Profitable Advertising for Small Industrial
Goods Producers*. Washington: Small Business Administration, 1956,
102 pp.

8.427 Wolfe, Charles H. *Modern Radio Advertising*. New York: Funk &
Wagnalls, 1949, 738 pp.

    A reader with a section on developmental trends.

"There will be some who will point to bound volumes of our very
excellent trade papers and to boundless pages of hand-picked
investigations. But compared to the law, medicine, engineering,
architecture, acting, plumbing, cab-driving, teaching, keeping
store, banking, contracting, farming, publishing or any other of
our sister professions, advertising has no more guide posts than
the Atlantic Ocean. With all the available data on tap, the
advertising man still has to answer a lot of questions by ear.
Putting it another way, the best guide he has is his common
sense."

                                        Roy Durstine
                                        (8.513, p 120)

8.500 COPYWRITING TEXTS

8.501 Barton, Howard A. *How to Write Advertising*. Philadelphia:
Lippincott, 1925, 275 pp.

    Singing words to inspire ad crafting.

8.502 Batten, Henry A.; Goodrich, Marcus; and Toogood, Granville. *The
Written Word: A Study of the Art of Writing, with Especial Reference to
Its Function in Advertising*. New York: Greenberg, 1932, 163 pp.

    As demonstration, rewrites of the Gettysberg Address in seven
    styles.

8.503 Bedell, Clyde. *How to Write Advertising That Sells*. New York:
McGraw-Hill, 1940, 524 pp.

    Primarily retail. "This wordy work ... is dedicated to glad and
    resolute young intellectuals - studious, loquacious, ... and
    plagued with versatility and an inner compulsion, (who) will likely
    be the leaders in greatly improving the copy of tomorrow."

8.504 Brooker, Bertram. *Copy Technique in Advertising, Including a
System of Copy Synthesis, a Classification of Copy Services, and a Section
on Copy Construction*. New York: McGraw-Hill, 1930, 297 pp.

8.505 Burt, Frank A. *Successful Advertisements and How to Write Them*.
New York: Harper, 1940, 194 pp.

    By a successful account man who doubled as a professor at Boston
    University. Includes bibliography of collateral reading.

8.506 Burton, Philip W.; Kreer, Bowman; and Gray, John B., Jr. *Advertising Copywriting*. New York: Prentice-Hall, 1949, 521 pp.

8.507 Caples, John. *Advertising for Immediate Sales*. New York: Harper,
1936, 281 pp.

    "How to" with discussion of the development of radio and comic
    strip style advertisements. Forward by Bruce Barton.

8.508 Chesboro, Ida. *A Streamlined Study of Advertising Copy*. Minneapolis: Burgess-Beckwith, 1966, 106 pp.

8.509 Clarke, George T. *Copywriting: Theory and Technique*. New York:
Harper, 1959, 523 pp.

8.510 Cowle, Jerome M. *How to Make Big Money as an Advertising Copywriter*. West Nyack, NY: Parker, 1966, 201 pp.

8.511 DeVoe, Merrill. *Effective Advertising Copy*. New York: Macmillan,
1956, 717 pp.

8.512 Dunn, Samuel W. *Advertising Copy and Communication*. New York:
McGraw-Hill, 1956, 545 pp.

8.513   Durstine, Roy S. *Making Advertisements and Making Them Pay*. New York: Scribner, 1930, 264 pp.

    Big print exhortation on getting the "right word in the right place," i.e. copywriting.

8.514   Dutcher, Le Grand. *5,555 Result Producing Advertising, Selling Phrases*. Philadelphia: Dewey & Catkins, 1912, 140 pp.

8.515   Fehlman, Frank E. *How to Write Advertising Copy That Sells: Principles and Practices*. New York: Funk & Wagnalls, 1950, 352 pp.

    Printers' Ink book, the bulk of which is 24 case histories.

8.516   Flint, Leon N. *Advertising Clinic*. Lawrence, KS: n.p., 1918, 10 pp.

    "Diagnosis and treatment for lame, blind, anaemic, dyspeptic, lying, crazy and dead ads." A speech on copywriting.

8.517   Frederick, Justus G. *Masters of Advertising Copy: Principles and Practice of Copy Writing According to its Leading Practitioners*. New York: Frank-Maurice, 1925, 392 pp.

    A symposium of great authors including Barton, Appel, Hopkins, McManus, Goode, Tippers, etc.

8.518   French, Elbrun, ed. *The Copywriter's Guide*. New York: Harper, 1959, 536 pp.

8.519   Goode, Kenneth M. *How to Write Advertising*. New York: Longmans, Green, 1936, 168 pp.

8.520   Hall, Samuel R. *Writing an Advertisement: An Analysis of the Methods and the Mental Processes That Play a Part in the Writing of Successful Advertising*. Boston: Houghton Mifflin, 1915, 216 pp.

8.521   Herold, Don. *Humor in Advertising, and How to Make It Pay*. New York: McGraw-Hill, 1963, 200 pp.

8.522   Herrold, Lloyd D. *Advertising Copy: Principles and Practices*. Chicago: Shaw, 1926, 525 pp.

8.523   Hopkins, Claude. *Scientific Advertising*. New York: Moore, 1952, 79 pp.

    A classic on copywriting.

8.524   Hotchkiss, George B. *Advertising Copy*. New York: Harper, 1924, 471 pp.

    Early text which explains early copy testing techniques.

8.525 Huntley, Edward L. *Huntley's Ready Advertiser*. Chicago: Camdron, Amberg, 1887, 55 pp.

> "A collection of quaint phrases, trite sayings, crisp sentences and startling ejaculations" for making up newspaper copy.

8.526 Kelley, Martin. *Theme Advertising*. Toledo: Caslon, 1918, 55 pp.

> In contrast to "Reason Why."

8.527 Kidd, Elizabeth. *Just Like a Woman! How to Tell the Girls*. New York: Appleton, 1945, 184 pp.

> Unindexed, rambling discussion.

8.528 Lockwood, Richard B. *Industrial Advertising Copy*. New York: McGraw-Hill, 1929, 328 pp.

8.529 Malickson, David L., and Nason, John W. *Advertising: How to Write the Kind That Works*. New York: Scribner, 1977, 233 pp.

8.530 Matthews, John E. *The Copywriter*. Glen Ellyn, IL: n.p., 1964, 180 pp.

8.531 Metzger, George P. *Copy*. Garden City, NY: Doubleday, Page, 1926, 163 pp.

> "To sell John Smith what John Smith buys, you must see John Smith with John Smith's eyes."

8.532 Miller, George L. *Copy: The Core of Advertising*. New York: McGraw-Hill, 1949, 258 pp.

> Also appears under pseudonym Aesop Glim.

8.533 Miller, George L. *How Advertising is Written and Why*. New York: McGraw-Hill, 1945, 150 pp.

> Also appears under pseudonym Aesop Glim. Revised in 1961.

8.534 Milton, Shirley F. *What You Should Know About Advertising Copywriting*. Dobbs Ferry, NY: Oceans, 1969, 89 pp.

8.535 Naether, Carl A. *Advertising to Women*. New York: Prentice-Hall, 1928, 340 pp.

> Emphasis on copywriting style.

8.536 Norins, Hanley. *The Complete Copywriter: A Comprehensive Guide to All Phases of Advertising Communication*. New York: McGraw-Hill, 1966, 326 pp.

8.537 O'Dea, Mark. *A Preface to Advertising*. New York: McGraw-Hill, 1937, 216 pp.

> A collection of short essays from *Printers' Ink* with copy as a central theme.

8.538 Opdycke, John B. *The Language of Advertising*. New York: Pitman, 1925, 493 pp.

8.539 Opdycke, John B. *News, Ads and Sales: The Use of English for Commercial Purposes*. New York: Macmillan, 1914, 193 pp.

8.540 Page, Edward T. *Advertisement-Writing, Theoretical and Practical*. New York: Page-Davis, 1915, 252 pp.

> "Especially adapted to the use of business promotion in the office, in colleges, academies, commercial and public schools."

8.541 Page, Edward T. *Advertising: How to Plan, Prepare, Write and Manage*. New York: Publicity, 1903, 255 pp.

> Emphasis on copywriting "especially adapted for use in business, colleges, academies, commercial and public schools."

8.542 Pesin, Harry. *Sayings to Run an Advertising Agency By*. New York: Perspective Publications, 1966, 71 pp.

> Pithy advice on copywriting, one piece of wisdom per page.

8.543 Raymond, Charles H. *Modern Business Writing: A Study of the Principles Underlying Effective Advertisements and Business Letters*. New York: Century, 1921, 476 pp.

8.544 Reiss, Otto F. *How to Develop Profitable Ideas*. New York: Prentice-Hall, 1945, 202 pp.

> Creativity in copy and merchandising.

8.545 Ris, Thomas F. *Promotional and Advertising Copywriters Handbook*. 2d ed. Blue Ridge Summit, PA: Tab Books, 1971, 64 pp.

8.546 Ronson, Harvey. *Advertising Dictionary of Selling Words, Phrases and Appeals*. New York: Ronald, 1949, 365 pp.

> An organized "swipe" file.

8.547 Schellhase, Betsy A. *How to Be a Successful Copywriter: Million-Dollar Job Tips*. New York: Arco, 1965, 155 pp.

> Pragmatic guide to organizational roles as well.

8.548 Schwartz, Eugene M. *Breakthrough Advertising: How to Write Ads That Shatter Traditions and Sales Records*. Englewood Cliffs, NJ: Prentice-Hall, 1966, 236 pp.

> Based on a psychology of persuasion; copywriters' library on pp. 227 - 28.

8.549 Seil, Manning D., and Senger, Frank D. *Advertising Copy and Layout*. 4th ed. Danville, IL: Interstate, 1966, 183 pp.

8.550 Stebbins, Harry A. *Copy Capsules*. New York: McGraw-Hill, 1957, 223 pp.

8.551 Stein, Ruth L. *Count Your Characters: A Guide To Beginners in Retail Advertising Copywriting*. New York: Harcourt, Brace, 1946, 191 pp.

8.552 Surrey, Richard (pseud.). *Copy Technique in Advertising, Including a System of Copy*. New York: McGraw-Hill, 1930, 297 pp.

    Author's true name: Bertram Booker.

8.553 Wainwright, Charles A. *The Television Copywriter: How to Create Successful TV Commercials*. New York: Hastings House, 1966, 318 pp.

8.554 Weir, Walter. *On the Writing of Advertising*. New York: McGraw-Hill, 1960, 206 pp.

    Copy advice from a 30 year veteran.

8.555 Wilson, Stanley K. *Winning and Holding in Advertising and Selling*. New York: Devin-Adair, 1930, 226 pp.

    Primarily on copywriting, with some chapters reprinted from trade press articles.

8.556 Wiseman, Mark. *Before You Sign the Advertising Check: A Handbook of Advertising Analysis for Business Executives*. New York: Harper, 1938, 115 pp.

    Director of the Laboratory for Advertising Analysis, but emphasis is on copy objectives and style.

8.557 Woolf, James Davis. *Writing Advertising*. New York: Ronald, 1926, 287 pp.

8.558 "Words That Sing to Your Pocketbook." *Atlantic Monthly* 124 (October 1919): 572 - 75.

    On poetry vs. "execrable blots on human consciousness."

See also 8.099, 8.160, 8.196.

    "It is easier to write ten passably effective sonnets, good enough to take in the not too inquiring critic, than one effective advertisement that will take in a few thousand of the uncritical buying public."

                          Aldous Huxley*

*as quoted in <u>What We Think of Advertising</u>, BBD&O, 1966, unpaged

8.600 CASE HISTORIES

8.601 *Advertising Case History, 1 - 10*. Philadelphia: Curtis, 1941, various pages.

> Folios complete with layouts, sample ads and memos for: 1) Western Electric, 2) Armstrong Cork, 3) Green Giant, 4) Carnu-Auto Polish, 5) Hat Research Foundation, 6) Arrow Shirts, 7) California Fruit Growers, 8) DeBeer's Diamond Mines, 9) unknown (missing from Baker Library), 10) International Nickel.

8.602 American Tobacco Co. *"Sold American": The First Fifty Years, 1904 - 1954*. New York: American Tobacco, 1954, 144 pp.

> Well produced vanity history. Well illustrated. Appropriate attention given to advertising.

8.603 Ash, Brian. *Tiger in Your Tank: The Anatomy of an Advertising Campaign*. London: Cassell, 1969, 166 pp.

> Campaign history based on market research studies, but primarily of England's and Europe's experience.

8.604 Bonns, Edward, and Carrier, C.E. *Putting it Over by Means and Methods of Exploitation*. New York: Sieber, 1925, 236 pp.

> Not very informative, but includes two chapters on "How Great Organizations..." They use the term "exploitation" positively, as a blanket term for all mass suggestion whether advertising, public relations, propaganda, etc. It didn't catch on.

8.605 Borden, Neil H. *Advertising: Text and Cases*. Chicago: Irwin, 1950, 1,050 pp.

> Sequel to *Problems in Advertising*. Later editions co-authored by Martin V. Marshall.

8.606 Borden, Neil H. *Problems in Advertising*. Chicago: Shaw, 1927, 677 pp.

> The first Harvard casebook on advertising.

8.607 Boyd, Harper W., Jr.; Fryburger, Vernon; and Westfall, Ralph. *Cases in Advertising Management*. New York: McGraw-Hill, 1964, 426 pp.

8.608 Brooks, John. *The Fate of the Edsel and Other Business Adventures*. New York: Harper & Row, 1963, 182 pp.

> Reprinted from the New Yorker, this also includes articles on the Piggly-Wiggly Stores.

8.609 Cahn, William. *Out of the Cracker Barrel: The Nabisco Story from Animal Crackers to Zuzus*. New York: Simon & Schuster, 1969, 367 pp.

> Commissioned by the National Biscuit Company, this is nonetheless

a good tale of N.W. Ayer's work for NBC to "usher in a new era" of packaged goods. Detailed text, interspersed with interesting photos.

8.610 Caples, John. *Advertising Ideas: A Practical Guide to Methods That Make Advertisements Work*. New York: McGraw-Hill, 1938, 205 pp.

Annotations of 100 full-page magazine advertisements, most with high Starch readership scores.

8.611 Carson, Gerald. "The Beards That Made Poughkeepsie Famous." *American Heritage* 24 (1) (1972): 22 - 25.

The Smith brothers and their pioneering brand identification.

8.612 Cherington, Paul T. *Advertising as a Business Force: A Compilation of Experience Records*. Garden City, NY: Doubleday, Page, 1913, 569 pp.

Early text by a Harvard professor, written for the Associated Advertising Clubs of America. Includes relatively detailed discussion of advertising by Carnation Milk, Encyclopaedia Britannica, Crisco, Victor Corp., United Cigar Stores, Hunt Fruits, Scott Paper, National Cash Register, H.J. Heinz and others.

8.613 Diamant, Lincoln. *The Anatomy of a Television Commercial: The Story of Eastman Kodak's "Yesterdays."* New York: Hastings House, 1970, 191 pp.

A detailed description, from concept formation to copywriting to production to media placement. A good briefing behind the scenes. Includes questions and answers from professional workshop attendees.

8.614 Engle, James F.; Talarzyk, W. Wayne; and Larson, Carl M. *Cases in Promotional Strategy*. Homewood, IL: Irwin, 1971, 382 pp.

8.615 *46 Outstanding Advertising Case Histories*. Southport, CT: Maytham, 1963, 107 pp.

"Practical ... explained by the ... men who developed them." Print campaigns. Half of space is facsimilies, other half a brief outline of objectives and theories.

8.616 French, George. *General Advertising Campaigns*. Management of General Campaigns, Parts 1 - 3. Scranton, PA: International Textbook Press, 1926, 103 pp.

At home study course material, including descriptions of several firms: Wells Fargo, Colgate, International Silver, Imperial Coffee and an especially interesting case history of Scott Paper products.

8.617 Greyser, Stephen A. *Cases in Advertising and Communications Management*. Englewood Cliffs, NJ: Prentice-Hall, 1972, 665 pp.

Harvard cases with detail of exhibits.

8.618   Griese, Noel L.   "A T & T: 1908 Origins of the Nation's Oldest
Continuous Institutional Advertising Campaign."   *Journal of Advertising*
6 (3):   18 - 23.

    N.W. Ayer's campaign in 1908 to portray A T & T as a natural and
beneficent monopoly is discussed.

8.619   Jacobs, Laurence W.   *Advertising and Promotion for Retailing: Text
and Cases*.   Glenview, IL: Scott, Foresman, 1972, 248 pp.

8.620   LaGodna, Martin M.   "Agriculture and Advertising: Florida State
Bureau of Immigration, 1923 - 1960."   *Florida History Quarterly* 46 (1968):
195 - 208.

    Florida's national advertising program was headed by Nathan Mayo,
who acted as commissioner of agriculture from 1923 until his
death in 1960.

8.621   Lewis, Henry H.   *How Fortunes are Made in Advertising*.   Chicago:
Publicity Publishing, 1908, 242 pp.

    From the pages of *Success* magazine, covering Kodak, Heinz and many
more.   All "chapters" are brief.

8.622   Printers' Ink.   *Case Histories of Successful Advertising: Problems, Solutions, Results*.   New York: Funk & Wagnalls, 1949, 296 pp.

    Each case history described in 2 - 3 pages of "cold hard fact ..
in place of academic theory."

8.623   Rheinstrom, Carrol.   *Psyching the Ads: The Case Book of Advertising: The Methods and Results of 180 Advertisements*.   New York: Covici, 1929, 362 pp.

    Mini case-histories, but includes brief data on sales results and
media costs and circulation.

8.624   Rowsome, Frank, Jr.   *Think Small: The Story Behind Those Volkswagen Ads*.   Brattleboro, VT: Greene, 1970, 128 pp.

    An amply illustrated case history of Doyle, Dane Bernbach's Crea-
tive work for VW from mid-fifties to 1970.

8.625   Rowsome, Frank, Jr.   "The Verse by the Side of the Road."   *American
Heritage* 17 (1) (1965):   102 - 05.

    Discusses the advertising rhymes used (first in 1925) to promote
the sales of Burma-Shave, a brushless shaving cream.

8.626   Rowsome, Frank, Jr.   *The Verse by the Side of the Road: The Story
of the Burma-Shave Signs and Jingles*.   Brattleboro, VT: Greene, 1965,
121 pp.

    Includes the text of each and every poetic exhortation, like
"Shaving Brush all wet and hairy, I've passed you up for sanitary -
Burma-Shave."

8.627   Ruxton, Robert. *Twenty Pamphlets on Advertising*. Cambridge: Harvard University Press, 1921 - 23, 316 pp.

> Includes one on "Sunny Jim" and another on "Gold Dust" campaigns.

8.628   *The Story of Phoebe Snow*. New York: Delaware, Lackawanna and Western Railroad, 1950, 10 pp.

> Some story, but mostly reproductions of all of the famous verse from the turn of the century and a revival in WWII.

8.629   Tittley, J.V.   "Fifty Years of Advertising and Sales Promotion." In *Marketing Canada*, pp.   277 - 284.   Edited by I.A. Litvak and Bruce E. Mallen. Toronto: McGraw-Hill, 1964.

> History of copy changes of Canada Cement Co. Ltd. Neither informative, nor illustrative.

8.630   Udry, J. Richard; Bauman, Karl E.; and Others. *The Media and Family Planning*. Cambridge: Ballinger, 1974, 232 pp.

> Evaluation of birth control advertising.

8.631   Wagner, Philip. "Cigarettes vs. Candy." *New Republic* 58 (13 February 1929): 343 - 45.

> Briefly on competitive responses to the "Reach for a Lucky Instead of a Sweet" campaign.

8.632   Wallace, Robert R. "A Lucky or a Sweet or Both!" *Nation* 128 (13 March 1929): 305 - 07.

> On George Washington Hill's celebrated campaign and reactions to it.

8.633   Watkins, Julian L. *The Best Advertisements from Reader's Digest and the Qualities That Made Them Effective*. New York: Random, 1962, 141 pp.

> 100 ads reproduced with general commentary.

8.634   Willis, Paul P. *Your Future is in the Air: The Story of How American Airlines Made People Air-Travel Conscious*. New York: Prentice-Hall, 1940, 171 pp.

For additional case histories, see also 2.094, 3.031, 3.052, 3.104, 3.115, 3.116, 3.125, 3.127, 5.019, 5.068, 5.078, 6.017, 6.024, 6.078, 6.079, 8.053, 8.065, 8.088, 8.144, 8.305, 8.340, 8.362, 8.398, 8.515, 9.050, 10.002, 10.028, 10.031, 10.041, 10.045, 10.052, 10.063, 10.064, 10.067, 10.070, 10.083, 10.104, 10.105, and cases listed by the Harvard Case Clearing House in marketing, consumer behavior, and marketing research case books, as well as advertising.

9.000
MISCELLANY

9.001 Advertising Council. *From War to Peace: The New Challenge to Business and Advertising*. New York: War Advertising Council, 1945, 9 pp.

9.002 Advertising Council. *Put Your Advertising to Work for More "Women at War" in War Plants, Essential Civilian Jobs and the Armed Forces*. New York: Advertising Council: 1944, 12 pp.

9.003 Advertising Federation of America. *Advertising's War Task and Post-War Responsibility*. New York: AFA, 1943, 67 pp.

Highlights of a war advertising conference.

9.004 *The Advertising Parade: An Anthology of Good Advertisements Published in 1928*. New York: Harper, 1930, 172 pp.

Planned to be an annual publication, this is all that was produced. Perhaps the depression rained on the parade.

9.005 American Newspaper Publishers Association. *Advertising Goes to War*. New York: ANPA, Bureau of Advertising, 1942, 74 pp.

Promo piece, with many facsimilies.

9.006 American Newspaper Publishers Association. *The Newspaper as an Advertising Medium: A Handbook of the Newspaper in North America: Its Beginnings, itd Development, its Services to the Public, and its Useful- ness to Buyers of Advertising*. New York: ANPA, Bureau of Advertising, 1940, 170 pp.

Basics for businessmen; some data.

9.007 *Annual (1st) of Advertising Art in the United States*. New York: Publishers Printing, 1921, 130 pp.

Published for the Art Directors Club of New York with winners of competition. Published annually since with varying titles; even- tually split into multiple volumes for print, tv, etc. Artistic, with many familiar ads, though generally not characteristic of what is seen or what sells.

9.008 Baker, Stephen. *Visual Persuasion*. New York: McGraw-Hill, 1961, unpaged.

Directed at art directors, it includes a lot of text giving rationale for the images portrayed by the ads of the 50's.

9.009 Baran, Paul A., and Sweezy, P.M. "Theses on Advertising." *Science and Society* 28 (Winter 1964): 20 - 30.

Prepared for a British Labour Party Commission on the Americaniza- tion of mass media, compactly reviewing the U.S. experience.

9.010   Barton, Bruce.   *The Man Nobody Knows: A Discovery of the Real*
Jesus.   Indianapolis: Bobbs, Merrill, 1924, 220 pp.

> Written by a well known advertising man, this is the portrayal of
> Jesus as the supersalesman of all times, a businessman who "picked
> up twelve men from the bottom ranks of business and forged them
> into an organization that conquered the world."

9.011   Bates, Charles Austin.   *Short Talks on Advertising*.   New York: By
the Author, 1898, 211 pp.

> In aid of business.

9.012   Behrman, S.N.   "The Advertising Man."   *New Republic* 20 (20 August
1919):   84 - 86.

> Includes a stereotype description of "sartorially perfect, with
> sleek hair and parti-colored shoes."

9.013   Bellamy, Francis, ed.   *Effective Magazine Advertising*.   New York:
Kennerley, 1909, 361 pp.

> 508 essays written by readers of the November 1907 issue of *Every-*
> *body's Magazine,* articulating their preference for the most effec-
> tive ads in the issue.   All of the original 111 ads are reproduced
> as well.

9.014   Berchtold, W.E.   "Men Who Sell You."   *New Outlook* 165 (January
1935):   27 - 33, 55.

> Biographical sketches of Resor, Rubicam, Lambert, Esty, Collins,
> Getchell, Barton, Groesbeck, Hill, Bowles, *et al*.

9.015   Bezanson, Anne.   *Help Wanted Advertising as an Indicator of the*
Demand for Labor.   Wharton School of Finance and Commerce, Research Study
no. 6.   Philadelphia: University of Pennsylvania Press, 1929, 104 pp.

> "A summary of the help wanted ads in daily and Sunday newspapers
> in Philadelphia and six other cities."

9.016   Biggers, W.W., and Stover, C.A.   *When the Billing Goes Up, Up, Up,*
and the Profits Go Down, Down, Down.   New York: Gaus, 1969, 48 pp.

> Arguing against committee think tanks and for freelance creative
> work - especially themselves.

9.017   Black, George.   *Listen, Mr. President*.   Philadelphia: Chilton,
1960, 130 pp.

> A series of monologues on advertising, publicity and the promotion
> of industrial products.

9.018   *The Book of Advertising Tests: A Group of Articles That Actually*
Say Something About Advertising.   Chicago: Lord & Thomas, 1905?, 117 pp.

> Impassioned articles addressed to Mr. Advertiser.

9.019 Borden, Neil H.; Taylor, Malcolm D.; and Hovde, Howard T. *National Advertising in Newspapers*. Cambridge: Harvard University Press, 1946, 486 pp.

> Detailed study of problems and prospects for newspapers retaining advertising revenue.

9.020 Borsodi, William. *The Advertiser's Cyclopedia of Selling Phrases*. New York: Advertiser's Cyclopedia, 1909, 1,360 pp.

> "A collection of advertising short talks as used by the most successful merchants and advertisement writers."

9.021 Boulder (pseud.). *Hidden Causes of Reckless Advertising Waste*. Chicago: Lord & Thomas, 1913, 112 pp.

> Reprinted from *Judicious Advertising*.

9.022 Brown, H.C. *Portraits: Some of the Men We Know: Advertisers, Publishers, and Representative Men of Allied Interests*. New York: By the Author, 1898, 101 pp.

> Lovely photographic portraits of 200 sundry men working in positions from bill-poster to publisher. No text or index, but includes many recognizable names including Bates, Powers, Ward, Rowell.

9.023 Buck, Glen. *The Cost of Confusion*. Chicago: By the Author, 1929, 32 pp.

> Pamphlet promoting author's knowledge of advertising.

9.024 Bursk, Edward C.; Clark, Donald T.; and Hidy, Ralph W. *The World of Business: A Selected Library of the Literature of Business from the Accounting Code of Hammurabi to the 20th Century "Administrator's Prayer."* 4 vols. New York: Simon & Schuster, 1962, 2,655 pp.

> A fascinating set of original source material drawn from a very eclectic base. The first volume is almost exclusively concerned with marketing and advertising.

9.025 *Business: How to Get It, How to Keep It*. Girard, PA: Society of Economic Research, 1892, 64 pp.

> Advertising is the answer, mostly in epigrams.

9.026 Calkins, Earnest E. "Now is the Time to Advertise." *Review of Reviews* 81 (March 1930): 52 - 56.

> To cure depression.

9.027 Campbell, Stanley. *Because of these Things Advertising Pays*. Dallas: Jaggars, Chiles & Stouall, 1939, 88 pp.

> "A simplified discussion ... for the edification of those who plan, write, sell or produce advertising." Originally performed as a

series of dramatic dialogues to Dallas Advertising League.   Text
in dialogue format.

9.028   Carlton, B.L.   *The ABC of Successful Advertising in Two Lessons.*
Jackson, Mich.:   n.p., 1896, 26 pp.

Promotional pamphlet.

9.029   Deleted.

9.030   Chapman, Clowry.   *How Advertisements Defeat Their Own Ends.*   New
York: Prentice-Hall, 1931, 43 pp.

On the value of trade marks.

9.031   Chisholm, Robert F.   *The Darlings: The Mystique of the Supermarket.*   New York: Chain Store Age Books, 1970, 192 pp.

"Offers the ideas and speculations of informed observers, rather
than facts, analyses or statistical data."   The darlings are the
women who buy at supermarkets.

9.032   Clark, Neil M.   "Making Wisecracks is Charlie Archbold's Business."
American Magazine 100 (November 1925):   68 pp.

The use of epigrams as a means of advertising a product.

9.033   Crow, Carl.   *Four Hundred Million Customers.*   New York: Harper,
1937.

A digest of letters written over 20 years in answer to queries
from clients of an advertising agency about selling goods in
China, 1915 - 1935.

9.034   Crum, William L.   *Advertising Fluctuations, Seasonal and Cyclical.*
Chicago: A.W. Simon, 1927, 308 pp.

9.034a Cushman, Helen B.   "Trade Cards -- Records of the Advertising
Department."   *American Records Management Association Quarterly* 4 #4
(October 1970):   17 - 21 pp.

9.035   Deland, Lorin F.   *Imagination in Business.*   New York: Harper,
1909, 107 pp.

Tales of merchandising success.   See also article with same title
in *Atlantic Monthly* 103 (1909); 433 - 447 pp.

9.036   "Dream World of Advertising."   *American Heritage* 16 (1965):   70 -
75 pp.

Pictorial essay on advertising in the 1920's.   "Modern advertising
took advantage of the revolution in morals and was openly hedon-
istic."

9.037   Eads, George W.   *Problems of Advertising: Addresses Delivered in
Journalism Week, 1918.*   Journalism Series, no. 17.   Colombia, MO: University of Missouri, 1918, 20 pp.

Also appears in *The University of Missouri Bulletin,* vol. 19, no. 27.

9.038 Elkin, Frederick. "Advertising in French Canada: Innovations and Deviations in the Context of a Changing Society." In *Explorations in Social Change,* pp. 522 - 46. Edited by George K. Zollschan and Walter Hirsch. Boston: Houghton Mifflin, 1964.

9.039 Elkin, Frederick. "Advertising Themes and Quiet Revolutions: Dilemmas in French Canada." *American Journal of Sociology* 75 (July 1969): 112 - 22.

9.040 Elkin, Frederick. "Bicultural and Bilingual Adaptations in French Canada: The Example of Retail Advertising." *Canadian Review of Sociology and Anthropology* 2 (August 1965): 132 - 48.

> Two large English department stores in downtown Montreal were studied. A content analysis was made for five sample periods, all in 1960.

9.041 Elkin, Frederick. *The Employment of Visible Minority Groups in Mass Media Advertising: A Report Submitted to the Ontario Human Rights Commission.* Downsview, ON: York University Press, 1971, 79 pp.

> Blacks, Asians and Indians are focused on.

9.042 Elkin, Frederick. "Mass Media, Advertising and the Quiet Revolution." In *Canadian Society: Pluralism, Change and Conflict,* pp. 184 - 205. Edited by Richard J. Ossenberg. Scarborough, ON: Prentice-Hall of Canada, 1971.

9.043 Elkin, Frederick. "A Study of Advertisements in Montreal Newspapers." *Canadian Communications* 1 (Summer 1961): 15 - 22.

> "A content analysis of all advertisements in the daily editions of the Montreal Star and La Presse. The advertising styles are no different in the two appers."

9.044 Ennis, David R. *The Emergence of Dramatic Advertising.* Groer, SC: Groer Citizen, 1932, 53 pp.

> Sample newspaper ads, without illustrations.

9.045 Ferguson, James M. *The Advertising Rate Structure in the Daily Newspaper Industry.* Englewood Cliffs, NJ: Prentice-Hall, 1963, 94 pp.

> A Ford Foundation dissertation prize winner from the University of Chicago. Examines the differences between rates charged by national and local advertisers.

9.046 Firestone, Otto J. *Broadcast Advertising in Canada: Past and Future Growth.* Ottawa: University of Ottawa Press, 1966, 358 pp.

> Not as historical as it might sound, but rather a typically competent economic analysis which includes data base from 1946 - 1965.

9.047 Firestone, Otto J. *The Public Persuader: Government Advertising.*
Toronto: Methuen, 1970, 258 pp.

> Academic, prepared for a Canadian government Task Force. A
> detailed study of Canadian activities, with a briefer review of
> U.S. and English experience.

9.048 Fowler, Nathaniel C., Jr. "A Conversation: Advertising, Past,
Present, and Future." *Arena* 29 (1903): 638 - 44.

> Brief interview, little history.

9.049 Freeman, William C. *One Hundred Advertising Talks*. New York:
Winthrop Press, 1912, 228 pp.

> Selected and arranged by George French, who comments on the
> writers' "convincing naivité."

9.050 Glatzer, Robert. *The New Advertising: The Great Campaigns From
Avis to Volkswagen*. New York: Citadel, 1970, 191 pp.

> Dates the "new advertising" as starting in 1949 with agencies
> formed by Ogilvy and Bernbach, the latter receiving most of the
> fulsome praise.

9.051 Goodman, Milton. "The Humanness of Advertising." *Harper's
Weekly* 62 (8 April 1916): 362 pp.

> Ads "spring from the soil" not from the "dry-as-dust" professor.

9.052 Greeley, Horace. "The Philsophy of Advertising." *Hunt's Merchants Magazine* 23 (1850): 580 - 83.

> Discussion of early advertising by the man whose advice to "go
> west, young man" was probably the best advertisement possible for
> the new communities on the expanding frontiers of early America.

9.053 Greer, Carl R. *Across with the Ad-Men*. Hamilton, OH: Beckett,
1924, 238 pp.

> Travel journal by the "Buckeye Cover Man" attending the Interna-
> tional Advertising Convention, London, 1924. Uninteresting, irre-
> levant to advertising except as the chronicle of a boondoggle.

9.054 Groome, Harry C., Jr. *This is Advertising*. Philadelphia: Ayer,
1975, 116 pp.

> The Ayer book on what advertising is all about, who does what and
> how to get a job in it.

9.055 *A Guide to Effective War-Time Advertising*. New York: Associated
Business Papers, 1942, 90 pp.

> Encouraging advertising in business papers.

9.056 Hammond, Dorothy M. *Advertising Collectibles of Times Past*. Des Moines: W.H. Books, 1974, 128 pp.

Discussion of advertiques.

9.057 Harriman, Lee. *The Dublin Letters*. New York: Washburn, 1931, 258 pp.

Fictional (?) letters from the office of the president of the Dublin Advertising Agency.

9.058 Harris, Miller, and Gosage, Howard. *Dear Miss Afflerbach: Or, the Postman Hardly Ever Rings 11,342 Times*. New York: Macmillan, 1962, 202 pp.

Amusing letters in response to a "give-away" ad by Eagle Shirts run in the *New Yorker*.

9.059 Heintz, Ann Christine. *Persuasion*. Chicago: Loyola University Press, 1970, 224 pp.

A workbook pamphlet "to bring the media world into the classroom."

9.060 Hornung, Clarence P. *Handbook of Early Advertising Art*. 2 vols. New York: Dover, 1956.

Quality reproduction of 19th Century American engravings in the public domain. The first volume is pictorial and the second typographic. A frequently used reference book by art directors.

9.061 Jenkins, John R., and Zif, Jay J. *Planning the Advertising Campaign: Players' Manual*. New York: Macmillan, 1971, 171 pp.

A complex role play simulation of ice cream and cottage cheese promotion.

9.062 Johnson, Samuel. "Art of Advertising," *Idler* 11 (20 January 1759).

Quotable on "the art being nearly perfected."

9.063 Karolevitz, Robert F. *Old Time Agriculture in the Ads*. Aberdeen, SD: North Plains Press, 1970, 120 pp.

A view of the changing farm life from 1875 - 1910.

9.064 Kaufman, Herbert. *The Clock That Had No Hands, and Nineteen Other Essays About Advertising*. New York: H. Doran, 1912, 116 pp.

Mini-essays testifying the author's faith in advertising.

9.065 Kelley, Stanley, Jr. *Professional Public Relations and Political Power*. Baltimore: Johns Hopkins Press, 1956, 247 pp.

Most of this is on the use of advertising methods by politicians running for office in the post WW II decade.

9.066   Kimball, Arthur R.   "Binding Advertisements in Serials."   *Library Journal* 28 (1903):   766 - 77.

   A Librarian of Congress encourages retention of advertisements, contrary to conventional practice of the time.

9.067   Knight, George M.   *How to Cut Your Advertising Costs, Yet Get Maximum Results*.   Leonardtown, MD: By the Author, 1954, 37 pp.

   Mimeographed book arguing for postcards, especially to publicize books to librarians.

9.068   Landauer, Bella C.   "A Short History of Trade Cards."   *Bulletin of the Business Historical Society* 5 (1931):   1 - 6.

9.069   Landauer, Bella C.   "Trade Cards: An Over-looked Asset."   *Bulletin of the Business Historical Society* 9 (1935):   33 - 38.

   A plea for using trade cards as a source for historical research from the owner of the world's largest collection, now managed by the New York Historical Society.

9.069a Larson, George.   *The Blimp Book*.   Mill Valley, CA: Squarebooks, 1977, 95 pp.

   Text and photographs of the classic speciality advertisements, the Goodyear Blimp.

9.070   McKee, Homer.   *Bread, Butter and Beefsteak*.   York, PA: Maple Press, 1943, 32 pp.

   How advertising prepared America for wartime.   Also appears in *Inland Printer* (July 1943).

9.071   MacManus, Theodore F.   *The Sword Arm of Business*.   New York: Devin-Adair, 1927, 188 pp.

   Based on experience in auto industry, especially with Dodge and Cadillac.   Pseudo text to attract business.

9.072   Marquis, J. Clyde.   "Advertising as an Aid to Direct Selling." *Annals of the American Academy of Political and Social Science* 50 (November 1913):   197 - 202.

   On agricultural markets, by an editor of *The Country Gentleman*.

9.073   Martin, Edward.   "Advertisement."   *Atlantic Monthly* 103 (January 1909):   36 - 39.

   Some material on political advertising.

9.074   *The Metropolitan Museum of Art Bulletin* 34 (Spring 1976):   52+.

   The entire issue of the Bulletin is devoted to the reprinting of examples of American printed ephemera drawn from the collections of Landauer, Burdick and the Met itself and displayed there as a bicentennial exhibit.   A lavish catalogue.

9.075 Meyerhoff, Arthur E. *The Strategy of Persuasion: The Use of Advertising Skills in Fighting the Cold War.* New York: Coward-McCann, 1965, 190 pp.

"Shows that the American advertising profession, master of the arts of persuasion, can reshape the American image, ... thereby reversing the disastrous losses of our timid and moribund information program."

9.076 Miller, Roger. *Advertising Tours and Exhibits.* Ashville, NC: n.p., 1927?, 23 pp.

Discusses Chamber of Commerce advertising and trade shows, prepared for the 13th Annual Convention of the National Association of Commercial Organization Secretaries.

9.077 *Money Makers: A Plea to be Measured by the Dollar Guage Only: A Master Salesman's Presentation of Salesmanship-in-Print.* Chicago: Lord & Thomas, 1913, 73 pp.

9.078 Morella, Joe; Epstein, Edward Z.; and Clark, Eleanor. *Those Great Movie Ads.* New Rochelle, NY: Arlington, 1972, 320 pp.

Little text and most reproductions are in black and white, but enough ads are reproduced to make this a good single source of primary materials unavailable in conventional libraries.

9.079 Munsey, Frank A. "Advertising in Some of Its Phases." *Munseys Magazine* 20 (November 1898): 476 - 86.

Originally a speech to Sphinx Club, it says much about magazine advertising and argues for the role of agents.

9.080 Nathan, George Jean. "Advertising." *American Mercury* 18 (December 1929): 496 - 97.

Dubious of wisdom of getting attention at any cost.

9.081 National Association of Secondary School Principles. *Learning to Use Advertising: A Problem of the Modern American Consumer.* Washington, DC: NASSP, 1944?, 67 pp.

A typescript unit for high school students.

9.082 Norbeck, Peter, and Norbeck, Craig, eds. *Great Songs of Madison Avenue.* New York: Quadrangle, 1976, 251 pp.

Song sheets for famous jingles of fifty years.

9.083 Norman, John B. *Mirth, Misery, Mystery of "Want" Advertisements.* St. Paris, OH: n.p., 1900, 28 pp.

Oddities experienced by the ad taker.

9.084   Nuechterlein, James A.   "Bruce Barton and the Business Ethos of the 1920's."   Paper presented at the Annual Meeting of the Canadian Association for American Studies, Waterloo, Ontario, October 1975.

A study of Barton's "inspirational" writings.

9.085   O'Dea, Mark.   *Adlandia: An Advertising Quiz.*   Dansville, NY: By the Author, 1941, 75 pp.

350 Q & A's designed for high school students for 50th anniversary of *The Instructor.*

9.086   Olsen.   Lester, ed.   *Advertising Work Told with Pictures.*   New York: Funk & Wagnalls, 1950, 160 pp.

Sponsored by the Milwaukee Advertising Club.

9.087   O'Neill, H.   "On Reading American Magazines: Advertising Section." *Living Age* 324 (7 February 1925):   301 - 03.

Ruminations provoked by advertising's stimulating imagery.

9.088   Osborn, Alexander F.   *Applied Imagination: Principles and Procedures of Creative Thinking.*   New York: Scribner, 1953, 317 pp.

The bible of creativity by the developer of brainstorming, and one of the founders of BBD&O.   Several other titles on this theme, including *Wake Up Your Mind,* and *Your Creative Power.*

9.089   Paschall, Irvin F.   *Selling It to the Advertiser: A Book of Facts for the Agent to Tell His Client.*   Philadelphia: Buchanan, 1915, 96 pp.

Promotes *The Farm Journal,* alternate pages blank.

9.090   Peabody, Nelson J.   *The Advertiser's Almanac, 1885 - 1946.*   Dayton, OH: Pflaum, 1946, 32 pp.

Commemorative for the *Young Catholic Messenger.*

9.091   Phelps, George H.   *Tomorrow's Advertisers and Their Advertising Agencies.*   New York: Harper, 1929, 256 pp.

Chatty, designed to inspire confidence and trade with the author's agency.

9.092   Pollay, Richard W.   "The Importance and the Problems of Writing the History of Advertising."   *Journal of Advertising History* 1 (December 1977):   3 - 5.

The keynote article for this journal.

9.093   Pollay, Richard W.   "Maintaining Archives for the History of Advertising."   *Special Libraries* 69 (April 1978):   145 - 54.

A guide and encouragement for records retention.

9.094   Pollay, Richard W.   "Wanted: Contributions to the History of
Advertising." *Journal of Advertising Research* 18 (October 1978):

        An argument to influence executives.

9.095   Pompian, Richard O. *Advertising*. New York: Watts, 1970, 90 pp.

        Discussion for juveniles.

9.096   Rank, Hugh, ed. *Language in Public Policy*. Urbana, IL: University of Illinois Press, 1974, 248 pp.

        Includes four articles on advertising rhetoric for high school
        teachers of English.

9.097   Rankin, William H. *Advertising and Its Relation to the Public*.
New York: n.p., 1925, 11 pp.

        "The first advertising address ever broadcast," from WEAF (New
        York) in 1922. Pamphlet promotes Rankin's advertising agency.

9.098   Reed, Vergil D., and Crawford, John. *The Teaching of Advertising
at the Graduate Level*. New York: Columbia Graduate School of Business,
1963, 70 pp.

        Sponsored by American Association of Advertising Agencies. See
        also Ross.

9.099   Roberts, Peter. *Any Color So Long as It's Black: The First Fifty
Years of Automobile Advertising*. New York: Morrow, 1976, 144 pp.

9.100   Robinson, Charles M. "Artistic Possibilities of Advertising."
The Atlantic Monthly 34 (1904): 53 - 60.

        On streets and highways.

9.101   Rorty, James. "Advertising and the Depression." *Nation* 137
(December 20, 1933): 703 - 04.

        Impact of the depression on the profession.

9.102   Roson, Ben. *The Corporate Search for Visual Identity: A Study of
Fifteen Outstanding Corporate Design Problems*. New York: Van Nostrand,
1970, 259 pp.

        Mostly facsimilies.

9.103   Ross, Billy I. *Advertising Education: Programs in Four Year
American Colleges and Universities*. New York: American Association of
Advertising Agencies & American Academy of Advertising, 1965, 188 pp.

        Sponsored by A.A.A., this reports a survey whose focus is on under-
        graduate education. Includes a chapter on the history and a
        bibliography, pp. 180 - 188. Focuses on education. See also Reed.

9.104   Salt, Enoch J. *Nuggets: A Book Written For the Use and Benefit of the Merchant, Manufacturer, and Advertiser in General.* Columbus, OH: n.p., 191?, 129 pp.

        Salt was advertising manager for F. & R. Lazarus & Co.

9.105   Sheafer, Henry C. "A Study in Advertising." *Arena* 29 (1903): 383 - 90.

        Incidental observations.

9.106   Shenck, J.C. *A Friend at Your Elbow: Being a Series of Hints and Helps to Those Who Appreciate the Benefits of Unique and Interesting Advertising.* New York: Dry Goods Economist, 1893, 128 pp.

        Advertising matter interspersed with tear out copy for retailers' use.

9.107   Spitzer, Leo. "American Advertising Explained as Popular Art." In *Essays on English and American Literature,* pp. 248 - 77. Princeton: Princeton University Press, 1962.

        An arcane discussion that also appears in Spitzer's *A Method of Interpreting Language.* Protracted discussion of Sunkist ads.

9.108   Stark, Saidee E. *How Schools Use Advertising Material.* New York: Association of National Advertisers, 1930, 184 pp.

        Also appears as Ph.D. thesis, Columbia, 1931, "The Development of Criteria For the Educational Evaluation of Advertising Material Used by Home Economics Workers."

9.109   Strable, Edward G. "The Origin, Development and Present Status of Advertising Agency Libraries in the United States." A.M. thesis, University of Chicago, 1954, 156 pp.

        Finds each to be idiosyncratic in collections and procedure.

9.110   Sullivan, John. *The Truth About Advertising.* New York: American Management Association, 1928, 11 pp.

        A speech encouraging good marketing to prevent "dumb advertising."

9.111   Sunners, William. *American Slogans.* New York: Paebar, 1949, 345 pp.

        "The world's greatest collection of slogans and phrases (13,000) to help agencies comply with the Lanham Act; to help copywriters ... and contestants."

9.112   Sunners, William. *How to Win Prize Contests.* New York: Arco, 1950, 393 pp.

        A good guide to the many varieties of contest promotions used by marketeers in the 30's and 40's but most interesting material is a list of health "conditions" created by advertising and curable by the advertisers' products, pp. 17 - 26.

9.113 Thompson, William A. *Making Millions Read and Buy: The Influence and Use of the Newspaper In Advertising*. New York: W. Drey, 1934, 248 pp.

> Endorsement of the virtues of newspaper advertising in the face of competition from radio. No index.

9.114 Tyler, Poyntz. *Advertising in America*. New York: Wilson, 1959, 214 pp.

> Good little reader on the institution as part of "The Reference Shelf" series.

9.115 Walsh, Richard J. *Selling Forces: A Study of the Basic Principles of Advertising and More Particularly Advertising in National Periodicals*. Philadelphia: Curtis, 1913, 280 pp.

> And more particularly still, in Curtis Publishing.

9.116 *The War and the Nation's Advertisers*. Chicago: Photoplay, 1918, 35 pp.

> Facsimiles of WWI ads.

9.117 Wheeler, John R. *An Advertising Manual for People Who Have to Write Their Own Advertisements*. Calgary: J.D. McAra, 1915, 35 pp.

> Sample press material promoting clothes.

9.118 Wisby, Hrolf. "Modern Advertising Methods." *Independent* 56 (1904): 260 - 64.

> Sees ads displacing commercial travellers. Miscellaneous data on size and rates of industry.

9.119 Wood, James Playsted. *This is Advertising*. New York: Crown, 1968, 186 pp.

> A book for young adults, descriptive primarily of the institutions.

9.120 Woodford, Jack. "Help Wanted." *American Mercury* (December 1928): 491 - 96.

> On copy in classified real estate ads.

9.121 Woodward, Helen. *The Lady Persuaders*. New York: Obolensky, 1960, 189 pp.

> Discussion of the changing roles of women's magazines.

9.122 Zeigler, Shirley K., ed. *Perspectives on Advertising Education*. Knoxville, TN: American Academy of Advertising, 1974, 524 pp.

> "Proceedings of 1974 conference of University Professors of Advertising.

9.200   VOCATIONAL GUIDES

9.201   Allen, Frederick J.   *Advertising as a Vocation.*   New York: Macmillan, 1919, 178 pp.

9.202   Beasley, Norman.   "Breaking into Advertising."   *Saturday Evening Post* 200 (30 July 1927):   35 pp.

> Suggests newspaper editorial and space selling experience is preferable to college.

9.203   Bell, Harrie A.   *Getting the Right Start in Direct Advertising.* New York: Graphic Books, 1946, 161 pp.

> First published in serial form in the *Reporter* of direct mail advertising.

9.204   Boland, Charles M.   *Careers and Opportunities in Advertising.*   New York: Dutton, 1964, 215 pp.

9.205   Calkins, Earnest Elmo, *The Advertising Man.*   New York: Scribner & Sons, 1922, 205 pp.

> Covers advertising as a vocation.

9.026   Clair, Blanche, and Dignam, Dorothy, eds.   *Advertising Careers for Women.*   New York: Harper, 1939, 268 pp.

> "22 lectures ... setting forth the fields of opportunity to which advertising beckons women."

9.207   Collins, Al.   *To Market ... To Market: A Book on Advertising and Marketing by Experts in the Profession.*   Highland Park, IL: By the Author, 1965, 223 pp.

> Description of roles and functions of members of the industry, including a brief description of the major research houses.   Vocational in tone.

9.208   Groome, Harry C., Jr.   *Opportunities in Advertising Careers.* Louisville, KY: Vocational Guidance Manuals, 1976, 126 pp.

9.209   Hall, Samuel R.   *Getting Ahead in Advertising and Selling.*   New York: McGraw-Hill, 1926, 100 pp.

> "A book of earnest counsel to ambitious men and women who are attracted to the field of promotional work or who, being in it, are eager to climb higher."

9.210   Hoyt, Charles Wilson.   *Training for the Business of Advertising.* New York: G.B. Woolson, 1922, 125 pp.

9.211   James, Alden, ed.   *Careers in Advertising and the Jobs Behind Them.* New York: Macmillan, 1932, 677 pp.

> Written by many varied practitioners.

9.212 Johnson, George. *Your Career in Advertising*. New York: Messner, 1966, 189 pp.

9.213 Kleppner, Otto. *Entering the Advertising Field*. Scranton: International Correspondence Schools, 1937, 84 pp.

9.214 Larison, Ruth H. *How to Get and Hold the Job You Want*. New York: Longman, Green, 1950, 264 pp.

>   Official textbook of the Job-Finding Forum of the Advertising Club of New York.

9.215 Larison, Ruth H. *Opportunities in Advertising*. New York: Vocational Guidance Manuals, 1950, 80 pp.

9.216 Larranaga, Robert D. *Advertising*. Minneapolis: Dillon, 1973, 196 pp.

9.217 Lewis, Norman. *How to Become an Advertising Man*. New York: Ronald, 1927, 185 pp.

9.218 Lowen, Walter A., and Watson, Lillian E. *How to Get a Job and Win Success in Advertising*. New York: Prentice-Hall, 1941, 382 pp.

>   Appendices include a collection of famous people writing on what qualities are most important for success, and recollecting how they got their start.

9.219 McBride, Mary M., ed. *How to Be a Successful Advertising Women: A Career Guide for Women in Advertising, Public Relations and Related Fields*. New York: Whittlesey House, 1948, 259 pp.

>   Done for Advertising Women of New York.

9.220 Moore, Sidney. *So This is the Ad Biz!* New York: Pageant, 1966, 118 pp.

>   Anecdotes designed to give the average reader a sense of the nuts and bolts of operations.

9.221 Pryor, William C., and Pryor, Helen S. *Let's Look at Advertising*. New York: Harcourt Brace, 1940, 243 pp.

>   Appears to be written for high school "civics" class. No index.

9.222 Pyle, Margory. *Advertising: A Field for Women*. Philadelphia: Bureau of Occupations, 1923, 48 pp.

>   Based on interviews in Philadelphia.

9.223 Ryan, Bernard. *So You Want to Go into Advertising*. New York: Harper, 1961, 178 pp.

9.224 Singer, Jules B. *Your Future in Advertising*. New York: Popular Library, 1961, 159 pp.

9.225 Woolf, James Davis. *Getting a Job in Advertising.* New York: Ronald, 1946, 103 pp.

See also 3.048, 3.077, 8.321, 9.204, 9.211.

"If I were starting life over again, I am inclined to think that I would go into the advertising business in preference to almost any other. This is because advertising has come to cover the whole range of human needs and also because it combines real imagination with a deep study of human psychology. Because it brings to the greatest number of people actual knowledge concerning useful things, it is essentially a form of education... It has risen with ever-growing rapidity to the dignity of an art. It is constantly paving new paths...The general raising of the standards of modern civilization among all groups of people during the past half century would have been impossible without the spreading of the knowledge of higher standards by means of advertising."

Franklin Delano Roosevelt*

*as quoted in <u>What We Think of Advertising</u>,BBD&O, 1966, unpaged

9.300   FACETIA AND SATIRE

9.301 Abe, Alan. *Crazy Ads*. New York: Citadel, 1960?, unpaged.

With drawings by Rudi Bass.

9.302 Anthony, Norman, and Delacorte, George T., Jr. *Ballyhoo*. New York: Simon & Schuster, 1931, 89 pp.

Selection of satirical pictures and ads from magazine of the same name published 1931 - 1939.

9.303 Benedict, Edward G. *The Wretchedness of Living in Town, or the Hallucinations of a City Man Who Ought to Know Better*. New York: n.p., 1900, 39 pp.

36 advertising pictures humourously illustrating one poem with 36 lines.

9.304 Case, Oliver F. *Fun for the Million and Business Ads Written in Verse*. New Haven: n.p., 1896, 128 pp.

The ad is bad and the verse is worse.

9.305 Dwiggins, Clare V. *Wants*. Philadelphia: J.C. Winston, 1909, 96 pp.

Cartoons illustrating newspaper want ads.

9.306 Farghor, George A. *The Log of a Sea-Going Advertising Solicitor*. Chicago: H.C. Wisnor, 1917, 20 pp.

Fantasy tales of "the world's greatest advertising solicitor."

9.307 Hartt, Rollin L. "The Humors of Advertising." *Atlantic Monthly* 93 (1904): 602 - 612.

Finding amusement in actual ads.

9.308 Johnson, Nunnally, "They Laughed!" *Harper's Magazine* 166 (December 1932): 119 - 122.

Fictional, humorous completion of stories typically used in advertising for correspondence courses.

9.309 Morgan, Henry, and Wagner, Gary. *And Now a Word From Our Sponsor*. New York: Citadel, 1960, unpaged.

Satirical ads and comments featuring Morgan, who mocked his own advertisers on his broadcasts as well.

9.310 Munson, Alexander D. *Lyrics of Trade for the Christmas and New Year's Holiday's, 1865 - 66*. New York: By the Author, 1865, 73 pp.

Verse on behalf of New York retailers. Alternative pages blank.

9.311 *Purely Personal*. New York. November 1935 - September 1942. No. 1 - 9.

> Numbering erratic; no. 4 lacks date. Reprints amusing personal newspaper ads.

9.312 Rollka, Arthur W. *Archibald Whootle on Advertising*. Tenafly, NJ: A.W. Publishers, 1962, 127 pp.

> Satirical on biographical reflections of ad men.

9.313 Rose, William G. *The Ginger Cure*. Cleveland: By the Author, 1911, 85 pp.

> Fictional portrayal of visit of ad man to retailer. Ginger: vigor, energy and push.

9.314 Shukle, Terrance. *Giraffe Raps: A Tale of Advertising in America*. Ann Arbor: Street Fiction Press, 1976, 112 pp.

> Slickly produced satirical ads, mocking current styles of advertising for drugs, tobacco, alcohol and sundry products of dubious social worth.

9.315 Simple Simon (pseud.). *The Simple Simon Series: Being a Collection of Adventures in the Life of ... "The Businessman Nobody Knows."* New York: Business Books, 1952, 110 pp.

> "Satirical tone reflects goodnatured and slight contempt for the tendency of big business to over-complicate its thinking." Copyright by E.B. Reeder.

9.316 Stokes, Charles W. "Simple Life - and How." *New Republic* 59 (10 July 1929): 203 - 05.

> Suggests (facetiously?) using advertising to promote the simple life.

9.317 Street, Julian L. *Sunbeams, Inc*. Garden City, NY: Doubleday, Page, 1920, 120 pp.

> Story of Belwyn Brown, advertising engineer. Fiction?

9.318 Thompson, T. Harry, ed. *Wilbur Waffle, Sloganeer: An Autobiography*. Philadelphia: Ayer, 1931, 83 pp.

> "A grin tale" -- mock biography and "who's whooey."

See also 9.032, 9.058, 9.083.

10.000
RELATED LITERATURE:
Marketing, Public
Relations, Broadcasting

10.001 Allen, James B. *The Company Town in the American West*. Norman, OK: University of Oklahoma Press, 1966, 205 pp.

Includes a brief chapter on company stores which draws heavily on Johnson's work. Supplemented with other information, especially on Phelps Dodge, the most persistent manufacturer-merchant.

10.002 Allyn, Stanley C. *My Half Century with NCR*. New York: McGraw-Hill, 1967, 209 pp.

Best for its description of flamboyant salesmanship pioneer, John H. Patterson, Allyn's predecessor as President.

10.003 Asher, Louis, and Heal, Edith. *Send No Money*. Chicago: Argus, 1942, 190 pp.

Readable anecdotal story of Sears and mail order business written by an insider to "set the record straight."

10.004 Assael, Henry, ed. *A Pioneer in Marketing: L.D.H. Weld, Collected Works, 1916 - 1941*. New York: Arno, 1978.

"Weld was one of the first writers to define marketing as an integrated set of activities separate from economics. In a series of articles in 1917 he defined the functional and institutional approaches to marketing." Weld analyzed costs and economic effects of marketing and advertising.

10.005 Assael, Henry, ed. *Early Development and Conceptualization of the Field of Marketing*. New York: Arno, 1978.

An anthology which "traces the development and conceptualization of marketing from the late 19th century writings of political economists on the processes of distribution to the earliest conceptualization of marketing into the commodity, functional and institutional approaches." See Bartels 10.014 - 17.

10.006 Atherton, Lewis E. *The Frontier Merchant in Mid-America*. Columbia, MO: University of Missouri Press, 1971, 183 pp.

A revised edition of *The Pioneer Merchant in Mid-America*. Pages 153 - 162 are specifically on advertising.

10.007 Atherton, Lewis E. *The Pioneer Merchant in Mid-America*. New York: De Capo, 1969, 135 pp. Originally published as vol. 14, no. 2 of the University of Missouri Studies, Columbia, 1939.

The evolution from peddlers to a mercantile class in U.S. frontiers from 1830 - 1860. Less readable than Carson's *General Store* but more suitable as a reference source.

10.008 Atherton, Lewis E. *The Southern Country Store, 1800 - 1860.*
Baton Rouge, LA: Louisiana State University Press, 1949, 227 pp.

> Scholarly discussion of the double function of goods distribution
> and cotton factor.

10.009 Bacon, Elizabeth M.   "Marketing Sewing Machines in the Post-Civil
War Years." *Bulletin of the Business Historical Society* 20 (3) (1946):
90 - 94.

> Brief article including material not in Andrew Jack's study of
> Singer.

10.010 Bailyn, Bernard. *The New England Merchants of the Seventeenth
Century.* Cambridge, MA: Harvard University Press, 1955, 249 pp.

> Scholarly work, often cited.

10.011 Barach, Arnold B. *Famous American Trademarks.*   Washington, DC:
Public Affairs Press, 1971, 192 pp.

> Drawn from a column in Kiplingers *Changing Times,* "The News
> Behind the Ads," this book has some 100 different 2 - 300 word
> mini-stories on trademarks. As poor as Lambert, which makes
> Campbell's *Why Did They Name It* the best of a poor competition.

10.012 Barger, Harold. *Distribution's Place in the American Economy
Since 1869.* Princeton, NJ: Princeton University Press, 1955, 222 pp.

> Commissioned by the National Bureau of Economic Research, assess-
> ing the changing costs of distribution, hours worked, productiv-
> ity, etc. Better than most economists' work in that it does
> describe real changes in institutional practice during the
> period covered, 1869 - 1949.

10.013 Barnouw, Erik. *A Tower in Babel: A History of Broadcasting in
the United States to 1933.* New York: Oxford University Press, 1966.

_____. *The Golden Web: A History of Broadcasting in the United
States, 1933 - 1953.* New York: Oxford University Press, 1968.

_____. *The Image Empire: A History of Broadcasting in the United
States from 1953.* New York: Oxford University Press, 1970.

> This trilogy is the definitive history of broadcasting, comparable
> to Mott's, *History of American Magazines.* A condensation of this
> work, the *Tube of Plenty: The Evolution of American Television,*
> was published in 1975.

10.014 Bartels, Robert. *The Development of Marketing Thought.* Homewood, IL: Irwin, 1962, 284 pp.

> A survey of the changing conceptualization of marketing activity
> in the twentieth century. Although critically reviewed (more for
> the shortcomings in marketing thought than for the author's fail-
> ures), this is nonetheless valuable if for nothing else than an
> extensive bibliography.

10.015 Bartels, Robert. *The History of Marketing Thought*. Columbus, OH: Grid, 1976, 327 pp.

A new edition of *The Development of Marketing Thought*. Contains a chapter specifically on advertising.

10.016 Bartels, Robert. "Influences on the Development of Marketing Thought, 1900 - 1923." *Journal of Marketing* 16 (July 1951): 1 - 17.

Biographical sketches included.

10.017 Bartels, Robert. *Marketing Literature: Development and Apprai-sal*. New York: Arno, 1978.

Republication of Ph.D. dissertation, Ohio State University, 1941. Bartel's hypothesis is that "early marketing scholars' research and writing resulted from external experience and internal per-ceptions." Reviews the literature between 1900 - 1940. Includes letters from 31 marketing theorists explaining why they studied marketing.

10.018 Beckman, Theodore N., and Nolen, Herman C. *The Chain Store Problem: A Critical Analysis*. New York: McGraw-Hill, 1938, 350 pp.

Prepared by academics as part of the often bitter depression controversy. Presents original research on prices, consumer attitudes, legislation and a chapter on the history of chain stores.

10.019 Bernays, Edward L. *Crystallizing Public Opinion*. New York: Liveright, 1961, 219 pp.

Another edition of a 1923 classic, "the first book-length dis-cussion of the scope and function of professional public rela-tions," this has a preface with the author's view of the histori-cal evolution and professionalization.

10.020 Bernays, Edward L. "Emergence of the Public Relations Counsel: Principles and Recollections." *Business History Review* 45 (1971): 296 - 315.

Combines the reminiscences of one of the "founding fathers" of public relations counseling for corporate clients with the same author's philosophy of his profession and a defense of its role against some criticism it has received. Includes experiences with American Tobacco during the era of George Washington Hill and Alfred Sloan's General Motors Corporation.

10.021 Bernays, Edward L., ed. *The Engineering of Consent*. Norman: University of Oklahoma Press, 1955, 246 pp.

Despite jacket cover claim to being social science, and a section on research by Sherwood Dodge, this is still a reader offering miscellaneous ideas and anecdotes. Notwithstanding, widely read and quoted.

10.022 Bolles, Joshua K. *The People's Business: The Progress of Con-*
sumer Cooperatives in America. New York: Harper, 1942, 170 pp.

> A journalistic history of consumer cooperatives.

10.023 Boorstin, Daniel J. "A. Montgomery Ward's Mail-Order Business."
Chicago History 2 (1973): 142 - 52.

> By tying his company to the Patrons of Husbandry (the Grangers),
> Ward could offer rural America goods in continuing competition
> with Richard Sears.

10.024 Boorstin, Daniel J. *The Americans: The Democratic Experience.*
New York: Random, 1973, 717 pp.

> One of an outstanding trilogy, this volume covers many aspects
> of marketing history including department stores, selling,
> franchising, installment buying and has a focus on "consumption
> communities." Author an outstanding historian, director of the
> Smithsonian Institute, and Librarian of Congress.

10.025 Bradshaw, T.F. "Superior Methods Created by the Early Chain
Store." *Bulletin of the Business Historical Society* 17 (April 1943):
35 - 43.

> Covers 1870 - 1914 and defends the chain store idea.

10.026 Brown, Les. *Television: The Business Behind the Box.* New York:
Harcourt, Brace, Jovanovich, 1971, 374 pp.

> Discussion of TV spot-buying practices and their implications.

10.027 Campbell, Hannah. *Why Did They Name It ...?* New York: Bell,
1964, 207 pp.

> Republication of a series of articles originally appearing in
> *Cosmopolitan* magazine, these are brief journalistic discussions
> of various firms and trade marks.

10.028 Carson, Gerald. *Cornflake Crusade: From the Pulpit to the*
Breakfast Table. New York: Rinehart, 1957, 305 pp.

> How food faddists put Battle Creek, Michigan on the map, written
> by an ex-advertising executive.

10.029 Carson, Gerald. "The Machine That Kept Them Honest." In *Great*
Stories of American Businessmen, pp. 334 - 347. New York: American
Heritage, 1972.

> The story of National Cash Register and its founder, super-
> salesman J.H. Patterson.

10.030 Carson, Gerald. *The Old Country Store.* New York: Dutton, 1965,
330 pp.

> Won a prize from the American Historical Association when it was
> first published in 1954.

10.031   Carson, Gerald. *The Roguish World of Doctor Brinkley*.   New York: Rinehart, 1960, 280 pp.

The story of one of the great radio medicine men, selling "goat-gland" sex rejuvenation true to the flamboyant style of his tradition. Essentially the story of successful promotion and mass merchandising via media.

10.032   Clark, Thomas D. *Pills, Petticoats and Plows*. New York: Bobbs-Merrill, 1944, 359 pp.

Not as informative as it might be about the history of general stores in America.

10.033   Clay, Floyd M. *Coozan Dudley LeBlanc: From Huey to Hadacol*. Gretna, LA: Pelican, 1973, 264 pp.

An annotated history of the last of the great patent medicine promoters whose Hadacol Caravan sold millions of dollars of merchandise.

10.034   Cohen, Ira. "The Auction System in the Port of New York: 1817 - 1937." *Business History Review* 45 (1971): 500 - 10.

An interesting description of the once dominant auction system, and how new channels of distribution rose to take its place.

10.035   Cole, Arthur H. "Marketing Non-Consumer Goods Before 1917." *Business History Review* 33 (1959): 420 - 28.

A review of secondary sources to highlight the development of branch sales offices (i.e. Singer), salesmanship (i.e. John Patterson, NCR) and sales promotion and advertising.

10.036   Deleted.

10.037   Converse, Paul D. *The Beginning of Marketing Thought in the United States: With Reminiscences of Some of the Pioneer Marketing Scholars*. Austin; TX: University of Texas, Bureau of Business Research, 1959.

Reprinted in 1978 by Arno.

10.038   Converse, Paul D. "The Development of the Science of Marketing: An Exploratory Survey." *Journal of Marketing* 10 (July 1945): 14 - 23.

Results of a survey of 45 scholars who began their careers before 1925. Presents their opinions as to the value of various books and articles. Good bibliographic leads for sources of measured importance in influencing the field.

10.039   Converse, Paul D. *Fifty Years of Marketing in Retrospect*. Studies in Marketing, no. 5. Austin, TX: Bureau of Business Research, 1959, 104 pp.

10.040 Coolsen, Frank G. *Marketing Thought in the United States in the Late Nineteenth Century.* Lubbock, TX: Texas Tech Press, 1960, 231 pp.

> Misleading title, this dissertation is concerned only with the thought of four economists: Atkinson, Wells and two Farquhars.

10.041 Daughters, Charles G. *Wells of Discontent: A Study in the Economic, Social and Political Aspects of the Chain Store.* New York: Newson, 1937, 370 pp.

> Hysterical and strongly anti chain store. A counterpart to Lebhar. A good section on lobbying methods and propaganda of chains.

10.042 Dietz, Lawrence. *Soda Pop: The History, Advertising, Art and Memorabilia of Soft Drinks in America.* New York: Simon & Schuster, 1973, 184 pp.

> Published for the gift market, nonetheless quite good. Focuses heavily on the Coca-Cola Co. despite the title, and was written with access to all of the Coca-Cola archival files.

10.043 Dolan, J. *The Yankee Peddlers of America.* New York: Potter, 1964, 270 pp.

> Excellent book, more readable than Richardson's.

10.044 Donovan, Richard, and Whitney, Dwight. "Painless Parker: Last of America's Tooth-Plumbers." *Collier's,* 5 January 1952, pp. 12 ff.

> Entrepreneurial promotion a la Barnum. Serialized, see subsequent issues.

10.045 Emmett, Boris, and Jeuck, John E. *Catalogues and Counters: A History of Sears, Roebuck and Company.* Chicago: University of Chicago Press, 1950, 788 pp.

> A thorough, competent piece of scholarship.

10.046 Fuller, Alfred C. *A Foot in the Door: The Life Appraisal of the Original Fuller Brush Man.* New York: McGraw-Hill, 1960, 250 pp.

> Paperback version given as a token reward to successful "Fullerettes."

10.047 Galambos, Louis. *Competition and Cooperation: The Emergence of a Modern Trade Association.* Baltimore: Johns Hopkins University Press, 1966, 329 pp.

> The history of the Cotton Textile Institute, 1880 - 1935, with particular attention on the last decade. Valuable as so few trade associations have been recorded by scholars.

10.048 Golden, Lou L. *Only by Public Consent: American Corporations Search for Favorable Opinion.* New York: Hawthorne, 1968, 386 pp.

> Public relations by major firms, American Telephone & Telegraph, Standard Oil of N.J., General Motors, and Dupont.

10.049 Goldman, Arich. "Stages in the Development of the Supermarket."
Journal of Retailing 51 (Winter 1975): 49 - 64.

        To the new Hyper-marchés.

10.050 Gras, N.S.B. "Shifts in Public Relations." *Bulletin of the
Business Historical Society* 19 (October 1945): 97+.

        Good pioneering historical effort.

10.051 Grether, E.T. "The First Forty Years." *Journal of Marketing* 40
(July 1976): 63 - 69.

        A history of the content of the *Journal of Marketing*, the leading
        journal in the field for both the professional and, for many
        years, the academic audience.

10.052 Hartley, Robert F. *Marketing Mistakes*. Columbus, OH: Grid,
1976, 147 pp.

        Case histories of the disasters of the Edsel, Dupont's Corfam,
        W.T. Grant, J.C. Penney, Montgomery Ward and others. The last
        two focus on the late 40's, while the remaining are from the late
        60's and 70's.

10.053 Henry, Kenneth. *Defenders and Shapers of the Corporate Image*.
New Haven: College & University Press, 1972, 240 pp.

        An academic study of the sociological history of public relations,
        addressing the question of whether an occupational group can
        professionalize in a bureaucratic setting.

10.054 Hollander, Stanley C. "Consumerism and Retailing: A Historical
Perspective." *Journal of Retailing* 48 (Winter 1972); 6 - 21.

        Focuses on food retailing.

10.055 Hollander, Stanley C. "Entrepreneurs Test the Environment: A
Long Run View of Grocery Pricing." Paper presented at the American
Marketing Association Conference, Chicago, 3 September 1966.

        "A review of grocery store pricing and merchandising practices,
        based upon examination of trade magazines, 1869 - 1949."

10.056 Hollander, Stanley C. *History of Labels: A Record of the Past
Developed in the Search for the Origins of an Industry*. New York: A.
Hollander, 1956, 46 pp.

        Detail of research findings, but mostly before the 20th century,
        and antiquarian in character.

10.057 Hollander, Stanley C. "Nineteenth Century Anti-Drummer Legislation in the United States." *Business History Review* 38 (1964): 479 -
500.

        Also includes material on the formation of commercial travellers'
        mutual benefit organizations.

10.058   Hollander, Stanley C. *The Rise and Fall of a Buying Club.* Marketing and Transportation Paper, no. 3. East Lansing, MI: Bureau of Business and Economic Research, 1959, 43 pp.

> The "club" is the oddly named Association of Army and Navy Stores, Inc., formed in 1916 as a buying club for discounts and liquidated in 1952. Thoroughly documented from primary sources.

10.059   Hollander, Stanley C. *Sales Devices Through the Ages.* New York: Meier, 1953, 32 pp.

> A pamphlet with accurately cited facts, but superficial in that its prime function was to promote sales promotion devices.

10.060   Hollander, Stanley C. "She Shops for You or With You." In *New Essays in Marketing Theory,* pp. 218 - 240. Edited by George Fisk. Boston: Allyn & Bacon, 1971.

> Discussion of the "professional shoppers," a minor role performed from 1850 - 1940 and suggestions about their possible resurgence.

10.061   Hollander, Stanley C., and Marple, Gary A. *Henry Ford: Inventor of the Supermarket?* Bureau of Business Research, Marketing Paper, no. 9. East Lansing, MI: Michigan State University, 1960, 56 pp.

> Story of the most sophisticated of "company stores," the Ford commissaries. Organized in assembly line concepts and in answer to public fear of chain stores.

10.062   Hotchkiss, George B. *Milestones in Marketing.* New York: Macmillan, 1938, 305 pp.

> A survey of the growth of marketing.

10.063   *How They Sell: The Successful Marketing Techniques of 13 Major American Corporations.* New York: Dow Jones, 1965, 208 pp.

> Includes Muntz TV, Mattel (Barbie Dolls), Levitt & Sons (Levittown), H.J. Heinz, Electrolux and State Farm Insurance among others.

10.064   Hower, Ralph M. *History of Macy's of New York,* 1858 - 1919. Cambridge, MA: Harvard University Press, 1943, 500 pp.

> An excellent academic study of a pioneer department store. Probably the best single source for detailed information.

10.065   Hower, Ralph M. "Urban Retailing 100 Years Ago." *Bulletin of the Business Historical Society* 12 (December 1938): 91 - 95.

> Discusses the specialization which predated department stores.

10.066   Hower, Ralph M. "Wanted: Material on the History of Marketing." *Bulletin of the Business Historical Society* 9 (1935): 79 - 81.

> A plea for original materials, but could equally be a plea for scholarly attention to such materials.

10.067 Hutchinson, William T. *Cyrus Hall McCormick*. 2 vols. New York:
Da Capo Press, 1968.

A scholarly reprint of the 1930 edition. Volume I, Chapter 14 is
on "Advertising the McCormick Reaper and Mower."

10.068 Jack, Andrew. "The Channels of Distribution for an Innovation:
The Sewing Machine Industry in America, 1860 - 1865." *Explorations in
Entrepreneurial History* 9 (3), February 1957: 113 - 41.

A scholarly description rich in data, but not much on promotion.

10.069 Johnson, Ole Simon. *The Industrial Store: Its History, Operations and Economic Significance*. Atlanta: University of Georgia Press,
1952, 171 pp.

A scholarly history of Pennsylvania coal town company stores.

10.070 Johnson, Roy W., and Lynch, Russell W. *The Sales Strategy of
John H. Patterson*. New York: Dartnell, 1932, 344 pp.

Patterson was the founder of National Cash Register, and has
been described as the "Napolean of Modern Sales Promotion." This
is the most detailed description of the specific sales techniques
used and the role of advertising. Includes the famous blueprint
sales plan.

10.071 Jones, Fred M. *Middlemen in the Domestic Trade of the United
States, 1800 - 1860*. Urbana: University of Illinois Press, 1937, 81 pp.

The best work until Porter and Livesay.

10.072 Jones, Fred M. "Retail Stores in the United States, 1800 - 1860."
Journal of Marketing 1 (October 1936): 134 - 42.

A review of general stores and early chain and department stores.

10.073 Kelley, Stanley, Jr. *Professional Public Relations and Political
Power*. Baltimore: Johns Hopkins Press, 1956, 247 pp.

Academic, including a little material on the use of advertising.

10.074 Kelley, Thomas P., Jr. *The Fabulous Kelley: Canada's King of
the Medicine Men*. Don Mills, ON: General Publishing, 1974, 149 pp.

Reminiscences of the son of the man who ran a medicine show from
1890 to 1931 and sold Shamrock Nerve Tablets, etc. But best
known for his tapeworm lecture to sell his New Oriental Discovery.
Includes sample pitches.

10.075 Kelley, William T. "The Development of Early Thought in Marketing
and Promotion." *Journal of Marketing* 21 (July 1956): 62 - 67.

In some ways more satisfying than Bartels' work, probably because
of its brevity.

10.076 Lambert, Issas E. *The Public Accepts: Stories Behind Famous Trade Marks, Names and Slogans*. Alberquerque: University of New Mexico, 1941, 253 pp.

> Despite an introduction by William Allen White, this is a very disappointing effort consisting of 110 1 - 2 page PR department vignettes. Much white space and large type.

10.077 Lebhar, Geoffrey M. *The Chain Store: Boon or Bane*. New York: Harper, 1932, 206 pp.

> Widely read defence of chains, but not very informative.

10.078 Lebhar, Geoffrey M. *Chain Stores in America, 1859 - 1962*. New York: Chain Store Publishing, 1963, 430 pp.

> Presents statistical data on major chains and a good discussion on the interwar lobbying against chains. Still the best historical overview.

10.079 Lloyd, Craig. *Aggressive Introvert: Herbert Hoover and Public Relations Management, 1912 - 1932*. Columbus: Ohio State University Press, 1973, 206 pp.

10.080 McNamara, Brooks. *Step Right Up: An Illustrated History of the American Medicine Show*. Garden City, NY: Doubleday, 1976, 233 pp.

> Well researched book, designed for the gift market. Covers many early 20th Century (pre WW II) characters. See also Young's *Toadstool Millionaires,* to which this is a fascinating companion piece.

10.081 Mahoney, Tom, and Sloane, Leonard. *The Great Merchants*. New York: Harper & Row, 1966, 375 pp.

> Despite the fact this is a second edition, and that the first was translated into several languages, this is a relatively poor collection of descriptions of the giants of American retailing. Generally written as if a vanity press operation.

10.082 Markin, Ron J. *The Supermarket: An Analysis of Growth, Development and Change*. Pullman: Washington State University, 1968, 164 pp.

> Much of the attention on history.

10.083 Marquette, Arthur F. *Brands, Trademarks and Goodwill: The Story of the Quaker Oats Company*. New York: McGraw-Hill, 1967, 274 pp.

> Many references to advertising in the index.

10.084 Michelman, Irving S. *Consumer Finance: A Case History in American Business*. New York: Fell, 1966, 336 pp.

> A well written history of the legitimization of lending by a member of the industry. Concerns primarily the Russell Sage Foundation reform movement of 1910 ff.

10.085   Deleted.

10.086   Mott, Frank L.   *History of American Magazines, 1865 - 1885.*   5 vols.   Cambridge: Harvard University Press, 1938.

>   Best source for information on magazines.   See also Mott's *History of United States Newspapers*.

10.087   Myers, Kenneth H., Jr., and Smalley, Orange A.   "Marketing History and Economic Development."   *Business History Review* 33 (1959):   387 - 401.

>   A report and commentary on two conferences concerning the need for a history of marketing in the United States.   Conferences instigated by Arthur H. Cole.

10.088   Pasdermadjian, Hrant.   *The Department Store: Its Origins, Evolution and Economics.*   London: Newman, 1954, 217 pp.

>   First three chapters are a good review of secondary literature on the evolution of the department store, but difficult to find.   Written for the International Association of Department Stores.   International and praising in perspective.

10.089   Porter, Glen, and Livesay, Harold.   *Merchants and Manufacturers: Studies in the Changing Structure of Nineteenth Century Marketing.*   Baltimore: Johns Hopkins Press, 1971, 257 pp.

>   An excellent study, focusing on the shift in the use of channels of distribution that made mass markets and hence mass production possible.

10.090   Raucher, Alan.   *Public Relations and Business, 1900 - 1929.*   Baltimore: Johns Hopkins University Press, 1968, 178 pp.

>   Scholarly treatment based in part on the papers of Ivy Lee and John Price Jones.   Selected and annotated bibliography, pp. 157 - 172.   Attributes growth of the PR function to the communications needs of a mass market, not political defensiveness.

10.091   Resseguie, Harry E.   "Alexander Turney Stewart and the Development of the Department Store, 1823 - 1876."   *Business History Review* 39 (1965):   301 - 22.

>   Good information on the formation of policies central to the emerging form of retailing now known as the department store.

10.092   Rich, Edwin Ernest.   *The History of the Hudson's Bay Co., 1670 - 1870.*   New York: Macmillan, 1958 - 59, 2 vol.

>   A very detailed account of early history and growth of the Bay by the company's archivist.   The best of many.

10.093   Rosenberg, Larry J., ed.   *The Roots of Marketing Strategy: A Collection of Pre-1950 Readings.*   New York: Arno, 1978.

>   Includes articles on marketing research and demand, buying be-

haviors, product pricing, distribution and advertising strategy, sales management, and marketing productivity.

10.094   Ross, Irwin. *The Image Merchants: The Fabulous World of Public Relations*. Garden City, NY: Doubleday, 288 pp.

A journalistic trip through the major PR firms. A good companion piece to Mayer's *Madison Avenue USA*.

10.095   Shapiro, Stanley J., and Doody, Alton F. *Readings in the History of American Marketing: Settlement to Civil War*. Homewood, IL: Irwin, 1968, 484 pp.

Covering many aspects of marketing including distribution, transportation, credit, advertising, pedlars, general stores, etc. Bibliography on marketing to 1860.

10.096   Silk, Alvin J., and Stern, Louis William. "The Changing Nature of Innovation in Marketing: A Study of Selected Business Leaders, 1852 - 1958." *Business History Review* 37 (1963): 182 - 99.

Drawing on secondary sources, the author's main thesis is that the risks of innovation used to be assumed with entrepreneurial boldness and naivete and are now assumed to be following rational managerial analysis.

10.097   Smalley, Orange A., and Sturdivant, Frederick D. *The Credit Merchants: A History of Spiegel, Inc*. Carbondale: Southern Illinois University Press, 1973, 336 pp.

An excellent job by competent marketing scholars, aided by Sturdivant's experience with "The History of American Hospital Supply," his dissertation. Pity the firm is not more interesting, being yet another mail order firm from Chicago.

10.098   Smith, Clayton L. *The History of Trade Marks*. New York: n.p., 1923, 71 pp.

10.099   Sobel, Robert. *The Manipulators: America in a Media Age*. Garden City, NY: Doubleday, 1976, 458 pp.

A one volume history of the media, but Barnouw's work makes a better reference source.

10.100 Stalson, Owen. *Marketing Life Insurance: Its History in America*. Cambridge, MA: Harvard University Press, 1942.

Considering the nature of corporate histories in this industry, this is a gem.

10.101   Tedlow, Richard S. "Keeping the Corporate Image: Public Relations and Business, 1900 - 1950." Ph.D. dissertation, Columbia University, 1976, 404 pp.

A well written and researched review, deserving of greater exposure.

10.102 Tedlow, Richard S.   "The National Association of Manufacturers and Public Relations During the New Deal." *Business History Review* 50 (Spring 1976): 24 - 45.

By using PR heavily in the depression, the N.A.M. helped make itself a permanent fixture in American corporate life. An excellent study.

10.103 Tonning, Wayland A.   "The Beginnings of Money-Back Guarantee and the One-Price Policy in Champaign-Urbana, Illinois, 1833 - 1880." *Business History Review* 30 (1956): 196 - 210.

Traces the history of these retailing practices.

10.104 Twyman, Robert W. *History of Marshall Field & Co., 1852 - 1906.* Philadelphia: University of Pennsylvania Press, 1954, 249 pp.

Scholarly study, second in importance only to Hower's *Macy's.*

10.105 Wagner, Susan. *Cigarette Country: Tobacco in American History and Politics.* New York: Praeger, 1971, 248 pp.

Much on advertising, but mostly in 50's and 60's.

10.106 Weil, Gordon L. *Sears, Roebuck, U.S.A.: The Great American Catalog Store and How it Grew.* New York: Stein & Day, 1977, 277 pp.

Treatment by an independent journalist. See also Emmet and Jeuck.

10.107 Westerfield, Roy B.   "Early History of American Auctions: A Chapter in Commercial History." *Transactions of the Connecticut Academy of Arts and Sciences* 23 (May 1920): 159 - 210.

Auction selling in New York, early 19th century.

10.108 Woodman, Harold D.   "Itinerant Cotton Merchants of the Antebellum South." *Agricultural History* 40 (April 1966): 79 - 90.

A discussion of itinerant merchants which reappears in a slightly different form as chapter eight of Woodman's *King Cotton and His Retainers.*

10.109 Wooster, Harvey.   "A Forgotten Factor in American Industrial History." *American Economic Review* 16 (March 1926): 14 - 27.

Reprinted in Shapiro and Doody as "The General Store: A Marketing Axis of the Period," it explores the role played by early 19th century general stores in helping New England's industry develop.

10.110 Wright, John S.   "A Brief Marketing History of the Jewel Tea Company." *Journal of Marketing* 22 (April 1958): 367 - 76.

An abstract of a Ph.D. dissertation (Ohio State, 1954) covering 1901 - 1951. Not very insightful.

10.111 Wright, John S., and Parks, B. Dimsdale, Jr., eds. *Pioneers in Marketing*. Atlanta: Georgia State University Press, 1974, 162 pp.

> A collection of 25 biographies of men who contributed to the growth of marketing thought. All originally appeared in scattered issues of the *Journal of Marketing*.

10.112 Wright, Richardson L. *Hawkers and Walkers in Early America*. Philadelphia: Lippincott, 1927, 317 pp.

> Early scholarly treatise on pedlars, medicine men, etc.

10.113 Young, James H. "The Hadacol Phenomenon." *Emory University Quarterly* 7 (June 1951): 72 - 86.

> Interesting account as Young is both an excellent historian and had the opportunity to travel with the Hadacol Caravan.

10.114 Young, James H. *The Medical Messiahs: A Social History of Health Quackery in Twentieth Century America*. Princeton: Princeton University Press, 1967, 460 pp.

> Were it not for the thorough scholarship displayed, this book would be labelled a muckraker. A sequel to *Toadstool Million-aires,* this story essentially follows the history of laws and prosecution for misleading advertising in the U.S. and the man-oeuvres of the comtemporary medicine men to avoid prosecution.

10.115 Young, James H. *The Toadstool Millionaires*. Princeton: Princeton University Press, 1961, 282 pp.

> The history of patent medicines and their selling.

10.116 Zimmerman, M.M. *The Challenge of Chain Store Distribution*. New York: Harper, 1931, 334 pp.

> Pro-chains and authored by a "chain store merchandising council." Nonetheless, informative.

10.117 Zimmerman, M.M. *The Supermarket: A Revolution in Distribution*. New York: Mass Distribution, 1955, 340 pp.

> Good source.

11.000
FICTION

11.001 Allen, Ralph. *Chartered Libertine*. New York: St. Martin's, 1955, 270 pp.

11.002 Amory, Cleveland. *Home Town*. New York: Harper, 1950, 310 pp.

    Ballyhoo in the publishing world.

11.003 Andrews, Robert D. *Legend of a Lady; The Story of Rita Martin*. NY: Coward-McCann, 1949, 342 pp.

    Woman executive of soap opera accounts.

11.004 Angell, Roger. *Stone Arbor and Other Stories*. Boston: Little, Brown, 1961, 245 pp.

    Short stories of the middleclass originally appearing in the *New Yorker*.

11.005 Asinof, Eliot. *Bedfellow*. New York: Simon & Schuster, 1968, 223 pp.

11.006 Aurthur, Robert A. *Glorification of Al Toolum*. NY: Rinehart, 1952, 244 pp.

    Common man makes good.

11.007 Bardin, John F. *Christmas Comes But Once A Year*. New York: Scribner, 1954, 241 pp.

    Personal reactions to death of a child.

11.008 Beauvoir, Simoine de. *Les Belles Images*. NY: Putnam, 1968, 224 pp.

    Set in Paris, but author widely read in U.S.

11.009 Bercovici, Rion. *For Immediate Release*. NY: Sheridan, 1937, 317 pp.

    On improbable press agentry.

11.010 Bernstein, Abraham. *Home is the Hunted*. NY: Dial, 1947, 308 pp.

    Anti-semitism in agencies.

11.011 Bissell, Richard. *Julia Harrington: Winnebago, Iowa, 1913*. Boston: Little, Brown, 1969, 84 pp.

    In the form of a diary of an adolescent girl, whose purpose is the painting of an historical scene not the telling of a dramatic story. This book is delightful and beautifully illustrated with advertising, trade cards, catalogue pages and other printed commercial ephemera "collected by Julia."

11.012 Boyle, Harry J. *The Great Canadian Novel*. Toronto: Doubleday, 1972, 343 pp.

Story of dissipation of ex-advertising man, with some flashbacks.

11.013 Brinkley, William. *Don't Go Near the Water*. New York: Random, 1956, 373 pp.

Public relations in WW II Navy made into a movie.

11.014 Brown, Lee D. *Destiny is a Woman*. NY: Egmont, 1938, 358 pp.

For a man who finds career meaningless.

11.015 Buck, Pearl S. *Other Gods: An American Legend*. New York: J. Day, 1940, 381 pp.

Impact of celebrity status on young mountain climber by Nobel Prize winner, although not for this.

11.016 Burlingame, Roger. *You Too*. NY: Scribner, 1924, 302 pp.

Copywriting compromises literary aspirations.

11.017 Burnett, John G. *Company Man*. NY: Harper, 1956, 248 pp.

Airlines advertising.

11.018 Constable, George. *What Shy Men Dream*. New York: Harcourt, Brace & World, 1969, 124 pp.

11.019 Corley, Eric. *Acapulco Gold*. New York: Dodd, Mead, 1972, 329 pp.

11.020 Daley, Joseph A. *Spicy Lady*. New York: St. Martin's, 1973, 210 pp.

11.021 De Mare, George. *The Empire*. New York: Putnam, 1956, 317 pp.

Public relations in the executive suite.

11.022 Dillon, Jack. *The Advertising Man*. New York: Harper's, 1972, 316 pp.

V-P, Doyle Dane Bernbach tells tale of copy chief who can't adjust to importance of market research.

11.023 DiMinno, Nicholas. *Half a Dollar is Better Than None*. NY: Doubleday, 1952, 250 pp.

Satirical.

11.024 Eichler, Alfred. *Death Of An Ad Man*. New York: Abelard-Schumann, 1954, 251 pp.

Detective, defective.

11.025 Eichler, Alfred. *Murder in the Radio Department*. New York:
Gold Label, 1943, 253 pp.

      Detective story.

11.026 Elsschot, William (pseud.). *Soft Soap*. In *Three Novels*. New
York: House & Maxwell, 1965, 252 pp.

      British setting.

11.027 Finney, Jack. *Time and Again*. New York: Simon and Schuster,
1970.

      Contemporary adman time travels to 1882 New York.

11.028 Foreman, Robert L. *The Hot Half Hour*. New York: Criterion,
1958, 190 pp.

      By head of Radio-TV for BBD&O, the fiction is poor but the detail
      "written with savvy and authenticity" - *N.Y. Herald Tribune*
      October 5, 1958, p. 11.

11.029 Freegood, Morton. *The Wall-to-Wall Trap: A Novel*. New York:
Simon & Schuster, 1957, 243 pp.

11.030 Gardner, Herb. *A Piece of the Action*. New York: Simon & Schuster, 1958, 313 pp.

      A light novel whose hero creates a commercialized character
      called "The Slob."

11.031 Gasner, Beverley. *Nina Upstairs*. NY: Knopf, 1964, 180 pp.

      By ex-copywriter of NY retail ads.

11.032 Goldsmith, Gene. *Layout For A Corpse*. New York: Mill, 1949,
245 pp.

      Detective story, obviously.

11.033 Greig, Maysie. *Heart Appeal*. NY: Doubleday, 1935, 300 pp.

      Romance in life of retail copywriter.

11.034 Gribble, Leonard R. *Don't Argue with Death*. New York: Roy,
1959, 190 pp.

11.035 Grumbine, E. Evalyn. *Patsy Breaks into Advertising*. NY: Dodd,
1939, 324 pp.

      Career advice for older juveniles.

11.036 Haberman, Helen L. *How About Tomorrow Morning?* NY: Prentice-
Hall, 1945, 264 pp.

      Heroine an advertising career woman.

11.037 Hannibal, Edward. *Chocolate Days, Popsicle Weeks*. Boston:
Houghton Mifflin, 1970, 376 pp.

> Publisher gave author a "literary fellowship award." Study in
> character egocentricity, not exposé of materialism.

11.038 Harrison, Charles Y. *Nobody's Fool: A Novel*. New York: Holt,
1948, 300 pp.

> Title refers to a "common man" found by a P.R. firm, to their
> regret.

11.039 Hartswick, Frederick G. *The Winning Line*. NY: Covici, 1934,
248 pp.

> Satire on a soap promotion contest.

11.040 Herber, William. *Death Paints A Portrait*. Philadelphia: Lippincott, 1958, 223 pp.

11.041 Hine, Al. *Birthday Boy*. NY: Scribner, 1959, 374 pp.

> Reflections on career of ad man by associates on his birthday.

11.042 Hobson, Laura Z. *The Celebrity: A Novel*. New York: Simon &
Schuster, 1951, 308 pp.

> Effects of a novelist's success on those near and far.

11.043 Hyams, Edward S. *The Slaughterhouse Informer*. Philadelphia:
Lippincott, 1955, 256 pp.

> English publicity and publishing world.

11.044 Hyams, Eric. *Into the Dream*. New York: Longmans, Green, 1957,
278 pp.

11.045 Iams, Jack. *Prematurely Gay*. New York: Morrow, 1948, 248 pp.

> Humorous, promotion of hair-oil.

11.046 Kazan, Elia. *The Arrangement: A Novel*. NY: Stein & Day, 1967,
444 pp.

> Author a prominent theatre director.

11.047 Keating, Henry R.F. *Death and the Visiting Firemen*. Garden City,
NY: Doubleday, 1973, 234 pp.

11.048 Kelly, James. *The Insider*. New York: Holt, 1958, 384 pp.

> Experienced author tells tales, particularly of management of
> drug accounts.

11.049 Kiefer, Middleton (pseud.). *Pax*. New York: Random, 1958,
279 pp.

> The marketing of Pax, a tranquilizer by two former drug industry
> P.R. men, Harry Middleton and Warren Kiefer.

11.050 Kirk, Jeremy (pseud.). *The Build-up Boys*. New York: Scribner,
1951, 242 pp.

> Public relations for Cloverleaf Milk Co.

11.051 Leinster, Murray (pseud.). *Operation: Outer Space*. Reading,
PA: Fantasy Press, 1954, 208 pp.

> Same as William F. Jenkins.

11.052 Leokum, Arkady. *Please Send Me, Absolutely Free...* NY: Harper,
1946, 337 pp.

> Satire on agency life viewed by a copywriter.

11.053 Leonard, John. *The Naked Martini*. Garden City, NY: Doubleday,
1964, 255 pp.

> A member of the lost generation from Harvard lost in New York
> decadence.

11.054 Livingston, Harold. *The Detroiters*. Boston: Houghton Mifflin,
1957, 342 pp.

> Automobile advertising careers.

11.055 Longstreet, Stephen. *The Flesh Peddlers: A Novel*. New York:
Simon & Schuster, 1962, 351 pp.

11.056 Longstreet, Stephen. *The Promoters: A Modern Novel*. New York:
Simon & Schuster, 1957, 373 pp.

> Story of Texas industrial tycoon, told by his publicity mail in
> robust, bad prose.

11.057 Longstreet, Stephen. *She Walks in Beauty: A Novel*. New York:
Arbor, 1970, 312 pp.

11.058 Loring, Emile. *As Long As I Live*. Philadelphia: Penn, 1937,
308 pp.

> Sentimental romance of commercial artist with heads of rival
> agencies.

11.059 McKay, Allis. *Women About Town*. NY: MacMillan, 1938, 279 pp.

> Heroine a Chicago commercial artist.

11.060 McLaughlin, Robert. *The Notion of Sin.* New York: Simon &
Schuster, 1959, 217 pp.

    Life among the savages in New York's advertising and publishing
    circles.

11.061 McMullen, Mamy. *Strangle Hold.* New York: Harper, 1951, 206 pp.

    Detective story.

11.062 Mannin, Ethel E. *Sounding Brass.* New York: Duffield, 1926,
340 pp.

    English advertising world.

11.063 Mano, D. Keith. *The Death of Henry Goth.* New York: Knopf, 1971,
505 pp.

    Black humor in the industrial sanitation biz.

11.064 Mead, E. Shepherd. *The Admen.* New York: Simon & Schuster, 1958,
309 pp.

    Authroed by V-P from ad agency on second career, with conflict
    over hard-sell vs. soft-sell, which seems a peculiarly dated
    theme.

11.065 Mead, E. Shepherd. *The Big Ball of Wax: A Story of Tomorrow's
Happy World: A Novel.* New York: Simon & Schuster, 1954, 246 pp.

    Set in 1992 with a benign big brother advertising, a commercial-
    ized utopia.

11.066 Meade, Everard. *The Golden Geese: A Fascinating Novel About
Hucksters and Not-so-hidden Persuaders.* New York: Dodd, Meade, 1968,
274 pp.

    Experienced author writes on a convention. Includes a character
    loosely based on George Washington Hill. See also Wakeman, *The
    Hucksters.*

11.067 Monsarrat, Nicholas. *Story of Esther Costello.* New York: Knopf,
1953, 269 pp.

    A slick shocker of promotional racket built around a severely
    handicapped girl, originally published in England.

11.068 Morgan, Albert. *The Great Man.* NY: Dutton, 1955, 319 pp.

    Behind the scenes of TV.

11.069 Morgan, Joe. *Amy Go Home.* New York: D. McKay, 1964, 307 pp.

11.070 O'Connor, Edwin. *The Oracle.* New York: Harper, 1951, 216 pp.

    Portrait of a bombastic radio personality.

11.071 Olesker, Harry. *Now, Will You Try for Murder?* New York: Simon & Schuster, 1958, 185 pp.

   Mystery novel by a TV producer.

11.072 Owen, John. *The Hoarding*. NY: Dutton, 1923, 370 pp.

   English advertising executive, a women artist, and a man of letters who advertises himself as opposing all forms of advertising; all in the cocoa industry.

11.073 Panetta, George. *Viva Madison Avenue*. New York: Harcourt, Brace, 1957, 250 pp.

   Adventures of two young Italians on the make.

11.074 Pohl, Frederick, and Kornbluth, Cyril M. *The Space Merchants*. New York: Ballantine, 1953, 179 pp.

   Well received science fiction by recognized authors.

11.075 Priestley, John B. *Thirty-First of June: A Tale of True Love, Enterprise and Progress, in the Arthurian and Ad-Atomic Ages*. NY: Doubleday, 1962, 168 pp.

   English humorous fantasy.

11.076 Priestly, John B. *Wonder Hero*. New York: Harper, 1933, 337 pp.

   English comedy on hero-making by media.

11.077 Raphaelson, Samson. *Skylark*. NY: Knopf, 1939, 225 pp.

   "Pithy sample of advertising psychology" - *New York Times,* July 9, 1939, p. 7. Adapted to a play published by Random House.

11.078 Raven, Simon. *The Rich Pay Late: A Novel*. NY: Putnam, 1965, 237 pp.

   Ambitious men in England's publishing world.

11.079 Samstag, Nicholas. *Come and See My Shining Palace*. Garden City, NY: Doubleday, 1966.

   Ad manager for *Time*. See other publications.

11.080 Sayers, Dorothy L. *Murder Must Advertise*. New York: Harcourt, 1933, 344 pp.

   English author, but widely read in North America, and still in print.

11.081 Schneider, John G. *The Golden Kazoo*. New York: Rinehart, 1956, 246 pp.

   Fictional political campaign of 1960.

11.082   Schoonover, Lawrence. *Quick Brown Fox*. NY: Macmillan, 1952,
234 pp.

       Story of art director by ex-copywriter.

11.083   Sedges, John (pseud.). *Bright Procession*. New York: J. Day,
1952, 305 pp.

       Character study of N.Y. public relations executive.

11.084   Sheldon, Michael. *The Personnel Man*. Toronto: McClelland &
Stewart, 1966, 173 pp.

11.085   Shulman, Max. *Anyone Got A Match?* New York: Harper & Row,
1964, 27 pp.

       Satirical character like George Washington Hill who fights against
Surgeon General's report.

11.086   Sinclair, Robert B. *It Couldn't Be Murder*. New York: Mill,
1954, 213 pp.

       Triple murder tale.

11.087   Skirrow, Desmond. *I'm Trying to Give it Up*. New York: Doubleday, 1969, 256 pp.

       Industrial spying, imported from England.

11.088   Slesar, Henry. *The Grey Flannel Shroud*. New York: Random,
1959, 212 pp.

       A first mystery novel.

11.089   Spence, Hartzell. *Radio City*. NY: Dial, 1941, 351 pp.

       "Vivid presentation of the background of radio entertainment"
including much on advertising. *NY Times* Oct. 26, 1941, p. 28.

11.090   Stein, Sol. *Living Room: A Novel*. New York: Arbor, 1974,
309 pp.

       A woman copywriter's career and sex life.

11.091   Stephens, Edward. *Twist of Lemon*. NY: Doubleday, 1959, 478 pp.

       First novel well received by reviewers.

11.092   Stout, Rex. *Before Midnight: A Nero Wolfe Novel*. New York:
Viking, 1955, 184 pp.

       Mystery novel of ad-execs and puzzle solvers.

11.093   Trevor, Elleston. *The Billboard Madonna*. New York: Morrow,
1961, 320 pp.

11.094   Van Rider, Robert A.   *Really Sincere Guy*.   NY: McKay, 1958, 370 pp.

On public relations.

11.095   Vansittart, Peter.   *Orders of Chivalry*.   NY: Adelard-Schuman, 1959, 320 pp.

English story on TV and advertising.   Reviewed as "disassociated hypercerebration."

11.096   Van Slyke, Helen.   *All Visitors Must Be Announced*.   Garden City, NY: Doubleday, 1972, 372 pp.

11.097   Wakeman, Frederic.   *The Hucksters*.   New York: Rinehart, 1946, 307 pp.

Popular and made into a movie starring Clark Gable.   Client character based on George Washington Hill.

11.098   Wells, Herbert G.   *Tono-Bungay*.   New York: Outfield, 1909, 400 pp.

Patent medicine business in England.

11.099   Werner, Carl A.   *A Man May Dream*.   NY: Sheridan, 1940, 246 pp.

Chronology and dreams of a successful advertising man.

11.100   Willock, Ruth.   *5:30 to Midnight*.   NY: Harper, 1941, 296 pp.

Department store advertising art department shenanigans.

11.101   Wilson, Harry L.   *Professor, How Could You!*   New York: Cosmopolitan, 1924, 340 pp.

Professor sabbaticals as a patent medicine trouper.

11.102   Wilson, Sloan.   *The Man in the Gray Flannel Suit*.   NY: Simon & Schuster, 1954, 304 pp.

A classic on the new community of corporate commuters.   The term became synonymous with admen, and the fashion fad was accompanied by pink linen shirts.

11.103   Woodward, Helen.   *Queen's in the Parlor*.   NY: Bobbs-Merrill, 1933, 316 pp.

Written by experienced author but not as disclosing as *Through Many Windows*.

11.104   Wouk, Herman.   *Aurora Dawn, or the True History of Andrew Reale*. New York: Simon and Schuster, 1947, 241 pp.

Similar to Wakeman's *The Hucksters*:   radio, soap, and a character like George Washington Hill.

11.105 Yates, Richard. *Disturbing the Peace: A Novel.* New York:
Delacourte/Seymour Lawrence, 1975, 278 pp.

Psychological descent of a media representative.

"They is a punchin' bag in our land that every highbrow
and scribbler swings at sooner er later -- and that's
advertisin'. Seems nobody with a college education has got
any more use fer advertisin' than they got fer a dead polecat
on a hot night -- 'ceptin' the fellers who make a livin'
advertisin', and even they get sorta bristly, like it's a
humpbacked kid o' theirs and they'll fight you if you speak
mean about it. Now if I use five-and-ten-cent words and
disappoint the perfessers and reformers who expect me to rip
up the business with hacksaws, I'm sorry. I don't think
advertisin' is no dead polecat and no humpbacked kid, neither.
I ain't even agin' it.
"When my pop he said, 'Let a hog in the house and he'll
crawl on yer table,' he wasn't agin' hogs, neither. Fact,
we was all pretty near raised on pork. Pop was jest statin'
a plain fact about hogs. All I aim to do tonight is state
plain facts...
"Signs is like hogs: nobody claims they's pretty, but
everybody knows you gotta have 'em....
"They is some wild-eyed folks likes to holler, 'Abolish
advertisin'.' Shucks, tryin' to stop advertisin' in this
land is like tryin' to stop freckles with a rubber eraser....
Only thing is, I look around our land and right now I say we
ain't got signs' by and large, we got a hog in the house."

Father Calvin Stanfield
(11.104, p 196-7)

IV.
Directories

20.000
ARCHIVES, MANUSCRIPTS
AND SPECIAL COLLECTIONS

20.001 Advertising Research Foundation - Information Center
       3 E. 54th St.   (212) 751-5656
       New York, NY   10022   Elisabeth R. Proudfit
                                              Mgr. Info. Center

       Holdings: Extensive collection of pioneering studies in
       media research. Access by members and qualified graduate
       students with prior permission of parent organization.

20.002 Ally & Gargano - Information Center
       437 Madison Ave.   (212) 688-5300
       New York, NY   10022   Susan Schofield
                                              Res. Info. Supervisor

       Holdings: 35 vertical file drawers of archives, including
       Ally & Gargano Archives, 1962- (press clippings, etc.).

20.003 American Marketing Association - Information Center
       222 S. Riverside Plaza   (312) 648-0536
       Chicago, IL   60606   Lorraine Caliendo
                                              Mgr./Librarian

       Holdings: 24 ft. of archives, including conference proceed-
       ings, AMA publications and official minutes. Materials date
       from 1940's and thus reflect changes in advertising tech-
       niques and philosophy. Access upon presentation to library
       director or by prior permission of library director (pre-
       ferred, but not necessary).

20.004 Audit Bureau of Circulation (ABC)
       123 N. Wacker Dr.   (312) 236-7994
       Chicago, IL   60606   T.J. Donnelly
                                              Supervisor of Communications

       Holdings: ABC is a repository for circulation reports on
       member publications from 1914 to the present. It verifies
       the circulation claim of member publishers and makes reports
       available to advertisers in the Audit Report, copies of
       which date from 1914 to the present and are available in
       bound volumes or on microfilm. Member firms and publications
       have access to these records at any time and university stu-
       dents and researchers by appointment.

20.005 Baker Library
       Harvard Business School   (617) 495-6361
       Soldiers Field Rd.   Robert W. Lovett
       Boston, MA   02163   Librarian/Manuscripts

       Holdings: Harvard Advertising Awards, 1924 - 30, ca. 1
       drawer and a collection of trade cards, trade catalogs,
       photos and examples of advertisements in Mss. & Archives
       Dept. as follows:

20.006   Adams & Hudson Records, (Boston), 1832 - 35 (2 vols.).

Accounts for advertisements which appeared for various firms in the *Centinel and Palladium*.

20.007   Allen, E.C. Papers, 1871 - 96 (472 vols., 33 boxes, 6 cases, 1 chest - 60 ft.). One of the persons who made Augusta, ME an important publishing center. He published farm magazines, books and developed a mail order business in variety items. The collection is unusually complete; it includes ledger accounts for the agents, cash books, records of subscription and of mailings and unbound papers and extensive files of copyright entries and of advertising circulars. The collection is important for a study of the beginnings both of the mail order business and of mass advertising. A fuller description may be seen in: Lovett, Robert W. "Publisher and Advertiser Extraordinary: The E.C. Allen Collection." *Bulletin of the Business Historical Society* 24 (December 1950): 210 - 215.

20.008   Benson, John Papers, 1952 (1 box). Draft of Benson's part of proposed book on advertising by Benson and Walter A. Gaw. Benson, who had been president of the American Association of Advertising Agencies, wrote on ethical standards in advertising.

20.009   Homer & Palmer Advertising Ledgers, 1830 - 36 (3 vols.). Contains accounts of advertisements appearing for individuals and firms in the *Daily Centinel* and *Gazette*.

20.010   Adams & Hudson, Account Books, 1830 - 36 (5 vols.). Accounts for advertisements in Boston newspapers.

20.011   Kress Library of Business and Economics. Has ca. 20 pieces of pre-1850 advertising ephemera.

20.012   Martineau, Pierre D. Papers, 1953 - 64 (3 vols.). Addresses and miscellaneous papers.

20.013   Means, James & Family Papers, 1869 - 1965 (ca. 2 ft.). Shoe manufacturer of Boston and owner of the James Means Company of Boston and Brockton, MA, and Kittery, ME. Letter books (1891 - 1904) of Means, advertising matter for the $3 shoe and minutes (1900 - 1904) of the James Means Company, Kittery, ME. Unpublished list in the library's manuscript division.

20.014   Noyes, Morillo Papers, 1859 - 77 (20 memorandum books and 1 box). The books show Morillo Noyes to have been a master peddler. In 1859 he employed 12 peddler-assistants and kept 18 horses for his business. His headquarters were at Burlington, VT where he maintained a warehouse. He and his assistants covered a large area of country in Vermont, New York and Massachusetts. They collected wool, pelts, hides, horn, hair, old metal, and rags, giving in trade such commodities as sold by a general store.

20.015   Ward & Gow Records, (New York), 1895 - 1919 (8 ft.). Account books and unbound business papers of an advertising firm, one

of the first to systematize streetcar advertising. Includes
records of the Inter-city Car Advertising Co., advertising
concessions at Coney Island and Brighton Beach, NY and
Brighton Beach Music Hall. Inventory in the library.

20.016   Bank Marketing Association - Information Center
         309 W. Washington   (312) 782-1442
         Chicago, IL   60606   Cynthia Porter
                                              Dir./Info. Services

         Holdings: *Best of TV* and *Best of Radio*. Not in the library,
         but available through another BMA dept.; *Golden Coin,* 1969-.
         Advertising campaigns by banks and public affairs campaigns;
         School Projects, 1950's-. Theses from BMA School of Market-
         ing, covering topics related to advertising. Access upon
         presentation to library director.

20.017   Boston University Libraries - Manuscript Division
         770 Commonwealth Ave.
         Boston, MA   02159

         Holdings: Lewis, William Bennett Papers, 1930 - 69 (8 ft.).
         Advertising executive. Business correspondence, diaries,
         personal and family records of travel and papers relating to
         Lewis' advertising career, in connection with the Columbia
         Broadcasting System and other institutions, with material,
         formerly restricted, of the U.S. Office of Facts and Figures
         and the Office of War Information during WW II. Inventory
         in the library. Information on literary rights available
         in the library.

20.018   Deleted.

20.019   Stern, Daniel Papers, 1953 - 68 (ca. 300 items). Advertising
         executive and author. Correspondence, typescripts of Stern's
         writings with holograph corrections, research notes, galleys,
         publicity materials and other papers. Inventory in the
         library. Information on literary rights available in the
         library. Additions to this collection are anticipated.

20.020   Business & Professional Advertising Association
         205 E. 42nd St.   (212) 661-0222
         New York, NY   10017   R.L. Coleman
                                              Managing Dir.

         Holdings: Records of this 58 yr. old Association, originally
         called Industrial Advertisers Association, then Association
         of Industrial Advertisers. Access upon presentation to
         library director.

20.021   Campbell-Ewald Co.-Reference Center
         30400 Van Dyke St.   (313) 574-3400
         Warren, MI   48093   Elizabeth L. Smith
                                              VP & Mgr. Reference Center

         Holdings: Trade association booklets, annual reports.

General Motors Corp. auto booklets and competitive auto ads
1920 to date; Campbell-Ewald archives, 1911 - present; and
client archives. Access with prior permission of library
director and materials must be used on premises.

20.022   Chicago Historical Society - Library
         North Ave. & Clark St.   Frank Jewell
         Chicago, IL   60614   Librarian

         Holdings: Chicago city, newspaper and advertising agent
         directories; trade, commercial, direct-mail, and premium
         catalogues; advertising pamphlets; early market studies;
         postal and advertising cards; printing specimens; adver-
         tising and commercial maps; advertising periodicals. The
         Graphics Collection contains posters, broadsides, prints, and
         photographs concerning advertising primarily related to busi-
         nesses and industries headquartered in the Chicago area, cat-
         alogued by subject and business name. The Manuscript Collec-
         tion holds the Leon Mandel MSS relating to retail newspaper
         advertising 1928 - 1950 and the Claude A. Barnett (Associated
         Negro Press and National Negro Business League) MSS which
         have material on black advertising, 1925 - 1955.

20.023   Cincinnati Art Museum - Library
         Eden Park   Patricia P. Rutledge
         Cincinnati, OH   45202   Librarian

         Holdings: A small collection of books and vertical file
         material on advertising art.

20.024   The Coca-Cola Company
         P.O. Drawer 1734   (404) 897-2121
         Atlanta, GA   30301   Wilbur George Kurtz, Jr.
                                             Archivist

         Holdings: Includes art and memorabilia collections; adver-
         tising and promotional material, audiovisual records and
         marketing research. The company's advertising files are an
         important portion of the records: an extensive print and
         negative file (ca. 10 ft.) contains glossy prints of all the
         illustrations used in advertising Coca-Cola since 1886.
         These are arranged by types: posters, magazine advertising,
         motion picture stills, calendars and historical photographs,
         each in chronological order. This section includes a special
         section on WW II advertising and photographs of early wagons,
         trucks, bottlers, executives and early homes of The Coca-Cola
         Company in Atlanta. The entire file is subject indexed.
         There is a complete collection of all advertising copy used
         since 1886, arranged chronologically and bound in scrapbooks.
             Comprehensive files are maintained on advertising and
         promotion for every phase of the company. A separate file
         covers overseas advertising copy and art. The company's
         four volume study, *A History and Analysis of Advertising for
         Coca-Cola,* offers an evaluation of advertising copy used in
         all media between 1934 and 1955. Tapes of radio commercials
         dating from "Singing Sam" in 1935, have been preserved and

and indexed as have both audio and video tapes of television advertising.

There are statistical records from the company's research in marketing and market psychology, fields in which The Coca-Cola Company has long been a leader. Summaries of this data are preserved in the archives, including records of distribution, sales, field programs and schedules for promotions from the company's earliest days.

In addition to the materials housed in the Coca-Cola USA building in Atlanta, records are preserved in two storage areas: the basement of the Coca-Cola USA building (Archives I) and a warehouse (Archives II), totaling ca. 3,200 sq. ft. of space.

Researchers from outside the company are allowed use of source materials in the archives on application. They must make appointments for use in advance and be prepared to discuss their specific research projects with the archivist. The archives in the past has assisted students of business administration, marketing and history and sociologists investigating the impact of advertising.

20.025 Columbia University Libraries - Manuscript Division
    801 Butler Library   Bernard C. Crystal
    New York, NY   10027   Librarian

Holdings: Actively collect in the area of printing, the graphic and book arts, publishing and literary agents; numerous examples of book advertisements and prospectuses, American type specimen catalogues, and catalogues of printer's equipment and supplies. Checklist of manuscript collections for journalists, editors, publishers, booksellers and literary agents is available from the library.

20.026 Benjamin, William E. Papers, 1884 - 1910 (4 boxes). Contains material on promotion and personal sales management of Stedman's *Library of American Literature*.

20.027 Schuster, Max Lincoln Papers, 1925 - 1969 (ca. 60,000 items). Contains the correspondence for the years 1951 - 1966 of Mr. Schuster, co-founder and chairman of the board of Simon & Schuster, Inc. Includes advertisements (2 boxes), and similar materials for Pocket Books, Inc., which was owned by Simon & Schuster.

20.028 Columbia University Libraries - Oral History Collection
    221 M. Butler Library   Elizabeth B. Mason
    New York, NY   10027   Librarian

Holdings: See *The Oral History Collection of Columbia University*, 1964 and its Supplement(s).

20.029 Arnold, Frank Atkinson Papers, 1867 - 1958 (101 pp.). Early advertising experiences, first contacts with radio, broadcasting and advertising, Director of Development for NBC, pre-recorded programs, early radio advertisers, advertising agencies, technical advances in radio, television and its problems.

20.030   Bernays, Edward L. Papers, 1891- (403 pp.). Psychological
                and legal ramifications of public relations, societal tech-
                niques, symbolism and propaganda, "engineering of consent,"
                social consciousness-raising and consumerism, Gallup polls,
                corporations and research, segmental approach, industrial and
                labor relations, politicians and pollsters, reminiscences of
                the Sigmund Freud family, the Franklin D. Roosevelt family,
                Senator Joseph McCarthy, opera and ballet personalities,
                impressions of many public figures. Closed during the
                lifetime of Mr. and Mrs. Bernays.

20.031   Bowles, Chester Papers (866 pp.). Material on his experi-
                ences in advertising, in product research and pricing, radio
                advertising and in Benton & Bowles, as well as information
                related to his numerous government appointments.

20.032   Book-of-the-Month Club, 1955 (21 items). Transcripts of
                tape-recorded interviews with the founders, members of the
                Selection Committee and executive and technical personnel,
                discussing the founding of the company, the selling of cur-
                rent books by mail to subscribers, the selection of titles,
                use of premiums, advertising, sales, subscribers, book design
                and calligraphy, book manufacture, publishers, opposition of
                book dealers and the Literary Guild and other book clubs.
                Persons interviewed include George Gallup and Maxwell Sack-
                heim.

20.033   Durstine, Roy Sarles Papers (49 pp.). Material on the elec-
                tion of 1912, William Howard Taft, Bruce Barton and adver-
                tising from 1912 - 49. Permission required to cite or quote.

20.034   Gallup, George Horace Papers (158 pp.). Family background
                and education; early newspaper readership surveys; journa-
                lism teaching 1929 - 1932; principles of effective adver-
                tising; magazine publishing: *Literary Digest, Reader's
                Digest, Saturday Evening Post, Look,* etc.; postcard polling;
                Gallup polls from 1933. Permission required to cite or
                quote.

20.035   Golenpaul, Dan Papers (205 pp.). Material on *Information
                Please Almanac;* the genesis and production of "Information
                Please;" Heywood Broun, Oscar Levant, Clifton Fadiman, John
                Kiernan and others on the program; relations with advertising
                agencies and sponsors. Permission required to quote or cite.

20.036   Hauptli, Albert Papers (103 pp.). Material on magazine work,
                McGraw-Hill, from 1920: paid vs. free circulation publica-
                tions; growth of advertising agencies, role of salesmen,
                special media publications; *American Machinist, Product
                Engineering;* automation. Permission required.

20.037   Lasker, Albert Davis Papers (180 pp.). Early adventures as
                a newspaper reporter; his career in advertising; George
                Washington Hill and others.

20.038   Paley, William S. Papers (67 pp.). Includes material on childhood and education in Chicago; experiences as an advertising manager, Congress Cigar Company; use of radio in advertising; CBS, 1928+.

20.039   Radio Pioneers Transcripts (94 items). Transcripts of tape-recorded interviews with directors, engineers, government officials, performers, station and network executives and writers discussing the early history of radio and television. Subjects include early advertising, operating methods in radio stations, radio's relations with government and the development of programming, especially audience participation, children's musical and newscasting programs.

20.040 Connecticut Historical Society - Library
1 Elizabeth St.   (203) 236-5621
Hartford, CT   06105   Dr. Christopher Bickford
                                    Library Director

      Holdings: Trade catalogs limited to Connecticut, listed in Romaine: *A Guide to American Trade Catalogs 1744 - 1900.* Bowker, 1960; trade cards; advertising cards; broadsides.

20.041 Cornell University Libraries - Department of Manuscripts and University Archives
John M. Olin Library   Kathleen Jacklin
Ithaca, NY   14853   Archivist

      Holdings: Scale Manufacturing Trade War Papers, 1898 - 1900 (1 box). Papers relating to a trade war between the National Computing Scale Company and the Computing Scale Company, manufacturers of scales in Ohio, including considerable material on business and advertising methods of the period.

20.042   Spencer, Leland Papers. 1930 - 67 (24 ft.). Professor of Marketing, 1924 - 64, senior research associate, 1964+, milk marketing consultant. Includes correspondence, memoranda, reports and printed matter concerning the economic aspects of pricing and distribution of milk, especially in New York and New Jersey; extension work and activities as an economic analyst and consultant for state and federal agencies, as well as farmer and dealer organizations in the milk industry; correspondence, memoranda, reports, minutes, financial statements and publicity material of the N.Y.S. Bureau of Milk Publicity (1934 - 42) and Milk for Health, Inc. (1949 - 58) and its successor, the Producers Milk Market Development Board (1958 - 60); and printed matter, reports, and correspondence relating to his testimony in the "Safeway Case" (1954 - 55) regarding milk prices in California.

20.043 Crain Communications Inc. - Editorial Library
740 North Rush St.   (312) 649-5328
Chicago, IL   60611   Margaret G. Maples
                                    Head Librarian

      Holdings: Bound volumes of *Advertising Age* and provides the

Advertising Age Cite Service. (Hopefully the corporate records of this significant publisher will someday become
available. This may also become the repository for Harry
Wayne McMahan's enormous collection of television ads - ed.).

20.044 D'Arcy, MacManus & Masius - Library Information Services
        Woodward at Long Lake Rd.   (313) 646-1000
        Blomfield Hills, ML   48013   Lois W. Collet
                                               Manager

        Holdings: Papers of principals mostly relating to company
        history. Access by prior permission of library director.

20.045 Detroit Public Library - Automotive History Collection
        5201 Woodward Ave.   James J. Bradley
        Detroit, MI   48202   Curator

        Holdings: Approximately 70 - 80,000 advertising pieces
        issued by American and foreign makers of: automobiles,
        buses, trucks, motorcycles, taxicabs, hearses, ambulances,
        horse-drawn vehicles, etc. These range in date from the
        late 19th century through 1978. Complete files of most
        important magazines concerned with auto industry; in many
        cases bound with ads.

20.046 Beecroft, David Papers, 1915 - 24 (3 ft.). Publisher of
        Automobile magazine and editor of *Automobile* trade journal.
        Correspondence files relating to early cars, companies and
        persons in the automobile industry. Correspondents include
        advertising men.

20.047 Duke University Library - Manuscript Department
        Durham, NC   27706

        Holdings: The advertising collection is composed chiefly
        of material from the U.S. (4,500 items divided into 60
        product categories). For additional information about adver-
        tising see a pamphlet in this library numbered 20434. It is:
        Garland B. Porter, "The Saga of Reuben Rink ..." (Atlanta,
        Dec. 1959), No. 35. "Reuben Rink" was Jules Gilmer Korner,
        Sr. of Kernersville, NC. See also: Jules G. Korner, Jr.,
        Joseph of Kernersville (Durham, 1958).

20.048 Duke (W.), Sons & Co. Papers, 1876 - 1904 (3 boxes & 3
        vols.). Consists of premiums and advertising devices used
        during the 1880's.

20.049 Gardner, Paris Cleveland Papers (3,156 items). Gardner was
        on the staff of the Federal Trade Commission and investigated
        possible cases of deceptive advertising. (He did similar
        work after transferring to the Division of Radio and Periodi-
        cal Advertising on Aug. 18, 1947). As attorney-examiner,
        Gardner's job involved uncovering the facts of a case and
        summarizing the evidence in a report recommending action, if
        any. Many of these cases did not ever get that far but show
        the routine complaints about misleading or false advertising

which consumed most of Gardner's energy. The advertisements investigated usually appeared in periodicals or newspapers, though occasionally they included radio broadcasts. Very few of the cases dealt with major companies. Most of the possible offenders were small proprietary establishments. These F.T.C. files (1941 - 1951) do illustrate well the procedures and work of the F.T.C. which remain unrecorded in its formal decisions. Of special note is an investigation of advertising techniques used by the American Tobacco Company,

20.050   Journalists, Editors and Publishers Papers, 1802 - 1951 (1,104 items & 3 vols.). Papers of this group mainly in Southern States. Includes 370 items relating to the advertising policy of the *Virginia Free Press*. Card index in the library.

20.051   Dwight D. Eisenhower Library
General Services Administration
National Archives & Records Service
SE 4th St.   John E. Wickman
Abilene, KA   67410   Director

Holdings: Advertising Council records appear in various holdings as follows: records of Dwight D. Eisenhower as President, 1953 - 61, (boxes 620 - 623), consists of ca. 1,600 pages of correspondence, memoranda and reports; Clarence Francis Papers, (box 11), ca. 20 pages of correspondence, memoranda and reports; John H. Hamlin Reports, (box 1), ca. 20 pages of correspondence and memoranda; James M. Lambie, Jr. Reports, relates to Mr. Lambie's work coordinating public service advertising campaigns as director of the U.S. Government liaison with the Advertising Council, Inc.; Howard Pyle Papers, (box 1), material on the Advertising Council, Washington Meeting, March 22, 1955, consists of ca. 80 pages of correspondence, memoranda and reports; U.S. President's Commission on National Goals Records, 1959 - 61, (Box 21), Advertising Council Booklet for National Goals Committee, consists of ca. 150 pages of correspondence, reports and printed matter, (box 33), Advertising Council Formats, consists of copies of Ad Council National Goals advertisements appearing in national magazines.

20.052   Lambie, James M. Papers, 1953 - 61 (2 ft. (ca. 4,800 items). Government official. Outgoing correspondence and memoranda, documenting Lambie's service as special assistant in the White House Office, 1953 - 1961. Includes material relating to his work coordinating public service advertising campaigns as director of the U.S. Government liaison with the Advertising Council, Inc. Unpublished finding aid in the repository. Access restricted. Information on literary rights available in the repository.

20.053   Young & Rubicam Records of "Citizens for Eisenhower," 1952 - 56 (ca. 4 ft. (ca. 2,400 items). Correspondence, reports, notes, memoranda, addresses, layouts, ad proofs, art work,

news releases, reprints, scripts, posters, newspaper clippings, cards, booklets, brochures and other material, relating principally to the public relations and advertising
firm's participation in the Republican nomination and
presidential campaigns of Dwight D. Eisenhower in 1952 and
1956. Correspondents include Sigurd S. Larmon, David Levy,
Preston Wood, and Frederick A. Zaghi. Unpublished finding
aid in the library. Open to investigators under restrictions
accepted by the library.

20.054 Fairleigh Dickinson University - Friendship Library
        285 Madison Ave.   James Fraser
        Madison, NJ   07940   Director

        Holdings: Outdoor Advertising Association Collection.
        Collection consists of ca. 400 reference books and bound
        vols. of periodicals devoted to the poster in outdoor
        advertising; site photographs and photos of 24 and 12 sheets,
        ranging from the 1920's to the present; papers and miscellany
        of and about individuals and companies engaged in outdoor
        advertising.

20.055 Foote, Cone & Belding Communications, Inc. - Library
        200 Park Ave.   (212) 880-9128
        New York, NY   10017   Ruth Fromkes
                                            Librarian

        Holdings: Completely catalogued collection of all print
        advertising in print and slide form. Access upon presenta-
        tion to library director.

20.056 George Johnson Advertising - Library
        755 New Ballas Rd.   (314) 569-3440
        St. Louis, MO   63141   Marianne Goedeker
                                            Librarian

        Holdings: 16 file drawers of clippings; 1 drawer personal
        papers; speeches by advertising personnel, 1953-, (local and
        national speakers, covering all areas of advertising); per-
        sonal correspondence between Mr. Johnson and Stanley Resor
        re: creativity and agency business; agency fee system,
        1960's (correspondence with Shelby Page of Ogilvy, Benson
        & Mather, Inc. Access upon presentation to library director.

20.057 Goodrich (B.F.) Co.
        500 S. Main St.
        Akron, OH   44318   Jeffrey J. Harig
                                            Corporate Comm. Intern

        Holdings: Advertisement invoices and actual advertisement
        samples 1895 - 1919, 23 boxes of advertisement material
        listed chronologically (before 1890 - 1959), "Starch"
        reports 1939 - 1950, 2 boxes of b&w slides for advertising
        presentations, special advertisements 1930's, product de-
        signs, corporate biographical sketches, minutes, financial
        records, correspondence, personal papers, reports, taped

oral history material. Special holdings: travel maps,
greeting cards, radio broadcasts (scripts for the "Detect &
Collects" broadcast series). Open to scholars.

20.058 Kenyon & Eckhardt Advertising, Inc. - Library
       200 Park Ave.   (212) 973-7894
       New York, NY   10017   Karen M. Bloomberg
                                 Head Librarian

Holdings: *Comparative Advertising: A Systematic and
Annotated Bibliography of Comparative Advertising from
1972 - 1976.* Access upon presentation to library director.

20.059 Knox College Library - Archives
       Galensburg, IL   61401

Holdings: Calkins, Earnest Elmo Papers, 1827 - 1964 (ca.
7 ft.). Author and advertising executive. Correspondence,
articles for the *Atlantic Monthly,* research materials for
They Broke the Prairie (1937), Calkin's book about the
founding of Galesburg and Knox College, sketches, photos and
memorabilia. Includes letters (1925 - 1931) relating to
Calkins' travels in Egypt, England, France, Italy, Scotland
and Switzerland and material relating The Islanders, a club
composed of artists and art staff of Calkins and Holden, New
York, and to the Art Directors' Club tribute to Calkins.
Other subjects include advertising, books and Knox College
affairs.

20.060 Library of Congress - Manuscript Division
       Washington, DC   20540

Holdings: Includes papers of Bingham, Robert Worth; Daniels,
Josephus; Kleine, George B.; Luce, Henry R.; Meyer, Eugene;
Pulitzer, Joseph (1847 - 1911); Pulitzer, Joseph (1885 -
1955); the Reid Family; and Watson, John B.

20.061 Bernays, Edward L. Papers, 1897 - 1965 (120 ft. (ca. 202,200
items). Family and general correspondence, diaries,
speeches, articles, scrapbooks, reports, surveys, clippings,
press releases, photos and other papers relating to Bernays'
career: Diaghileff's Ballet Russe, the United Fruit Company,
the tobacco industry, Procter & Gamble and other soap companies, broadcasting companies, government agencies and
other clients. Includes Freud family correspondence, drafts,
galleys and notes for Bernays' book, *Biography of an Idea*
(1965) and public relations papers and writings of Doris
Elsa (Fleischman) Bernays. Correspondents include Homer
Capehart, Jacques Cartier, Willoughby S. Chesley, Norman Bel
Geddes, Eric Frederick Goldman, Hubert H. Humphrey, Alfred A.
Knopf, H.L. Mencken, Henry A. Wallace, Edmund Spurr Whitman,
American Tobacco (16 scrapbooks & 17 boxes), Dodge Bros.
(1 scrapbook & 9 boxes), Mack Trucks (5 scrapbooks & 13
boxes), Nash-Kelvinator (18 scrapbooks & 9 boxes), Philco
(115 scrapbooks & 5 boxes), Procter & Gamble (30 scrapbooks
& 19 boxes), United Fruit (17 scrapbooks & 36 boxes). Papers

restricted until after the death of Mr. and Mrs. Bernays.
Unpublished finding aid in the library.

20.062   Ogilvy, David Mackenzie Papers, 1935 - 66 (29 ft. (30,450
            items). Advertising executive, chairman and chief executive
            of Ogilvy, Benson & Mathers, Inc., New York. Correspondence
            with Rosser Reeves, Fairfax Cone and Raymond Rubicam; adver-
            tising proposals; market research reports; articles;
            speeches; and printed matter, primarily 1945 - 64; 26 boxes
            of account files including General Dynamics, General Foods,
            Rubenstein and Sears, which emphasize use of research in
            advertising, 1950 - 64; and the drafts and proofs of Ogilvy's
            published work, "Confessions of an Advertising Man." Also
            material related to Ogilvy's advertising career, as an exe-
            cutive and businessman in the U.S.; his work with the found-
            ing of Hewitt, Ogilvy, Benson & Mathers, Inc., a subsidiary
            of two British advertising agencies: S.H. Benson, Ltd. and
            Mather & Crowther, Ltd.; and his research in advertising.
            Also a manuscript of a brief autobiographical sketch (1911 -
            57), including draft elements for what became *Blood, Brains
            & Beer*. Literary rights public after death. Written per-
            mission required until 1990.

20.063   McGraw-Hill Publications Co. - Marketing Information Center
         1221 Ave. of the Americas   (212) 997-3222
         New York, NY   10020   Ranulph F. Norman
                                              Director

            Holdings: *McGraw-Hill Keys to Marketing Techniques*, biweek-
            ly, Dec. 1945- (abstracts from ca. 140 sources monthly); and
            60 vertical file drawers of relevant marketing & advertising
            material catalogued by subject -- some of it abstracted.
            Access upon presentation to or by permission of library
            director.

20.064   Metropolitan Museum of Art - Dept. of Prints and Photographs
         5th Ave. & 82nd St.   879-5500, ext. 254
         New York, NY   10028

            Holdings: Burdick, Jefferson R. Collection: trade and
            souvenir cards and other paper Americana. Consists of over
            300,000 items, housed in 394 numbered albums and boxes,
            dating from 1630. Most advertising items from late 19th
            century. Includes posters, calendars, tags, catalogs,
            banners, etc. Bulk of material from the private collection
            of Joseph R. Burdick, with a principal supplement by Bella
            Landauer. Collection mounted and numbered in conformity
            with the 1960 edition of the *American Card Catalog*. Print
            room open to visitors M-F, 2:00 to 5:00 P.M. Albums are
            large and bulky so the directory cautions readers to budget
            time generously and to provide the staff with advance notice
            as possible. Printed directory available on request.

20.065   Michigan State University - Historical Collections & Archives
         East Lansing, MI   48824

            Holdings: Ewald, Henry Theodore Papers, 1911 - 61 (16 fol-

ders). Founder and president of the Detroit advertising
agency, Campbell-Ewald Company, Inc. Biographical notes and
articles and a biography of Ewald, advertising materials and
newspaper clippings.

20.066   Miles Laboratories - Library Resources & Services
      1127 Myrtle St.   Charlotte S. Mitchell
      Elkhart, IN   46514   Director

      Holdings: Miles *Almanacs* and *Booklets;* and files of pharma-
      ceutical product advertising pieces, literature files on
      company related drugs and domestic marketing files.

20.067   Minnesota Historical Society - Division of Archives & Manuscripts
      1500 Mississippi St.   (612) 296-6980
      St. Paul, MI   55101   Dallas Lindgren Chrislock
                              Head/Reference Services

      Holdings: Better Business Bureau of Minneapolis Papers,
      1912 - 25 (60 boxes & 11 vols.). Correspondence and reports
      on fraudulent advertising in connection with prices, trade
      names, imitation products, patent medicines, investments
      and publications.

20.068   Blodgett, Harvey Alvaro Papers, 1888 - 1944 (12 items). A
      short reminiscence by Blodgett, president of the St. Paul
      firm of Brown-Blodgett, Inc.; the first payroll on which
      Blodgett is listed; and samples of advertising by Brown,
      Treacy and Company.

      Brown, Blodgett & Sperry Co. Records, 1917 - ca. 1945? (16
      vols.). Customer record book and samples (15 vols.) of the
      work of a printing and lithography firm owned by Harvey A.
      Blodgett and associates and its successors. A predecessor
      firm included E.O. Brown and Ernest D.L. Sperry.

20.069   Chester-Kent, Inc. Records, 1905 - 59 (5 ft.). Correspon-
      dence, minutes, clippings, sales reports, advertisements,
      testimonials and other records of Chester-Kent, Inc. and its
      predecessor and related firms, including the Adlerika Co.
      The firms manufactured and marketed Adlerika, a laxative
      and a treatment for appendicitis; Adla tablets for stomach
      ailments; Daru liver pills; and Vinol, a vitamin tonic.
          In addition to information on the manufacture and mar-
      keting of these products, particularly Adlerika, there is
      data on the Canadian (Toronto) branch of the Adlerika Co.;
      Frederick Stearns and Co. Ltd., Canadian (Windsor) manufac-
      turers of Adlerika; the Proprietary Assn.'s fair-practice
      code; fairtrade legislation and practices in 30 states;
      federal legislation regulating the drug industry; the
      National Wholesale Druggist Assn.; the Minnesota Taxpayers'
      Assn.; recovery measures and business policies during the
      depression of the 1930s; and rationing and price controls
      during WW II. Correspondents include Archie L. Gingold and
      Carl Weschcke.

20.070   Dollenmayer, Albert Papers, 1865 - 1938 (2 vols. & 7 boxes).
              Correspondence, diaries, scrapbooks and account books,
              chiefly 1880 - 98. Information on his career in Minneapolis
              as a writer of advertising and the owner of an advertising
              agency. Includes family papers.

20.071   Minnesota Association of Cooperatives Records, 1944 - 74
              (92 ft.). Restricted until 1994. Correspondence, reports,
              minutes, financial records, promotional literature, printed
              materials, news releases, clippings, questionnaires, legis-
              lative bills, and related materials documenting the admini-
              stration, membership, and activities of the Minnesota Assn.
              of Cooperatives (MAC), a trade group organized in 1946 to
              advance the interests of Minnesota co-operatives. Its
              members and affiliates include electric, health, agricultural
              marketing, insurance, credit, and consumer co-operatives.
                   It was formed to promote co-operatives and to counter
              adverse tax measures, primarily through overt political and
              legislative activity and often in association with the
              Democratic-Farmer-Labor party and various labor unions.
              During the 1950s, its emphasis shifted to public relations
              and public education to further the co-operative movement
              through conferences, institutional advertising programs,
              and instructional and promotional materials.
                   The records focus on MAC's activities in public rela-
              tions, education (especially vocational), legislation,
              rural economic development, services to farmers, workshops
              and conferences, and relations with local co-operatives and
              related organizations.

20.072 National Advertising Review Board (NARB)
        845 3rd Ave.   (212) 832-1320
        New York, NY   10022   Kenneth A. Cox
                                                  Chairman

              Holdings: files containing advertising matters adjudicated
              by NARB which are available upon request and the following
              Consultive Panel reports, published by NARB: *Product
              Advertising & Consumer Safety, Advertising and Women* and
              Identifying Competitors in Advertising. These are available
              for $1.00 each, plus postage.

20.073 National Archives of the United States
        8th Pennsylvania St.
        Washington, DC   20408

              Holdings: Committee on Public Information, 1917 - 1919,
              George Creel, Chairman (Record Group 63,110 ft.). Includes
              correspondence and records of chairman and associate chair-
              man, documents on nearly all domestic activities, preparation
              and distribution of information, use of film and photography,
              new release and other prepared copy and records of the "four
              minute men." See James R. Mock and Cedric Larson, *Words That
              Won the War* and George Creel's *How We Advertised America*.

20.074   Federal Trade Commission, 1903 - 59 (Record Group 122, 5,324 ft.). Includes records of the Special Board of Investigation created in 1929 to examine charges of false and misleading advertisings. Consists of radio program scripts and periodical ads passed by the Board, 1936 - 1938 (201 ft.). Except for this radio script material, no one may examine FTC records or be given information from them or copies of them except by permission of the FTC. See Estelle Rebec, comp. *Preliminary Inventory of the Records of the FTC,* (1948).

20.075   Food and Drug Administration, (Record Group 88). General Records, 1937 - 1946, (1.688 ft.). Includes records concerning Consumers Research, Inc., 1922 - 40 and advertising material for patent medicines and health devices, demonstrating the need for regulations 1933 - 37. Bureau of Chemistry, 1877 - 1920, (40 ft.). Includes copies of correspondence, articles and speeches by Dr. Harvey W. Wiley, Chief and minutes of the Committee on Business Methods, 1906 - 1914.

20.076   Office of the Postmaster General, records, 1773 - 1953 (877 ft.). Consists of case files with indices, registers and transcripts of hearings concerning the use of the mail for fraud, false advertising and other violations of the Postal Law and Regulations, 1905 - 51.

20.077   Nebraska State Historical Society
          1500 R. St.
          Lincoln, NE 68508   David H. Hoober
                                Manuscripts Curator

         Holdings: Advertising-Selling League of Omaha Papers, 1922 - 26 (ca. 35 items). Businessmen's organization. Publications, correspondence and clippings.

20.078   Chicago, Burlington & Quincy Railroad Company, Lines West Band Records, 1928 - 67 (ca. 1,800 items). Administrative correspondence and financial records of a band organized for advertising purposes.

20.079   Tanner, Richard Jerome Papers, 1866 - 1955 (ca. 4,000 items). Physician and Wild West showman of Norfolk, Neb. Correspondence, advertising material, printed matter, scrapbooks and other papers. Includes Tanner's advertisements for his medical practice and patent medicines and dime novels.

20.080   Needham, Harper & Steers Advertising, Inc. - Information Services Center
          401 N. Michigan Ave.   (312) 527-3400
          Chicago, IL   60660   Belle Mest
                                Mgr./Info. Services

         Holdings: NH&S data, 1950-, eg. all internally generated memoranda, speeches and publications. Access upon presentation to library director.

20.081   Needham, Harper & Steers of Canada Ltd. - Information Services
             Centre
         101 Richmond St. W. #300   (416) 364-1492
         Toronto, Ont. M5H 1T3   Margaret K. Imai
                                            Res. Librarian

             Holdings: NH&S Lifestyle reports, 75-. Product/user pro-
             files used in consumer and market research. Access by
             written permission of parent organization.

20.082   New York Historical Society
         170 Central Park W.   Wendy Shadwell
         New York, NY   10024   Curator of Prints

             Holdings: Bella C. Landauer Collection of Business and
             Advertising Art. Vast collection of early American adver-
             tising, including bookplates, theatre programs, posters,
             billheads, trade cards, catalogs, calendars, matchboxes,
             labels, promotional literature and objects. The collection
             establishes a picture of American business and industry from
             mid-twentieth century back to mid-nineteenth century.

20.083   New York Public Library - Economic & Public Affairs Division
         5th Ave. & 42nd St.   Mary M. Regan
         New York, NY   10018   Specialist, Hist. of
                                                 Advertising

             Holdings: Strong in the history of advertising, with works
             by Henry Rush Boss, Edgar Robert Jones, Henry Sampson, Play-
             sted Wood, Leo Burnett, David Ogilvy and others; actual maga-
             zine and newspaper advertisements from 17th century to
             present; publications of American Marketing Ass., Advertising
             Council, Advertising Federation of America, Advertising
             Research Foundation, Association of National Advertisers and
             American Association of Advertising Agencies; periodical
             resources such as *Advertising Agency, Journal of Marketing,*
             Mediascope, Printers' Ink, Tide, etc.; bound volumes of
             magazine advertisements, from 1911 - 1921; large collection
             of advertising art & layout, including a number of adver-
             tising posters for books, magazines and newspapers made by
             American artists from 1893 - 1924 (in Art & Architecture
             Division); and approx. 60 American posters illustrating
             brands of cigarettes and tobacco of late 19th century (in
             Arents Collection); contains Edward L. Bernays Collection on
             public relations. (This latter is a modest collection of
             titles bought with a small donation. Good P.R. for Bernays,
             but poor collection for research. The libraries aggregate
             collection is superb, however. The contrast between NYPL
             and Chicago Public Library is staggering - ed.).

20.084   Bennett, Paul Arthur Papers, 1925 - 66 (ca. 33 ft.). Person-
             al and professional correspondence, research materials, type-
             scripts of writings and other papers relating to Bennett's
             career as director of typography, Fuller & Smith, Cleveland,
             OH, art director and production manager, Dunlap-Ward Agency,
             Cleveland, advertising manager, Chandler Motor Company,

Cleveland Typographic and Advertising Depts., then typographic promotion manager, Mergenthaler Linotype Company,
New York, and secretary, The Typophiles, New York. Preliminary inventory available in the library.

20.085 Northwestern University Library - Archives
        Evanston, IL   60201   (312) 492-3354
                                            Patrick M. Quinn
                                            Archivist

        Holdings: Scott, Walter Dill Papers, ca. 1908 - 39 (45
        boxes). Material on pioneers in psychology and advertising
        and papers of the University president, 1920 - 39.

20.086 Ogilvy & Mathers, Inc. - Research Library
        2 E. 48th St.   (212) 688-6100
        New York, NY   10017   Wendy Kimball
                                           Librarian

        Holdings: Files of newspaper clippings and speeches con-
        cerning or by David Ogilvy. Presently closed to all out-
        siders.

20.087 Ohio Historical Society
        1982 Velma Ave.
        Columbus, OH   43211

        Holdings: Records of Radio Ohio, Inc., 1933 - 73, 55 ft.
        (reproduction copies only by express permission of legal
        agent for WBNS-TV); records of Sun (Gus) Booking Agency,
        Inc., 1926 - 55, 41 ft. (includes advertising for various
        vaudeville acts and acts for county and state fairs);
        records of WBNS-TV (Columbus, OH), 1949 - 75, 146 ft. (repro-
        duction copies only by express permission of the legal agent
        for WBNS-TV); records of WGSF-TV (Newark, OH), 1963 - 76,
        47 ft. (includes material relating to public service ads);
        large no. of broadsides, posters, trade cards and trade
        catalogues; largest collection of Ohio newspapers in the U.S.

20.088 Forbes, Benjamin P. Papers, 1850- (20 ft.). Includes adver-
        tising material for various chocolate companies (Forbes
        Chocolate Company, Hershey Chocolate Company, etc.) and
        manufacturing companies.

20.089 Nationwide Communications, Inc. Records, 1949 - 70 (57 - 62
        ft.). Advertising correspondence and files, public affairs
        and religious programming files, newscast scripts, editori-
        als, radio logbooks, advertising copy and reference files of
        a broadcasting company. Under no circumstances may any
        person or organization other than the Ohio Historical Society
        or its staff make reproduction copies without the express
        written permission of an officer of Nationwide Communica-
        tions Inc. Information on literary rights available in the
        repository.

20.090   Pet Incorporated - Corporate Library
         400 S. 4th St.   (314) 621-5400 x308
         St. Louis, MO   63166   L.R. Walton
                                                Corporate Librarian

         Holdings: Parent company advertising materials and company
         history, 1885-. Access by prior permission of library
         director.

20.091   Radio Advertising Bureau - Marketing Information Center
         485 Lexington Ave.   (212) 599-6659
         New York, NY   10017   Stephanie Sanders
                                                Dir./Marketing Info. Ctr.

         Holdings: Media advertising (radio, TV, newspapers, maga-
         zines); demography (consumer buying); broadcasting yearbooks,
         1935- ; and *Sponsor Magazine,* 1947 - 67. Access by prior
         permission of library director.

20.092   The Roper Center
         Yale University
         Box 1732 Yale Station   (203) 436-8186
         New Haven, CT   06520   Everett C. Ladd, Jr.
                                                Executive Director

         Established in 1946, the Roper Center is the oldest and
         largest archive of sample survey data in the world. There
         are more than 9,000 separate studies, dating from 1936 and
         covering 75 countries. The data is that of public opinion
         poll results and occasionally has data on public attitudes
         toward advertising, but contains little commercial research
         results. Data available for a fee.

20.093   Schlesinger Library on the History of Women in America
         Radcliff College
         10 Garden St.
         Cambridge, MA   02138

         Holdings: Advertising Women of New York Records, 1912 - 70
         (105 items). Letters, speeches, articles, resumes, newspaper
         clippings and photos, concerning women in advertising career
         training, consumer relations and consumer work, publicity and
         public relations, good advertising practices, and the history
         of the activities and achievements of the club, founded in
         1912 as the League of Advertising Women of New York. A
         review of women in advertising, and a large number of resumes
         of club activities, are by Dorothy Dignam.

20.094   Cumming, Adelaide Fish Hawley Papers, 1922 - 67 (2 - 1/2 file
         boxes & 1 oversize vol.). Correspondence, scripts, articles
         and stories, promotional literature, etc. of a broadcaster
         who portrayed Betty Crocker on television and radio, deliver-
         ed speeches to diverse organizations and served as a fashion
         commentator.

20.095   Dignam, Dorothy Papers, 1878 - 1946 (addition 1876 - 1960)
(250 items). Articles by Miss Dignam on women in advertising, home appliances, European goods, the market for
American goods in Europe and advertising work in the field of
fashion and beauty. Includes histories of the member of
the Advertising Women of New York, covering activities and
achievements of the club (1911 - 1930's), with yearly chrono-
logical highlights of the club's activities (1935 - 1960).
Unpublished inventory in the library. Information on literary rights available in the library.

20.096   Pinkham (Lydia E.) Medicine Company Papers, 1776, 1859 -
1968 (194 boxes, 601 oversize vols., 32 oversize folders,
61 oversize items & 3 poster rolls). Financial, advertising and general records of the Pinkham Co. at Lynn, Mass.
and its branches in Mexico and Canada. Advertising records
include studies, correspondence and contracts, test copy,
Pinkham Pamphlets and the *Text-Book Upon Ailments Peculiar
to Women*. There are numerous posters, novelties and samples
and 3 boxes of restricted material.

20.096a Sears, Roebuck and Co. - Archives
        Dept. 703, Public Relations, Sears Towers
        Chicago, IL   60684   (312) 875-8321
                                                 Lenore Swoiskin
                                                 Director of Archives

        Holdings: A collection of Sears' catalogues from 1888 to
        date (6,000 volumes). Open only to qualified researchers
        for reference use with prior approval.

20.097 Smithsonian Institution - Archives
        14th & Constitution
        Washington, DC   20560

        Holdings: Ayer (N.W.) Co. Collection, ca. 1889 - 1960 (200
        ft.). Donated by N.W. Ayer Co. of New York, contains more
        than 400,000 proofs of advertisements prepared by the firm
        and published in U.S. newspapers and periodicals. Arranged
        by client. Partial indexes. Access restricted; appointment
        necessary.

20.098 Warshaw Collection of Business Americana, 19th century (1,600
        ft.). The Collection contains advertisements, catalogs,
        price lists, bills, receipts, posters, magazines and other
        material related to American business and advertising his-
        tory. Arranged by subject &/or size of material. Partial
        indexes. Access restricted; appointment necessary.

20.099 Spitzer, Mills & Bates
        790 Bay St.   (416) 597-1616
        Toronto, Ont. M5G 1N9   J.C. Bramm
                                                 VP Communications

        Holdings: Early advertisements in Canadian magazines and
        newspapers, dating from 1926. Access by prior permission of
        library director.

20.100   State Historical Society of Wisconsin - Archives
          816 State St.   Josephine L. Harper
          Madison, WI   53706   Reference Archivist

              Holdings: Since 1955 the Society has collected the papers
              of prominent individuals and organizations in radio and
              television broadcasting, journalism, public relations,
              advertising and other communications media.
                 Broadcasting collections include those of Barnouw,
              Eric; Crossley, Archibald - partly restricted and presently
              unprocessed; and the National Association of Broadcasters -
              presently unprocessed.

20.101   Advertising Women of New York Papers, 1912 - 55 (35 vols. &
              1 box). Includes a history of the club, materials on the
              club's war work, surveys of job opportunities for women,
              the book, *How to be a Successful Advertising Women* and
              scrapbooks of historical, printed, special project, publicity
              and award materials. Inventory.

20.102   Barton, Bruce Papers, 1881 - 1965 (143 boxes, 12 vols. & 1
              pkg.). Includes correspondence with politicians, business-
              men, journalists, publishers, religious leaders, philanthro-
              pists, educators and others; articles, speeches and book
              manuscripts; papers of his father William E. Barton, Congre-
              gational minister and Lincoln authority.

20.103   Bates (Ted) & Company, Inc. Sound Recording, Dec. 12, 1965
              (1 disc on 2 sides & printed program). Recording of the
              lyrics of the 25th anniversary show of Ted Bates and Company
              at the Plaza Hotel, New York, NY.
                 Tape Recording, July 29, 1965 (2 reels). Recording by
              Rosser Reeves and associates concerning the history and
              personalities involved in the growth of the advertising
              agency.

20.104   Braucher, Frank Papers, 1920 - 68 (1 pkg.). President of
              Periodical Publishers Association and of the Magazine Adver-
              tising Bureau. Consists of testimonial letters on his re-
              tirement, two speeches and biographical articles.

20.105   Brophy, Thomas D'Arcy Papers, 1921 - 67 (76 boxes). Includes
              personal correspondence and speeches, client records and
              advertising programs and correspondence, minutes, reports,
              financial statements, press releases, clippings and brochures
              relating to civic and business organizations such as American
              Heritage Foundation, the Advertising Council and his adver-
              tising firm, Kenyon & Eckhardt.

20.106   Buchen, Walter Papers, 1932 - 42 (1 folder). "Buchen Books,"
              1932 - 1942, pamphlets distributed to midwest industrial
              manufacturers stressing the importance of advertising to
              business and discussing other current business topics;
              written by Walter Buchen and employees of the Buchen Company,
              Chicago, an industrial marketing and advertising company
              which he headed.

20.107 Burnett, Leo Papers (1 folder). Published speeches, essays and interviews by Leo Burnett, chairman of the Leo Burnett Company advertising agency; including the book *Communications of an Advertising Man* (1961); several pamphlets, 1963 - 1967, concerning advertising; and two *Good Citizen* pamphlets, 1948 and 1951, published by the American Heritage Foundation of which Burnett was a member.

20.108 Desmond, Robert W. Newspaper & Magazine Clippings, 1900 - 68 (175 boxes). Clippings collected by Robert W. Desmond, journalist and educator, relating to the field of mass communications including such topics as advertising, censorship, management, war correspondents and famous newsmakers and news stories.

20.109 Dignam, Dorothy Papers, 1907 - 59 (1 box, 1 vol. & 3 pkgs.). Advertising copywriter. Correspondence, memoranda, reports, notes, scripts, clippings, and other papers concerning Miss Dignam's work in the early days of advertising directed to women, for cosmetics, feminine necessities, clothing and fabrics, home appliances, food and Ford automobiles. Includes many samples of printed advertisements with the material related to their preparation. Unpublished inventory in the repository.

20.110 Heverly, John P. Recordings (2 discs). A transcribed recording, "The End of the Oregon Trail," used as an advertising sample for the Olympia Brewing Company on September 30, 1946.

20.111 Hill, John W. Papers, 1931 - 64 (46 boxes). Papers of the public relations counsel, writer, and founder of Hill and Knowlton, New York public relations firm, consist of his correspondence with people in public relations, advertising, journalism, and politics; memoranda and related business materials; articles, speeches, and interviews; drafts of Hill's two books, *Corporate Public Relations* (1958) and *The Making of a Public Relations Man* (1963); a file of newsletters for Hill and Knowlton staff, 1948 - 50; pamphlets, leaflets, and news releases issued by Hill and Knowlton; a folder of booklets and clippings pertaining to the operations of Hill and Knowlton International; and files which relate to general policies governing public relations projects. Inventory. Restricted. Unprocessed additions.

20.112 Hill & Knowlton Papers, 1956 - 57 (1 folder). Papers of Hill and Knowlton include a history of the firm prepared by the Harvard Business School, and printed materials about smoking and lung cancer compiled and released for the Tobacco Industry Research Committee by Hill and Knowlton.

20.113 Horlick's Corporation Records, 1873 - 1974 (6 boxes & 2 reels of microfilm). Material of the Racine, Wis. company which produced Horlick's Malted Milk. Consists largely of promotional materials, including testimonials from several explorers, but also containing historical sketches of the

business and family, corporate minutes and other documenta-
tion and a diagram of a double malt kiln printed in 1873.

20.114   James, Edgar Percy Howard Papers, 1922 - 69 (20 boxes & 1
tape recording). Advertising and broadcasting executive.
Includes a wide variety of materials on the commercial development of radio and television.

20.115   Meyer, Alfred Wallace Papers, 1905 - 46 (5 boxes). Chicago
advertising executive. Materials relating to advertising
accounts, mainly three: American Chain and Cable Company,
Western Railroads and Kimberly-Clark. Annotations by Meyer
show the development of advertising campaigns. Inventory.

20.116   National Broadcasting Company Papers, 1930 - 60 (261 boxes
& 1 vol.). Correspondence, reports, scripts, floor plans
for sets, promotional material, and other miscellaneous
materials from various departments of the Company. Unpublished inventory in the repository.

20.117   Page, Arthur Papers, 1908 - 60 (67 boxes & 1 vol.). Public
relations and business consultant of New York. Correspondence and other papers chiefly pertinent either to Page's
work in public relations and fundraising for educational
institutions and foundations or his activities as a business
consultant after 1948. Includes articles and addressed
(1923 - 1960), reports, minutes of meetings, press releases
and publicity kits, appointment books, pamphlets, a Page
family history and his public relations clients. Correspondents include Bruce Barton. Unpublished inventory in the
library. It is expected that additions will be made to the
collection.

20.118   Public Relations Society of America Papers, 1949 - 69 (93
boxes incl. 46 vols., 4 tapes & 4 films). Consists of
scrapbooks on the Society and the field of public relations;
examples of winners in the Society's Silver Anvil Award
competition for public relations projects, 1954 - 1967 and
other miscellaneous items.

20.119   Radio Executives Club Records, 1944 - 51 (1 box). Proceeding
of the club's television seminars, the first important series
of meetings held to prepare the broadcasting industry for the
postwar development of television and papers concerning the
role of television as a medium of mass communication and its
relationship to the other advertising media, presented at the
Media Group Meeting of the American Association of Advertising Agencies, 1951.

20.120   Reeves, Rosser Papers, 1927 - 71 (28 boxes incl. 26 vols.,
1 disc recording, 4 films & 4 tape recordings). Papers of
the major theoretician of hard sell advertising, including
correspondence, writings and speeches, materials on Dwight
Eisenhower's 1952 election campaigns, photographs and frag-
mentary records of Ted Bates and Company. Also contains
files on his book, *Reality in Advertising,* which illustrate
his hard-sell advertising theories. Partly restricted.

20.121   Shaw, John M. Papers, 1930 - 59 (3 boxes). Former public
          relations and marketing executive for the American Telephone
          and Telegraph Company. Includes correspondence, internal
          memoranda, articles and addresses and report summaries and
          recommendations.

20.122   Wittner, Fred Papers, 1928 - 72 (16 boxes). Papers of the
          founder of an advertising firm noted for its comprehensive
          services to industrial clients. Includes correspondence,
          materials on early advertising clients including Amelia Ear-
          hart and George Palmer Putnam and records concerning the
          Fred Wittner Company including client and personnel lists,
          publications, a diary and other materials.

20.123   Wolfe, H.D. Papers (1 box). Typescript of *Essentials of the
          Promotional Mix,* a marketing textbook by Professor Wolfe
          concerning with the promotional methods used in personal
          selling, media advertising, sales promotion, packaging and
          publicity.

20.124   Young, James W. Papers (1 folder). Memo, January 6, 1959,
          from James W. Young, advertising consultant, concerning the
          development of the "product image" type of advertising.

20.125   Other relevant papers include those of Baldwin, William H.,
          1922 - 63 (16 boxes, 9 vols., 2 charts, 1 pkg. & 1 file box);
          Benham, Frederick Darius, 1915 - 60 (3 folders); Bliss, Rob-
          ert L., 1950 - 70 (4 boxes incl. 6 vols. & 1 filmstrip);
          Bruno, Harry, 1919 - 69 (9 boxes incl. 10 vols.,
          6 pkgs., 3 tape recordings, 22 discs & photographs); Church,
          David, June 9, 1964 (2 tape recordings of interview); Hooper,
          C.E., Inc.; Lichtenberg, Bernard, 1917 - 40 (15 vols.);
          Mason, Frank E., 1931 - 45 (7 boxes); Page, Arthur, 1908,
          1913 - 60 (51 boxes incl. 6 vols., 1 vol. & 1 pkg., 1 disc
          recording); Starch, Daniel; Swinehart, Gerry, 1903 - 66
          (2 boxes).

20.126   State University of New York - Archives
          420 Capen Hill   Shonnie Finnegan
          Suny at Buffalo   University Archivist
          Amherst, NY   14260

          Holdings: Records of the University of Buffalo Endowment
          Fund Campaigns of 1920 and 1929, as well as later fund
          raising campaigns with employed advertising methods to "sell"
          the University to the public; and records showing the
          development of public relations at the University.

20.127   Osborn, Alexander Faickney Papers, 1948 - 66 (11 ft.).
          Author and advertising executive of Buffalo. Mss. of books
          written by Osborn: *Applied Imagination* (1953), *Wake Up Your
          Mind* (1952) and *Your Creative Power* (1948); and records of
          the Creative Education Foundation (1954 - 1964). Finding
          aid in the repository. Information on literary rights avail-
          able in the repository.

20.128   Walter, Thompson J. Company - Information Center
         875 N. Michigan Ave.   (312) 664-6700 x 6151
         Chicago, Il   60611   Edward G. Strable
                                               V.P., Mgr./Info. Services

         Holdings: *The JWT File,* 1902-. Information on JWT with
         emphasis on the Chicago Office, includes JWT profile index
         to *JWT News,* 1943- covering people in the company, and *JWT
         Chicago Office Print Ads,* 1902-. Ads produced by this
         office 1902 - 59 on film, since that time in hard copy.

20.129   Walter, Thompson J. Company - Information Center
         420 Lexington Ave.   (212) 867-1000
         New York, NY   10017   Mary Gegelys
                                               Dir./Info. Center

         Holdings: 2,000 sq. ft. of records and archives including:
         client advertising, late 1880's- (proofs, etc. in varying
         degrees of completeness); competitive advertising (tear-
         sheets from selected consumer magazines, covering most pro-
         duct categories); material covering JWT history, late 1880's-
         (letters, memoranda, photos, memorabilia, articles and
         speeches). Access by prior permission of library director.

20.130   Tracy-Locke Advertising and Public Relations, Inc.
         1407 Main Street   Mr. Ernest Blakey
         Dallas, Texas   75202   Manager, Information Ser-
                                                     vices
                                               (214) 742-3131 ext. 446

         Holdings: As agency library was started in 1967, most of
         the material is relatively current, but they have 12 verti-
         cal file drawers of clippings and pamphlets and 120 micro-
         film reels of research reports, client reports, and other
         data. Current adv. and marketing journals subscribed to.
         Interlibrary loans, photocopying for fee and reference assis-
         tance available. Access with prior permission of library
         director.

20.131   University of Arizona - Archive Collection of Television Commer-
             cials
         Dept. of Marketing, College of Business and Public Administration
         Tucson, AZ   85721

         Holdings: Collection of 1,400 commercials, starting in 1971;
         available for educational purposes only. Commercials have
         been donated by major advertising agencies and advertisers
         themselves. Donors include J. Walter Thompson Co.; Batten,
         Barton, Durstine & Osborne; N.W. Ayer & Son; Doyle, Dane,
         Bernbach; and SSC & B. Advertisers who have donated include
         William Wrigley Co.; Mobil; and Colgate Palmolive. Archive
         also serves as a depository for the public service commer-
         cials of the Advertising Council. An index to the
         commercials is in preparation.

20.132   University of Chicago Library - Manuscript Division/Special
         Collections
         1100 E. 57th St.
         Chicago, IL   60637

>   Holdings: Asher, Louis E. Papers, 1894 - 1918 (2 boxes).
>   Contains correspondence, advertising materials and other
>   documents related to Sears advertising campaigns. Asher
>   worked closely with Richard W. Sears on many of the great
>   promotion schemes of Sears, Roebuck and Co. A 3 page inven-
>   tory with introduction is available.

20.133   Cone, Fairfax M. Papers, 1945 - 71 (147 boxes). Includes
         correspondence, speeches and photographs. There is a 92
         page inventory of the Cone collection which is available
         for consultation in the Dept. of Special Collections.

20.134   University of Illinois at Urbana-Champaign - Archives
         Room 19
         University Library
         Urbana, IL   61801

>   Holdings: Announcements of the Advertising Department of the
>   College of Journalism and Communications; seminar programs of
>   the Advertising Department; occasional papers of the Adver-
>   tising Department; subject file of the Institute of Communi-
>   cations Research of the College of Communications; Jeffrey
>   O'Connell Papers.

20.135   Abrams, Samuel Scrapbook. 1902 - 6 (2 vols.). Includes
         materials from a correspondence course in advertising taken
         by Mr. Abrams before attending Illinois in 1907 - 10; promo-
         ional literature; correspondence; exercise sheets; and sam-
         ples of advertising and related material issued by the Page-
         Davis Correspondence School of Advertising Writing in Chica-
         go. Some material relates to Abrams' violin school and other
         Chicago businesses.

20.136   Evans, James F. Papers, 1924 - 67 (4 ft.). Professor of
         agricultural communications and journalism, University of
         Illinois. Advertising proofbooks (1924 - 1949) of the
         Aubrey, Moore and Wallace agency for International Harvester
         Company trucks and industrial power equipment. Unpublished
         finding aid in the repository. Information on literary
         rights available in the repository.

20.137   Sandage, Charles Harold Papers, 1930 - 63 (2 ft.). Professor
         of advertising at the University of Illinois. Correspond-
         ence, newsletters and programs (1938 - 1948) relating to the
         American Marketing Association, the Dept. of Marketing,
         Miami University, Oxford, Ohio where Sandage was on the
         faculty and the U.S. Office of Price Administration in Ohio,
         of which Sandage was an officer; surveys and reports on radio
         listening in the area of Bloomington, IL (1947), Champaign
         Co., IL (1946-47, 1949-50, 1963), and Butler Co., Ohio
         (1945-46) and scripts of radio broadcasts (1937 - 39) on

consumer education. Unpublished finding aid in the repository. Information on literary rights available in the repository.

20.138 University of Illinois at Urbana-Champaign - Communications
        Library
        122 Gregory Hall   (217) 333-2216
        Urbana, IL   61801   Eleanor Blum
                                                Communications Librarian

        Holdings: Young, James Webb Papers, 1957 - 59 (154 items).
        Letters from recipients of Young's books.

20.139 University of Iowa Libraries - Manuscript Division
        Iowa City, IA   52242   Robert M. McCown
                                                Manuscripts Librarian

        Holdings: The Donald G. Padilla Collection of Advertising
        Cards.

20.140 Springer, John Papers, 1866 - 1936 (ca. 7 ft.). Advertising
        agent, printer and newspaper editor of Iowa City. Correspondence, clippings, printed matter, memorabilia and other
        material relating to printing and advertising. Unpublished
        guide in the library. Information on literary rights available in the library.

20.141 University of Michigan - Bentley Historical Library - Michigan
        Historical Collections
        1150 Beal Ave.   Mary Jo Pugh
        Ann Arbor, MI   48105   Reference Archivist

        Holdings: Detzer, Karl L. Papers, 1916 - 1967 (2 boxes).
        Roving editor of *Reader's Digest* since 1939, he also has
        worked for advertising agencies, newspapers and the motion
        picture industry. Correspondence touches on all these
        careers. Manuscripts and published articles also are
        included.
            Note: materials may be used only in the reading room
        of the Bentley Historical Library. Researchers should
        write to the Reference Archivist to obtain information about
        hours and policies. Duplicating facilities are available
        for those using the Collections.

20.142 Johnson, Axel Petrus Papers, 1908 - 39 (ca. 250 items).
        Journalist and author. Correspondence and papers dealing
        with Johnson's position as advertising manager of the
        "Chicago Record-Herald" and publisher-owner of the "Grand
        Rapids Times." Includes materials used in teaching courses
        in advertising.

20.143 University of Oregon Library - Special Collections
        Eugene, OR   97403

        Holdings: Baker (Frederick E.) & Associates Account Records
        (Seattle), 1946 - 47 (12 ft.). Account records of a public
        relations firm.

20.144   Bensing, Frank C. Papers, 1926 - 51 (6 ft.). Commercial
          artist and illustrator. Correspondence with advertising
          agencies and magazines, 54 illustrations and other papers.

20.145   Brown, Lyndon Osmond Marketing Research Reports, 1930 - 47
          (ca. 2 ft.). Business executive and professor of marketing
          and advertising at Northwestern University. Market and dis-
          tribution analyses for specific clients of the various agen-
          cies with which Brown was associated, general analyses for
          agency use and agency internal files. Organizations
          represented include Lord and Thomas, Foote, Cone and Beldin;
          and Dancer-Fitzgerald-Sample. Inventory in the library.

20.146   Jackson, Charles Samuel Correspondence, 1902 - 6 (79 items).
          Journalist and newspaper publisher of Oregon. Correspondence
          with Fred Lockley relating to the practical aspects of
          selling advertising, among other subjects.

20.147 Western Reserve Historical Society
        10825 E. Boulevard   Dennis Harrison
        Cleveland, OH   44106   Curator of Manuscripts

          Holdings: Collection of advertising cards mounted in 2
          scrapbooks, one of which belonged to Else (Schweitzer) Ger-
          stenberger and contains ads from mostly Cleveland firms;
          and records of the Cleveland Shopping News Co. and its
          publication, *The Cleveland Shopping News,* 1922 - 50.

20.148   Raddatz, William Joseph Scrapbooks, 1904 - 40 (4 vols.).
          Advertising and printing executive of Cleveland. Corres-
          pondence, newspaper clippings, pamphlets, magazine articles,
          photos and programs relating to Raddatz' business career
          and his presidency of the Cleveland Advertising Club (1916 -
          1917).

20.149 Yale University Libraries - Manuscripts & Archives
        New Haven, CT   06520   Judith A. Schiff
                                                Chief Research Archivist

          Holdings: Century of Progress-World's Fair Collection,
          (39 ft.), consists of printed matter and publicity material
          related to the exhibits at the Century of Progress Interna-
          tional Exposition in Chicago (1933 - 34) and the New York
          World's Fair (1939 - 40).

20.150   Rogers, James Gamble, Jr., correspondence (Jan. - Oct. 1943)
          with associates at the advertising firm of Benton and Bowles
          while Rogers was serving with the Office of War Information
          in Washington. Also a memorandum (1942) and sample posters
          for an advertising campaign for the Can Manufacturers Insti-
          tute.

20.151 Yale University Libraries - Sterling Memorial Library
        New Haven, CO   06520

          Holdings: Sampter, E. Lawrence Collection of Printed Ephe-
          mera, 19th century (10,000+ examples of non-book printing).

The Collection, now in the Arts of the Book Room, consists
of early American bookmarks, calling cards, tickets, packaging labels, greeting cards and trade cards.

20.152 Young & Rubicam, Inc. - Library
        285 Madison Ave.   (212) 953-3075
        New York, NY   10017   Celestine Frankenberg
                                            Dir./Library Services

        Holdings: *House Advertising,* 1926 - 69. Examples of Y&R's,
        advertising of its own services; and *Annuals of Advertising,*
        1923-. Examples of the best in print and television.
        Access by prior permission of library director.

20.153 History of Advertising Archives
        Faculty of Commerce   R.W. Pollay, Curator
        University of British Columbia   (604) 228-2568
        Vancouver, B.C.   V6T 1W5

        Holdings: The majority of the titles listed within this
        Guide and catalogued accordingly, including many rare and
        obscure titles. Materials also include original materials
        not in this *Guide,* such as a special collection on Father
        Coughlin, related literature in marketing and consumer
        behavior, and sundry corporate histories.
             The archival and manuscript collection includes a large
        collection of advertising artifacts, particularly curious
        specialty items, advertiques illustrative of junctures in
        advertising history, and is extensive on patent medicine
        artifacts, including much printed ephemera. The collection
        also includes 2,500 35mm slides on advertising and business
        history and 6 ft. of videotapes of television ads.
             Access is open to all researchers, although circula-
        tion is controlled. Office space available for extended
        visits, as is colleague assistance and advice. Facilities
        include all necessary video and audio tape equipment.
        Mail inquiries as to holdings answered promptly.
             Aggressive acquisitions efforts include purchase of
        new titles, receipt of donations from benefactors, and
        patient scrounging in second hand bookstores from coast to
        coast. Potential contributions of libraries and archival
        material evaluated and, of course, gratefully received.
             Consultation on the establishment of archives and
        museums available for a nominal fee.

21.000
PROFESSIONAL ASSOCIATIONS

21.001   Advertising Club of New York
         23 Park Ave.   (212) 685-1810
         New York, NY   10016

         Founded in 1906 and sponsors educational and public service
         activities, promotion and public relations projects and
         meetings to hear various speakers in the field, personali-
         ties and celebrities. Arranges regular and special name
         brand promotions and programs and exhibits. Holds annual
         advertising and marketing course which offers classes and
         clinics in advertising production, sales promotion, marketing
         management, etc. Sponsors annual job-finding forum. Main-
         tains Advertising Hall of Fame; gives Andy Awards for excel-
         lence in media advertising. Affiliated with American Adver-
         tising Federation.

21.002   Advertising Council, Inc.
         825 3rd Ave.   (212) 758-0400
         New York, NY   10022

         Founded in 1942 and supported by American business to con-
         duct public service advertising programs. Encourages adver-
         tisers and advertising media to contribute time and space;
         advertising agencies to supply creative talent and facilities
         to further timely national causes. Bestows an annual public
         service award. Specific campaigns include: Aid to Higher
         Education; American Red Cross; Continue Your Education; Drug
         Abuse Information; Food, Nutrition and Health; Forest Fire
         Prevention; Help Prevent Crime; Help Fight Pollution; Jobs
         for Veterans; Pakistan Relief; Rehabilitation of the Handi-
         capped; etc. Publishes the *Public Service Advertising
         Bulletin,* bimonthly.

21.003   Advertising Research Foundation (ARF)
         3 E. 54th St.   (212) 751-5656
         New York, NY   10022

         Founded in 1936 to further scientific practices and promote
         greater effectiveness of advertising and marketing by means
         of objective and impartial research; develop new research
         methods and techniques; analyze and evaluate existing methods
         and techniques and define proper applications; establish
         research standards, criteria and reporting methods. Pub-
         lishes the *Journal of Advertising Research,* bimonthly.

21.004   Advertising Women of New York (AWNY)
         153 E. 57th St.   (212) 593-1950
         New York, NY   10022

         Founded in 1912 and is composed of women engaged in an exec-
         utive or administrative capacity in advertising, publicity,
         marketing, research or promotion for at least two years.
         Membership concentrated in New York area. Sponsors business,
         dinner and luncheon meetings and a career clinic to provide

personal job counseling to AWNY members. The affiliated
Advertising Women of New York Foundation conducts an annual
career conference for college women in their junior and
senior years and an annual one-day conference designed to
inform women consumers on the way advertising can help them.
Affiliated with the American Advertising Federation.

21.005   The American Advertising Federation (AAF)
         1225 Connecticut Ave., N.W.   Howard H. Bell
         Washington, DC   20036   President

The AAF traces its origins from the Advertising Federation
of America, founded in 1905, and the Advertising Association
of the West, founded about the same time. The present name
was adopted when the two organizations merged in 1967.
     The primary objectives are:
1) To promote a better understanding of the function of
advertising and of its values.
2) To promote higher standards of advertising practice
through a program of industry self-regulation.
3) To recognize outstanding accomplishments in the further-
ance of advertising as a profession and in its service to
the community.
4) To encourage young people to enter advertising as a
career, and to advance educational programs designed to
strengthen the skills of advertising practitioners.
5) To reflect industry views and concerns on public issues
affecting advertising at the state and federal levels.

21.006   American Association of Advertising Agencies (AAAA)
         200 Park Ave.   William R. Hesse
         New York, NY   10017   President

AAAA is the national association of the advertising agency
business. Founded in 1917, its membership now consists of
411 advertising agencies and accounts for three-fourths of
advertising volume placed by advertising agencies. The
fundamental purpose of the AAAA is to improve, strengthen
and interpret the advertising agency business in the U.S.A.
and abroad and to provide counsel and expertise on matters
of agency: finance, operation, organization, personnel and
other pertinent business matters.
     The Association works with media, research, supplier
groups, other associations and, when required, with member
clients to improve performance, efficiency and conduct of
the agency business.
     The AAAA represents the advertising agency business
with government to support the government in national
policy; to advise and help direct national policy where
possible; to help resist unwise, unfair or arbitrary regulation and legislation, and to bring agency expertise to bear
on government problems in an effort to solve them.

21.007 American Marketing Association (AMA)
        222 S. Riverside Plaza, Suite 606   (312) 648-0536
        Chicago, IL   60606

> Fosters research; sponsors seminars, conferences, and student marketing clubs; maintains educational placement service and doctoral consortium. Publishes *The Marketing News,* semimonthly; *Journal of Marketing,* quarterly; and *Journal of Marketing Research,* quarterly. Formed by merger of American Marketing Society and the National Association of Marketing Teachers.

21.008 Association of Canadian Advertisers (ACA)
        Suite 620, 159 Bay St.   (416) 363-8046
        Toronto, Ont. M5J 1J7

> Founded in 1914, ACA is the advertisers' spokesman in Canada. Its service to members and the advertising industry at large have been and are designed to help the advertiser by providing news and information that would not otherwise be readily available; upgrading the image of advertising by showing how it benefits consumers and producers; and speaking out for the advertiser with the strength of the combined voices of its more than 250 members. It also intercedes on behalf of the advertiser with federal ministers and members of the House of Commons and Senate Committees whenever legislation is proposed that affects advertising.

21.009 Association of National Advertisers, Inc. (ANA)
        155 E. 44th St.   Peter W. Allport
        New York, NY   10017   President

> Devoted exclusively to serving the needs of advertisers, the Association of National Advertisers is a non-profit organization, founded in 1910. To its membership of over 400 major U.S. corporations including 90 of the 100 largest users of advertising, the ANA provides information, assists in the training of member marketing and advertising executives and helps members drive maximum benefit from their advertising dollars. Member companies' advertising investments represent three-quarters of the total national advertising expenditures. The ANA also serves as a liaison for advertisers in communicating their practices and attitudes to agencies and media, as well as to the public and government.
>
> The basic long-term objectives of the ANA include the preservation of free and responsible advertising and to generate and assure sound policies and practices in the advertising community.

21.010 Automotive Advertisers Council (AAC)
        230 North Michigan Ave.   (312) 236-8720
        Chicago, IL   60601

> Founded in 1941. Advertising and/or sales promotion executives of manufacturing concerns, a substantial portion of whose products are sold through independent automotive whole-

salers. Provides forum for interchange of views and opinions
on needs of automotive trade, and encourages study research to increase advertising effectiveness. Co-sponsors
AAC Advertising Awards.

21.011 Bank Marketing Association (BMA)
        309 W. Washington   (312) 782-1442
        Chicago, IL   60606

        Provides printed materials and visual aids on all phases of
        banking and marketing; conducts research and educational
        workshops and seminars; co-sponsors summer sessions of
        fundamental and advanced courses in marketing at the Univer-
        sity of Colorado at Boulder and the University of Wisconsin
        at Madison; offers placement service; maintains Information
        Center, housing materials on public relations, marketing,
        advertising, business development, etc.; publishes *Bank
        Marketing Journal,* monthly. Formerly the Financial Adver-
        tisers Association, then Financial Public Relations Associa-
        tion, then Bank Public Relations and Marketing Association.

21.012 Business & Professional Advertising Association (B/PAA)
        205 E. 42nd St.   (212) 661-0222
        New York, NY   10017

        Organization of business communications professionals in the
        fields of advertising, marketing, and marketing communica-
        tions. Sponsors annual "Pro-Comm Awards Competition;"
        conducts seminars directed toward business communicators;
        compiles statistics; maintains Hall of Fame and Marketing
        data library containing over 200,000 documents (housed at
        McGraw-Hill). Originally called the National Industrial
        Advertisers Association, then the Association of Industrial
        Advertisers.

21.013 Canadian Advertising and Sales Association (CASA)
        Suite 400, 42 Charles St. E.
        Toronto, Ont. M4Y 1T6

        Formed in 1944 as an umbrella organization of all Adver-
        tising and Sales Clubs across Canada. Until 1953 known as
        the Federation of Advertising and Sales Clubs.

21.014 Canadian Advertising Research Foundation (CARF)
        Suite 620, 159 Bay St.   (416) 363-8046
        Toronto, Ont. M5J 1J7

        Founded in the late 1940's by the Association of Canadian
        Advertisers and the Canadian Association of Advertising
        Agencies (now the Institute of Canadian Advertising).
        Previously membership was restricted to representatives from
        these two groups. Now it is opened to the industry. At
        present all advertiser, agency, media, research, government
        and academic organizations are eligible for membership
        either on a full membership or associate membership basis.
        CARF publications include: *Toward Better Media Comparisons;*

Copy Testing - an Annotated Bibliography; Measuring Payout - an Annotated Bibliography; and *Media Research Standards and Full Consultation Procedure and Requirements.*

21.015 Council of Better Business Bureaus, Inc.
1150 17th St., N.W.
Washington, DC   20036

845 3rd Ave.   William H. Tankersley
New York, NY   10022   President

The BBB movement had its start early in the 20th century when groups of businessmen banded together under the name of "vigilance committees" to combat the fraudulent and misleading advertising of that day.

The movement became national in 1912 and in 1921 the name was changed to the National Better Business Bureau of the Advertising Clubs of the World (later simply National Better Business Bureau).

The Association of Better Business Bureaus emerged in 1946 as the national representative of the local bureau and operated separately from the National Better Business Bureau until the two were consolidated in 1970 to form the Council of Better Business Bureaus.

The BBB movement became international in 1928 and now has bureaus in Canada, Mexico, Puerto Rico, Venezuela and Israel.

The Council of Better Business Bureaus essentially is supported by memberships of major national businesses. Its goals are: to restore consumer confidence in the market-place and to regain for business its prerogative of self-regulation. The Council's functions: to give consumers a valid reason to believe that the business community -- or a sizable portion of it is trying to do the right thing, to protect businesses against illegal and unethical practices of competitors, to serve as an interface between business and the consumer and between business and government.

The Council's major activities include:
1) BBB Arbitration Panels throughout the BBB system.
2) Trade Practice Codes.
3) Consumer education programs.
4) *Do's and Don't's in Advertising Copy* (a subscription service).
5) Philanthropic Advisory Services.

21.016 Institute of Canadian Advertisers
8 King St. E., Suite 401
Toronto, Ont. M5C 1B5

Formerly called the Canadian Association of Advertising Agencies (CAAA).

21.017 Institute of Outdoor Advertising (IOA)
        625 Madison Ave.   (212) 755-4157
        New York, NY   10022

           Founded in 1965 to serve as a central source of information
           on outdoor advertising research, creativeness, promotion and
           effective use. In 1971 the Institute became the marketing
           division of the Outdoor Advertising Association of America.

21.018 Magazine Publishers Association (MPA)
        575 Lexington Ave.   (212) 752-0055
        New York, NY   10022

           Founded in 1919 and composed of publishers of 450 consumer,
           agricultural, business, educational and religious magazines
           issued not less than 4 times a year (does not include daily
           or weekly newspapers). Departmental activities include a
           Marketing Department which promotes magazines as an adver-
           tising medium. Houses and administers Publishers Informa-
           tion Bureau, a separate association which provides statisti-
           cal information about general magazine advertising.

21.019 Media Research Directors Association (MRDA)
        c/o James P. Burke
        The New Yorker
        25 W. 43rd St.
        New York, NY   10036

           Association of research directors of leading national print
           and broadcast media, founded in 1947.

21.020 National Advertising Review Board (NARD)
        845 Third Ave.   Kenneth A. Cox
        New York, NY   10022   Chairman

           NARB functions as the "appeals body" of the advertising
           industry's voluntary self-regulatory mechanism, formed to
           sustain truth and accuracy in national advertising. Does
           not maintain a library but has files containing advertising
           matters. See 20.072.

21.021 National Association of Broadcasters (NAB)
        1771 N. St., N.W.   (202) 293-3500
        Washington, DC   20036

           Represents radio and TV stations and all eight national
           radio and TV networks and associate producers of equipment
           and programs. Administers voluntary codes for radio and TV
           which provide broadcasters with guidelines in determining
           acceptable programming and advertising practices; upholds
           the American system of broadcasting, free from government
           censorship; combats discriminating legislative proposals
           against broadcasting and advertising. Formerly the National
           Association of Radio & Television Broadcasters; absorbed
           the Television Broadcasters Association.

21.022   National Federation of Advertising Agencies (NFAA)
         Sarasota Bank Bldg.   (813) 366-2902
         Sarasota, FL   33577

         Cooperative national network of non-competing local adver-
         tising agencies, founded in 1910. Organized to provide
         national facilities and branch office service for affiliated
         agencies.

21.023   Newspaper Advertising Bureau (Of the American Newspaper Publishers
            Association)
         485 Lexington Ave.   (212) 687-9300
         New York, NY   10017

         Founded in 1913 to sell the advantages of newspapers as a
         national advertising medium. Concerned with the daily
         newspapers in the U.S., Canada, Puerto Rico and the Philip-
         pines. Publishes *Expenditures of National Advertisers in
         Newspapers,* annual, and *Time Table of Retail Opportunities,*
         annual. Formerly called the Bureau of Advertising of ANPA.

21.024   Outdoor Advertising Association of America (OAAA)
         485 Lexington Ave.   (212) 986-5920
         New York, NY   10017

         Consists of firms owning, erecting, and maintaining stand-
         ardized poster parcels and painted display advertising fac-
         ilities. In 1971, the Institute of Outdoor Advertising
         became the marketing division of OAAA.

21.025   Point-of-Purchase Advertising Institute (POPAI)
         60 East 42nd   (212) 682-7041
         New York, NY   10017

         Founded in 1938. Represents producers and suppliers of
         point-of-purchase advertising signs and displays. Associate
         members are national and regional advertisers and retailers
         interested in use and effectiveness of signs, displays, and
         other point-of-purchase media. Sponsors merchandising
         awards contest, exhibit, and symposium. Conducts student
         education program; maintains library.

21.026   Radio Advertising Bureau (RAB)
         555 Madison Ave.   (212) 688-4020
         New York, NY   10022

         Founded in 1951 to promote the sale of radio time as an
         advertising medium. Sponsors regional conferences on sub-
         jects such as promotion, programming, sales and general
         management. Conducts extensive research programs into all
         phases of radio listening, commercial awareness and trends
         in other media. Formerly called the Broadcast Advertising
         Bureau.

21.027   Television Bureau of Advertising (TVB)
         1345 Avenue of the Americas   (212) 757-9420
         New York, NY   10019

         Founded in 1954 and concerns itself with improving and
         expanding the use of television as an advertising medium.
         Conducts audience composition studies, maintains television
         commercial film library, sponsors research on processes of
         communications studying all media and personal communica-
         tions. Publishes the *Spot Television Expenditures,* annual,
         and *TV Basics,* annual.

"During the last ten years, and particularly during the last
five years, the quality of advertising has passed through a
fiery revolution.
     The brilliant minds of the country are now giving attention
to the preparation of advertising.
     Advertising has become a science.
     Advertising has reached the platform of art.
     The great artists, who but a few years ago threw their entire
talent into historical themes, are today assisting the advertiser,
in making his goods known throughout the world.
     The greatest newspaper writers, and the most intellectual
authors, are not above giving their time to the preparation of
advertisements, which people will read, and therefore are
profitable to the advertiser.
     There is more real grey matter expended in the preparation of
the advertising pages in the average leading publication, than
there is spilled in the make-up of the literary department.
     The man with the power to write a telling advertisement may
have as fine a quality of brain excellence as he who can build
literature, and create romance.
     The man who knows how to direct advertising so that twenty-
five per cent. of it is guaranteed to return in positive profit,
will by and by find his monument in the same field with the
memorials of the men who discovered the composition of electricity,
or were able to regulate the sunshine."

                                        Nathaniel Fowler, Jr.*

_____

*Building Business: A Manual for Aggressive Businessmen, 1893.

Index to Bibliographies
and Directories

ABOUT THE EDITOR

Richard W. Pollay is Associate Professor of Marketing and Business History at the University of British Columbia in Vancouver. He has published in *Business and Society, Journal of Communication, Journal of Marketing, History of Medicine Quarterly,* and other publications.